WILLIAM AND KATE

WILLIAM
AND
KATE

A Royal Love Story

Christopher Andersen

G
GALLERY BOOKS
NEW YORK   LONDON   TORONTO   SYDNEY

GALLERY BOOKS
A Division of Simon & Schuster, Inc.
1230 Avenue of the Americas
New York, NY 10020

First Gallery Books trade paperback edition June 2011

GALLERY BOOKS and colophon are trademarks of Simon & Schuster, Inc.

For information about special discounts for bulk purchases, please contact
Simon & Schuster Special Sales at 1-866-506-1949 or business@simonandschuster.com.

The Simon & Schuster Speakers Bureau can bring authors to your live event.
For more information or to book an event contact the Simon & Schuster
Speakers Bureau at 1-866-248-3049 or visit our website at www.simonspeakers.com.

Designed by Joseph Rutt

Manufactured in the United States of America

10 9 8 7 6 5 4 3 2 1

Library of Congress Cataloging-in-Publication data is available.

ISBN 978-1-4516-2145-7
ISBN 978-1-4516-2146-4 (pbk)
ISBN 978-1-4516-2147-1 (ebook)

PHOTO CREDITS

Alpha/Globe Photos: 1, 2, 5, 9, 10, 11, 21, 29; Collections of the author: 3; Associated Press: 4,
6, 17, 19, 20, 22, 34, 35, 37, 38, 41, 48, 58; Rex USA/BEImages: 7, 12, 23, 25, 26, 27, 28, 31, 32,
33, 36, 39, 40, 42, 43, 44, 45, 46, 47, 50, 52, 53, 55, 56, 57, 59, 60, 63; Tim Graham/Getty Images:
8; INFGoff: 13; PRPhotos: 14; AFP/Getty Images: 15; Tim Clarke/AFP/Getty Images: 16; Getty
Images: 18; BEImages: 24; Xposure Photos: 30; Bauer-Griffin: 49; AP Photo/Gareth Fuller: 51;
AP Photo/Dominic Lipinski: 54; Andrew Winning/PA via AP Images: 61, 62; Chris Ison/PA via
AP Images: 64; AP Photo/Hugo Burnand, Clarence House: 65; AP Photo/John Stillwell, PA:
66, 67; AP Photo/Martin Meissner: 68

For my mother, Jeanette Andersen

I put it to William, particularly, that if you find someone you love in life, you must hang on to that love and look after it. . . . You must protect it.

—*Diana*

Preface

Theirs was destined from the very start to be one of the most celebrated unions of the twenty-first century. He was the dashing, charismatic young prince who would someday be crowned king of England. She was the stunningly beautiful commoner from working-class stock who won his heart when they were both barely out of their teens. Together, Prince William and Kate Middleton somehow managed to defy all odds to forge and sustain an enduring love amidst the scandals, power struggles, tragedies, and general dysfunction that are the hallmarks of Britain's Royal Family.

Along the way, they became the most written-about, gossiped-about, admired, and envied young couple of their generation. Just as a global audience of more than 800 million people tuned in to watch live coverage of the Wedding of the Century in 1981—the marriage of Prince Charles to Lady Diana Spencer—the marriage of their elder son to his college sweetheart would captivate the world.

With good reason. Not only is William heir to the British throne, but he is also heir to the compelling and complicated legacy of Diana, arguably the most celebrated woman of the modern age. Three times as many people—an estimated 2.5 billion—watched Diana's 1997 funeral as watched her wedding, and the image of William and his brother, Prince Harry, walking behind her horse-drawn casket through the streets of London was burned indelibly into the minds of a generation.

Their grief was ours as well, for we felt we knew Diana's boys—William in particular. His birth was breathlessly heralded on front pages and magazine covers around the world, and we watched "Wills" grow from naughty enfant terrible to gangling adolescent to dynamic adult—all while his parents' stormy marriage and then Diana's death in a Paris car crash sent shock waves through Buckingham Palace and around the world. The bittersweet truth was that we got to see William grow to become the impressive young man his mother never knew.

Yet for most of their decade-long romance, William and Kate managed to conduct their love affair largely away from the unremitting media glare. It certainly helped that Fleet Street, still acutely aware that William believed the press had literally chased his mother to her death, was inclined for a time to keep a somewhat more respectful distance from the prince. As a result, even as the wedding approached, the true nature of William's royal relationship remained a tantalizing mystery.

They are both impossibly attractive, disarmingly charming, young, athletic, elegant, *exciting.* More than any other couple in memory, William and Kate stand astride the yawning chasm that separates centuries of tradition from the ever-shifting realities of the electronic age.

Glamour, power, sex, wealth, betrayal, scandal, tragedy, adventure, history, heartache, duty, and of course tradition—not to mention the dreams and aspirations of a generation—are all embodied in the handsome future king and his stunning commoner queen.

It remains to be seen whether they will follow Diana's lead and connect with their subjects in a way no Windsors ever had before. For now, what William and Kate have given us is more than enough: part glittering fairy tale, part searing family drama, part political potboiler, part heart-stopping cliff-hanger—and, in all ways, an affair to remember.

There is only one Princess of Wales in people's minds. And only when Prince William gets married will it be time for another one.

—*Diana's friend Vivienne Parry,*
on the marriage of Prince Charles and Camilla

I

She steps into the sultry August night air, clutching her Longchamp bag to her side with one hand while trying to shield her eyes with the other. The flashes seem to be coming from every direction this time, and in the white-hot glare she feels as if she is about to lose her balance. Guided by the firm hand of her driver, or perhaps just a concerned friend, she somehow angles her way through the maelstrom of photographers until she reaches the waiting car. In one smooth motion, she lowers her head, ducks in, and slides across the backseat.

Before the door slams shut behind her—and before anyone inside has had the chance to buckle up their shoulder belts—the driver floors the accelerator, pressing his passengers back into their seats. They speed down one narrow side street, turn abruptly, then hurtle down another, but these maneuvers are not enough for them to elude her pursuers; she can see their headlights in the side-view mirrors, vanishing as they round a corner, only to reappear a split second later.

Suddenly, the car swerves and stops at a traffic light. A dozen paparazzi in cars and on motorcycles surround her now, waiting for the light to change. She turns and looks directly into the eyes of a photographer who sits astride a 600 cc Honda motorbike. Instinctively, she smiles out the window at him. He guns his engine, and even though *his helmet only allows her to see his eyes, she knows he is smiling back.*

It's not as if they are strangers. Over the last several years, she has become adept at disarming reporters with an easy, winsome charm. More important, she has learned how to manipulate them—how, as others had so skillfully done before, to use the press to further her own agenda.

But then at times like this, in the pursuit of a story and that million-dollar photograph, the sometimes-friendly press becomes the enemy. And everything spins wildly out of control.

Without warning, she is thrust back again as her driver jumps the light, making a hard right onto the main avenue paralleling the river. Glass-domed boats filled with tourists pass one another, and occasionally their spotlights fall on the architectural treasures for which the city is famous. She sees none of this. Instead, she stares straight ahead, at the back of her driver's brilliantine-slathered head, and prays that he knows what he's doing.

No more traffic lights are ahead, and the car zigzags through traffic even as it picks up speed. Tearing along at seventy miles an hour—the speed limit here is thirty miles an hour—it pulls far ahead of the pack. But two of the paparazzi riding on motorcycles manage to keep up, and the driver of the limousine presses down even harder on the gas pedal.

Now she can see the illuminated gardens on the opposite bank and just up ahead the giant carousel bathed in pink and purple lights— all a blur as the car rockets down the boulevard. "Slow down!" she finally cries, terror etched on her classically beautiful face. "Please, slow down. Oh, PLEASE!"

———

For years after his mother was killed in history's most famous car crash, he relived her horrific death in dreams. With time those dreams faded, only to be replaced by new nightmares that he described in varying degrees of harrowing detail to his closest friends, to his brother, Harry, to his father, and even to trusted members of his staff. In these terrifying visions, the river is not the Seine but the Thames, the city not Paris but London, and the victim not Diana but the love of his life: Kate Middleton.

The cause of the accident in which thirty-six-year-old Diana and her then lover Dodi Fayed died on August 31, 1997, was, in the end, as mundane as it was obvious. Operation Paget—Scotland Yard's official, three-year-long investigation into Diana's death—ultimately concluded that the blood alcohol of her car's driver was over three times the legal limit, and that Diana was the victim of a drunk-driving accident.

Her sons felt otherwise. They blamed the press for literally chasing their mother to her death—"the hounds of hell," William called them then—and polls at the time showed that most Britons agreed. Unwilling to risk the wrath of the public—or a crackdown by the government's powerful Press Complaints Commission—Fleet Street agreed to keep its distance from Diana's boys until they turned eighteen and had graduated from Eton, the elite prep school. Later, when William enrolled at St. Andrews University in Scotland and Harry pursued his dream of becoming a career army officer at Sandhurst Academy, the press grudgingly agreed to extend this hands-off policy, allowing the princes breathing room as they grew into manhood.

Thanks to this unusual arrangement with Britain's notoriously insatiable press, William and Kate were free to meet, fall in love, and—under the guise of simply being college roommates—live together for three full years. By the time they received their degrees from St. Andrews in June 2005—his in geography and hers in art history—the couple had never even been photographed together.

Overnight, the gloves came off—and with them, William's fragile peace of mind. At first, he took some solace in knowing that, whenever they were together as a couple, his security detail could hold the press at bay. But when they weren't together, Kate was an easy target: wherever she went—whether it was going out with friends, heading for the gym, or simply wheeling a cart into a supermarket, Kate was trailed by at least a half dozen reporters. They sprang from doorways and popped up from bushes, startling her while she tried to start her Audi or as she walked up to the front door of her apartment opposite a bus stop in Chelsea.

When a German magazine ran photos of William leaving Kate's flat in the early-morning hours—along with a red arrow pointing to their "Love Nest"—the young prince was, in the words of one courtier, "livid." He demanded action and got it in the form of a threatening letter from the royal law firm of Harbottle & Lewis. It was only the first in a string of stern warnings and blistering reprimands aimed at forcing Fleet Street to back down.

It may all have had as much to do with William's obsessive need for control. "I don't go around and expect everyone to listen to me the whole time," he once said. "But I like to be in control of my life. . . . If I don't have any say in it, then I end up losing complete control and I don't like the idea of that. I could actually lose my identity. . . . If you don't stick to your guns, then you lose control."

When it quickly became apparent that the press was one thing he could not control, William pulled Kate under the umbrella of royal protection. Yet even hulking bodyguards with

Glock 9 mm automatic pistols bulging beneath their jackets could not assuage the palpable fear he had that something frightening could—*would*—happen.

During the summer of 2010, plans were secretly under way in London for William's wedding to the only woman he had ever loved. For months, the Queen's advisers at Buckingham Palace had been hammering out the details with senior staff members at Clarence House, part of St. James's Palace and the official residence William shared with Harry, their father Prince Charles and their stepmother, Camilla. "I think," Camilla cracked to one of her neighbors at Highgrove, the Prince of Wales's country estate in Gloucestershire, "it must be very like negotiating a nuclear arms treaty."

The critical question was timing. The year 2012 was to be an extraordinarily busy one for the Royal Family. London was not only hosting the Summer Olympics that year, but the country would be celebrating the Queen's sixtieth year on the throne—her Diamond Jubilee.

Prince Charles, who married Diana when she was twenty and he was thirty-two, saw nothing wrong with postponing William's marriage until his thirty-first birthday in 2013. But that would mean stretching their courtship out to a full thirteen years, and that was something William was not prepared to ask Kate—already branded "Waity Katie" by the press—to do. "It's humiliating," William said when the idea was floated at a Clarence House planning session. "She's been very patient, but there are limits."

The sooner the better, as far as the Queen was concerned. Despite the fact that Kate was a commoner from decidedly middle-class roots, Her Majesty—"Granny" to William—had long ago embraced Miss Middleton as a suitable mate for her favorite grandson. The public was unaware that, in fact, the Queen had privately rooted for Kate to win back William after their highly publicized split in 2007.

The Queen had always taken a special interest in William. Given the increasing likelihood that Charles would ascend to the throne in his sixties, she realized early on that the future of the monarchy rested squarely on the shoulders of her grandson. So when he was five, she began a ritual that would last until he enrolled in college. Every week, he would join Granny for tea, invariably at Windsor Castle or Buckingham Palace. During these bonding sessions Her Majesty would chat with the boy about school and sports, the movies he liked and the music he listened to—all the while trying to deftly slip in a history lesson now and again. To illustrate a point, she might pull out a letter from Henry VIII or perhaps a note from Disraeli to Queen Victoria—originals, of course.

William cherished these moments with Granny—tutorials in kingship that she had never bothered to give her own son. In recent years, William had also come to increasingly rely on Prince Philip for advice and counsel. When the Palace began openly talking about plans to celebrate Philip's ninetieth birthday on June 10, 2011, it was left to Kate to state the obvious. "I can't think of a better birthday present," she told one of her closest friends since girlhood, "than to see your grandson get married. Not," she added with wink, "that I want to rush things . . ."

The sentiment was not lost on the groom. Even as he began arduous training as a search-and-rescue helicopter pilot at a remote air base off the coast of North Wales, William—fully cognizant that his most personal of matters was still very much an affair of state—consulted daily with St. James's Palace over when, where, and how his engagement would be announced.

Far more important, William pondered the moment when he would actually, finally ask Kate for her hand in marriage. In the days after Diana's death, when it came time to choose mementos, Harry had picked his mother's much photographed sapphire-and-diamond engagement ring, while William chose her favorite Cartier Tank watch. In 2009, William asked his brother if he'd be willing to trade. "It means a great deal to me," William told an old Eton classmate, "and I don't think Harry is getting married any time soon."

When thinking about the pomp and circumstance ahead, all the daunting logistics and screaming headlines and frenzied crowds, England's future king has never been able to erase the mental images of Kate being chased to her doom through London traffic. "Pure terror" is the way he described the nightmares. "I wake up shaking." Nor can he forget how his mother described what it was like being hounded by the press. "It's worse," Diana once said, "than sexual abuse."

This gnawing sense of dread, the prince told one of his royal protection officers, became even more intense than before. Whenever William thought back to the terrible fate that befell his mother, he faced the undeniable fact that any wife of his would spend the rest of her life being hunted the way Diana was.

Now just one question reverberated in his head: "Do I really have the right to marry Kate at all?"

———

You must believe me when I tell you that I have found it impossible to carry the heavy burden of . . . my duties as King as I would wish to do without the help and support of the woman I love.

—*William's great-great-uncle*
Edward VIII, in his emotional
1936 abdication speech

I do not want a husband who honors me as a queen, if he does not love me as a woman.

—*Queen Elizabeth I*

———

2

September 6, 1997

A sun-drenched Saturday in England

"Oh, God," said Carole Middleton, choking back tears as the caisson drawn by six horses of the King's Troop Royal Artillery pulled to a stop before Kensington Palace. In a spectacular outpouring of emotion, oceans of flowers lapped at the gates of all the royal palaces, monuments, and important government buildings. But none was so moving as the simple arrangement of white lilies and white roses atop the flag-draped coffin. The BBC camera zoomed in, and letters on the card—painstakingly printed by the young Prince Harry—became legible on the television screen. The card read, simply, MUMMY.

"How terribly, terribly sad," Carole muttered, shaking her head. "Those poor boys." Kate, sitting next to her on the Middletons' chintz-upholstered living room sofa, could not remember the last time she saw her mother so upset. Like millions of other students throughout the United Kingdom, Kate—who at fifteen was the same age as Prince William—had delayed her return to boarding school so she could mourn with her family the shocking death of Diana, Princess of Wales.

The outpouring of grief was as global as it was unprecedented. Sixteen years earlier, an estimated 750 million people watched the fairy-tale wedding of "Shy Di" to Prince Charles—including millions of bleary-eyed Americans who set their alarms at 5:00 a.m. to catch the happy event as it happened. Now, many of those same people were among the worldwide audience of 2.5 billion—by far that largest audience for any live event in television history—who joined in mourning the loss of a princess.

Nowhere, of course, was the pain—or the outrage—more keenly felt than in England. Although she had captured the world's imagination with her glittering sense of style, her personal warmth, and a playful sort of charisma, Diana had long been a thorn in the side of Britain's establishment. Unwilling to bend to the will of the Royal Family and accept her husband's infidelity, she embarked on her own series of love affairs that scandalized the nation and led to her bitter divorce from Charles in 1996.

The shock of her death—so violent, so unexpected, and so senseless—reminded the public that Diana, who connected with the average person in a way no other royal ever had, was still "the People's Princess." It was a lesson the Windsors were learning the hard way. The Queen's initial reluctance to return from her customary summer holiday in Scotland, to fly the Union Jack at half-staff in honor of Diana, or even to speak publicly of the tragedy, all betrayed the Royal Family's disregard for what Diana meant to the British people.

The Queen's intransigence led to the most serious threat to the monarchy since Edward VIII's abdication to marry the American divorcée Wallis Simpson. While headlines in the *Sun* blared WHERE IS OUR QUEEN? WHERE IS HER FLAG? and the *Mirror* pleaded SPEAK TO US MA'AM—YOUR PEOPLE ARE SUFFERING, angry crowds gathered outside Buckingham Palace demanding action. Even the staunchly pro-monarchy *Daily Express* implored the Queen SHOW US YOU CARE.

Heeding Prime Minister Tony Blair's pleas to act, the Queen finally returned to London, lowered the flag over Buckingham Palace to half-staff, and delivered a televised address aimed at winning back her subjects. "What I say to you now as your Queen and as a grandmother," she began, "I say from my heart. First, I want to pay tribute to Diana, myself. She was an exceptional and gifted human being. . . . I admired and respected her for her energy and commitment to others, especially for her devotion to her two boys."

Watching the Queen's speech from the Middletons' country estate in the tiny Berkshire parish of Bucklebury, Kate and her parents were unmoved—as were so many other British families. "We were all pretty fed up with the way the Royal Family was acting," Kate's grandmother Dorothy Goldsmith later recalled to a friend. Kate was no exception. "She didn't sound terribly sincere to me," she said at the time. "It's too little, too late."

Even those close to the Queen were surprised by her inability to grasp the magnitude of the tragedy. Within an hour of learning that Diana had died, she asked the British counsel general in Paris, Keith Moss, to find any royal jewels that Diana may have had among her things and return them to England immediately. "The Queen wants to know," Moss had told Beatrice Humbert, one of the nurses at the Paris hospital where Diana was taken, "where are the jewels?"

There were no royal jewels, and since she was no longer married, not even a wedding ring. But Her Majesty did not stop there. Since Diana had been stripped of her title after the divorce, the Queen turned down Charles's initial request for a royal jet to be dispatched to Paris to return the body to London. The Queen relented, but it would be far more difficult to convince her that Diana, who was no longer technically entitled to any special consideration, deserved a state funeral.

Bowing to the colossal weight of Diana's worldwide popularity, the Queen made a desperate eleventh-hour attempt to salvage what she could of the public's long-standing affection for the Crown. The ploy defused what was fast becoming a constitutional crisis, but the Middletons remained unmoved. "The Queen really doesn't get it, does she? None of them seem to get it," Kate told one of her classmates at Marlborough College, the elite $35,000-a-year coed boarding school she attended eighty miles west of London in Wiltshire. "The Royal Family is a pretty heartless bunch. But I feel so sorry for Prince William and Prince Harry."

Diana's boys were, in fact, the glue that seemed to be holding not only the monarchy but the entire nation together. The streets of central London teemed with more than 1.5 million people who had come to honor Diana's memory, but along the cortege route from Kensington Palace to Westminster Abbey, there was only the sound of muffled hoofbeats.

Flanking Diana's younger brother Earl Spencer, William, Harry, Prince Philip, and Prince Charles walked behind the caisson as it made its way through the eerily silent streets. Unbeknownst to Spencer, who objected to subjecting the boys to such an emotionally arduous ordeal, William and Harry had not asked to take part in the melancholy procession. Palace officials, with the Queen's blessing, had essentially ordered the boys to make the excruciating mile-long walk behind their mother's coffin, then "tricked" their uncle into believing that they had asked to participate. This was going "too far," said Spencer, whose eulogy for Diana at Westminster Abbey would constitute nothing less than a blistering attack on the Royal Family.

For most people lining the streets of London that day, the mere sight of Diana's boys walking slowly in the late-summer sun, their arms rigid at their sides, was almost unbearable. Most touching of all was solemn-faced twelve-year-old Harry, who seemed small and vulnerable as he tried to keep up with the long strides of the towering Windsor menfolk.

Sorrow was perhaps most evident on the face of William, who at fifteen seemed more man than boy. Walking with head down and hands clenched, his eyes glued to the ground directly in front of him, William looked up only for a moment outside Westminster Abbey—to shoot a withering look at photographers.

"He looks," Kate said as she watched the drama unfold on television, "so much like his mother." Blond and blue-eyed like Diana, William would soon grow to a full six foot three inches, which will eventually make him the tallest English monarch ever. (Henry VIII was six foot two.) Then there was the unmistakable downward tilt of the head followed by the upward glance that was at once guileless and seductive.

William was more than just a princely version of his celebrated mother, however. He brought a sense of dignity, calm, and courage to the equation at a time when the monarchy's popularity was at its nadir. As they had for years, polls were showing that a majority of the British people wanted William—not his father, Prince Charles—to succeed Elizabeth as king. Unfortunately for the Prince of Wales, that sentiment continued well into the twenty-first century.

By the time he marched behind the gun carriage bearing Princess Diana's body, William had already proven himself to be more
temperamentally suited to cope with the strain than any other
royal. Years before he faced the shock and anguish of his mother's
death, William had dealt with his parents' calamitous marriage—
and those lessons in forbearance began in the womb.

Diana was three months pregnant with William when, in a
jealous fit over her husband's long-term affair with the married
Camilla Parker Bowles, she hurled herself down the main staircase at Sandringham, the Queen's privately owned, twenty-
thousand-acre estate a hundred miles north of London in
Norfolk. The Queen herself came running and found Diana
sprawled on the marble floor at the foot of the stairs. Her mother-
in-law sent for Diana's physician, but it was left to the Queen's
sister, Princess Margaret, to help Diana to her feet. The Queen,
Diana later said, was "physically shaking, absolutely horrified. . . .
She was so frightened."

William's delivery was not easy. Diana was in labor for sixteen hours, but at 9:03 p.m. on June 21, she finally gave birth to
a seven-pound, one-and-a-half-ounce boy. William Arthur Philip
Louis Windsor was ushered into the world to the accompaniment
of thundering cannons, cathedral bells, and—in keeping with
centuries-old English custom—a town crier stationed outside
Buckingham Palace ringing a bell as he announced the birth of
the future king.

Charles and Diana were both besotted with their son, and for
a brief time it seemed as if they might be able to repair their damaged relationship. Since neither had experienced anything resem-
bling a happy childhood—Charles later described his mother as
"repressed" and his father as a sadistic bully; Diana's parents de-

spised each other—Charles and Diana doted shamelessly on their newborn. "We were all thrilled," Diana recalled of those first few weeks after bringing William home from London's St. Mary's Hospital. "Everyone was absolutely high as a kite."

Not for long. A passing comment by Charles when he put his arm around her waist during their engagement ("Oh, a bit chubby here, aren't we?") turned Diana into a full-fledged bulimic overnight. Now the princess, who stopped breast-feeding William at just three weeks so that she could resume losing weight, was back to making herself vomit daily.

Coupled with a case of full-blown postpartum depression, Diana's binge-and-purge cycle "threw off my hormones completely," she later said. "I was a total wreck." The mood swings reached epic proportions—"There would be crying, sobbing, wailing for two or three hours" at a time, recalled her friend Lord Palumbo—further fueling despair over her husband's infidelity. Moreover, Diana rightly believed that the powers that be at Buckingham Palace—the faceless "Men in Gray," she called them—were convinced she was mentally unbalanced and a danger to the monarchy. "Crazy as they come—damaged goods," Diana told her close friend Lady Elsa Bowker at the time. "That's me."

For Diana, who routinely upstaged her husband and the rest of the royals with her dazzling style and undeniable human touch, this meant being subjected to a battery of psychiatric examinations leading to heavy medication, including large doses of Valium. If anything, palace attempts at taming the vexsome princess only made things worse. "She was not about to just shut up and go along," Palumbo said. "Not Diana."

Upset by the way she was shunned by her in-laws at William's christening, Diana washed down a handful of pills with a half bottle of Scotch. After she was rushed by ambulance to the hospital and had her stomach pumped—an event that was incredibly, magically kept out of the press—a remorseful Diana vowed that she would never again jeopardize William's future by attempting to take her life.

Self-abuse was another matter. Before William reached the age of seven, Diana had at different times used a razor to slash her wrists, cut herself by intentionally running headlong into a glass display cabinet, inflicted deep gashes on her arm with a lemon peeler, and plunged a pocketknife into her own chest.

Diana felt she was being "scrutinized, analyzed, criticized" round the clock. The result, she told Lady Bowker, was "tears, panic"—the feeling that she was "sinking into this black hole."

Just four months after William's birth, Diana struck back at her husband by embarking on a scandalous extramarital affair of her own. Diana later insisted that she had not met Captain James Hewitt, the dashing cavalry officer who became her sons' riding instructor, until 1986. But in a startling 2005 interview conducted under hypnosis, Hewitt confessed that they had in fact met at a polo match in June of 1981, six weeks before she married Charles. They kissed a few days later, but did not actually consummate the relationship until four months after William was born.

Although the affair with Hewitt—which he later described in the tell-all book *Princess in Love*—lasted almost nine years, it did little to assuage Diana's anger. She continued to eavesdrop on Charles's furtive phone conversations with Camilla, and the atmosphere inside Kensington Palace grew increasingly toxic. "There was so much anger, so much screaming and door-slamming," royal housekeeper Wendy Berry said. "At times, it was sheer bedlam."

Diana worried about the effect all this was having on her impressionable toddler. William, she later conceded, "must have felt the tension even then."

If he did, he showed no sign of it at the time. Happy and outgoing, William was just nine months old when he accompanied his parents on a six-week tour of Australia and New Zealand. During a packed press conference in Auckland, New Zealand, television cameras captured the moment when William—already dubbed Wombat by Diana—stood on his own two feet for the first time. "You could see that Charles and Diana were just as surprised and delighted as the rest of us," said a reporter who was there. "They seemed to be just about as happy a little family as you could possibly imagine. Of course, at the time none of us had any idea about all that other stuff that was going on."

The tour was such a huge success that, less than a month later, Charles and Diana were dragooned into a two-week tour of Canada—this time sans William. Sadly, William was left behind at Kensington Palace to celebrate his first birthday with his nanny, Barbara Barnes. "William won't care," Charles reassured his wife. "He's too young to know the difference." But Diana suffered "guilt—tons of it" at the thought of not being there to watch William try to blow out his first birthday candle.

By the time they flew back from Canada, Wombat was already showing signs of becoming, in Diana's words, "a holy terror—dashing about, bumping into tables and lamps, breaking everything in sight." Before long, the prince exhibited a knack for trying to flush various personal items—his mother's toothbrush, his father's shoes—down the toilet, sliding down banisters, climbing up bookcases, and venturing out onto window ledges. While visiting his grandparents at Balmoral Castle in the Scottish highlands, William tripped an alarm that resulted in bodyguards racing to the royal quarters, weapons drawn.

Their son's antics provided some comic relief at home, but not enough to mask the mounting tension between Charles and Diana. Publicly, they maintained a sufficiently convincing facade, but at Kensington Palace they were living separate lives under the same roof. "The only words they exchanged," Lady Bowker said, "were angry ones."

It was then, Diana said coyly, that she found herself pregnant again "as if by a miracle." Tellingly, Hewitt was the first person she shared the news with outside the Royal Family. Her tone, Hewitt said, was both "anxious" and "matter-of-fact." He later confessed that he got the sense that Diana was "stopping short of saying more."

Once again, all England welcomed the arrival of the new prince, six-pound, fourteen-ounce Henry Charles Albert David, on September 15, 1984. But Charles was anything but pleased; he had wanted a girl, and for some reason Harry's coloring disturbed him. Later, at Harry's christening in Windsor Castle, Charles grumbled about the infant's "rusty" hair—a comment that clearly annoyed Diana's mother, Frances Shand Kydd. "You should just be thankful," she snapped, "that you had a child that was normal."

Charles's initial reaction to Harry's birth could only be explained by the fact that Diana and her husband had been at war with each other for more than a year. Opportunities for intimacy were, she conceded to Lady Bowker, "limited." At the time, Bowker said, "I took her to mean nonexistent."

Over the years, as Harry's physical resemblance to James Hewitt became more and more pronounced and the timeline of their affair changed dramatically, there would be rampant speculation about Harry's paternity. But for now, "the Heir and the Spare," as the tabloids promptly dubbed William and Harry, rounded out what appeared to be the perfect nuclear family.

Charles in time came to be as affectionate and caring a father to Harry as he was to William. But immediately after Harry's birth, the behind-the-scenes battles between Mummy and Papa resumed with a new ferocity. Coupled with the sudden appearance on the scene of a sibling rival, the pressures on William began taking their toll. No longer was he simply a mischievous scamp running circles around the archbishop of Canterbury and barking like a dog; William was now karate-chopping his mother, kicking the servants, and throwing cringe-making tantrums in public. Worst of all, by the age of four he was all too aware of where he stood in the royal pecking order. "You'll be sorry!" he would tell his exasperated nanny whenever she scolded him for breaking a Staffordshire figure or careering down the wide corridors of Kensington Palace screaming at the top of his lungs. "No one tells *me* what to do! When I'm king, I will have you punished!"

The Queen, Prince Philip, and Charles were not amused. Although Diana joked about Wombat's talent for wreaking mayhem—she called him "my mini-tornado" and "the Basher"—she was mortified by his bratty antics and the headlines (THE BASHER STRIKES AGAIN! WILLIAM THE TERRIBLE GOES BERSERK!) they inevitably provoked.

Diana had already gone to Buckingham Palace and begged "Mama"—the name the Queen had decided was most appropriate for her grown children and their spouses to use—for help in repairing her marriage. Even after Diana collapsed in the royal study and, in Mama's words, "cried nonstop," the Queen insisted she was powerless to get rid of Camilla. Now, in addition to appearing emotionally unstable, Diana worried that she would be portrayed as an unfit mother.

"William was obviously hurting," Berry said. "If your parents are going at it tooth and nail, you're going to act out in some way. William was angry and hurt, and that's how he coped with it." Lady Bowker agreed, "Children sometimes lash out when they are confused about things."

Convinced that William needed to interact with other children, Diana bucked centuries of tradition and rejected the notion that he should be educated by a governess inside the walls of Buckingham Palace. Instead, she enrolled him in Mrs. Mynor's Nursery School, in a terraced Victorian house in London's multiracial Notting Hill district.

As would be the case for the remainder of his life, William was accompanied each day by an armed security detail. While one bodyguard waited outside in the hallway, another sat in the back of the classroom, trying to be inconspicuous in a classroom full of preschoolers.

William's behavior at Mrs. Mynor's continued to raise eyebrows, even among his bodyguards. Quickly proving the tabloid headlines to be accurate, William routinely picked fights with other children and refused to take part in any activity that didn't interest him. He clenched his teeth and put up fists to any teacher courageous enough to try to discipline him. "He was always threatening to have us sent to the Tower," said one. "Either that or just executed by one of his bodyguards. Charming."

Nanny Barnes, who actually spent more time with William and Harry than either of their overscheduled parents did, would have none of it. She brushed aside all criticism of the princes, preferring to characterize them as simply "high-spirited" and "full of fun." When Prince Philip suggested that perhaps a new nanny would be able to tame William, Diana, who was also wary of anyone becoming too close to her boys, took his advice.

The new nanny—this time armed with the authority to spank the Basher—had little effect. William upheld his reputation as Britain's flesh-and-blood answer to Dennis the Menace with more tantrums, schoolyard tussles, and threats to have bodily harm done to the teaching staff. As king, William began telling anyone who would listen, he would have the power to have his knights "do anything I want them to—like killing *you*." In the fall of 1987 William departed for Wetherby, a prekindergarten school at Notting Hill Gate that was even closer to Kensington Palace. Mrs. Mynor and her teaching staff breathed a collective sigh of relief—until they were told that Harry would be replacing his older brother at the nursery school.

At Wetherby, Wills continued to run roughshod over children and adults alike. If he didn't like what was being served for lunch—and frequently he didn't—the prince screamed and threw his plate on the floor. If he raised his hand and wasn't called on first, he stormed out of the classroom. "I wanted to put him over my knee and spank the hell out of him," one of his protection officers said. "We all did. And I think that's probably what he was asking for someone to do—care enough to set some limits, you know? He was wild, uncontrollable."

The one person who did have the power to spank the boys, the new nanny, Ruth Wallace, did not hesitate to use it. Particularly unacceptable to "Nanny Roof" was William's high-handed manner with the staff. The prince, perhaps taking his cue from his notoriously curt father, showed outright contempt for many of the men and women who had served the Royal Family for years, even decades. She asked him to think about how it felt when someone hurt his feelings, then asked him to think about what others felt when he treated them badly. It was then, Diana said, "that a bulb went off in his head. Oh, other people have feelings, too!"

Wetherby's teachers never touched William, but they did what they could to turn the prince's behavior around. They punished William with verbal reprimands, time-outs, and—worst of all—banishment from his favorite games.

Just as often, they found themselves struggling to contain their laughter. After he turned six, William decided it was time to settle down. When five-year-old Eleanor Newton burst into tears, they asked what it was the prince had said to make the little girl so upset. "If you don't marry me," he had told her, "I'll put you in jail."

Nevertheless, by Christmas 1987 there was a noticeable change in William. Suddenly he was a mannerly young gentleman, saying please and thank you, extending his hand to introduce himself, and even rushing to open doors for others. "I think it was the whole idea of just being kind that appealed to him the most," Nanny Roof once explained. "Having good manners, being well behaved, is a way of being kind to others." Wallace's ace in the hole was William's own mother. "She was an excellent example, really. She went out of her way to be kind to average people, those who were less fortunate." According to Elsa Bowker, Diana had always "wanted the Royal Family to be human. There was no kindness there, and she was a kind person."

Diana was also irrepressibly mischievous, and William inherited that quality, too. He ambushed his mother, Prince Charles, and even the Queen with his squirt gun, pinched the backsides of titled ladies and chambermaids alike just to get a laugh (a practice that ended when the mother of a schoolmate found it anything but funny), and dropped water balloons from palace balconies.

At Highgrove, he careened around the grounds on his bicycle or a skateboard, climbed so high up in trees that he had to be rescued by the local fire department, and totaled his miniature Jaguar XJS cabriolet—a birthday present from the manufacturer.

While his city-loving mother disliked the countryside in general and horses in particular, Wills—a Windsor to the core—seemed, Charles observed, as if he had been "born in the saddle." By the time he was six, he not only was able to ride his pony, Trigger, bareback—he could do it standing up.

The Queen, who began riding at about the same age and would continue riding well into her eighties, was willing to look the other way when her grandson risked his neck on horseback. So was the Prince of Wales, who, ignoring Diana's objections, often took both boys to watch him compete in polo matches.

Indeed, Charles's connection to the boys seemed strongest when he was roughhousing with them on the floor—Papa played the title role in their wrestling game called Big Bad Wolf—or indoctrinating them in the rural pursuits that had defined the Royal Family for centuries. Shooting parties at Sandringham, fishing at Balmoral, foxhunting in the hills and valleys surrounding Highgrove—over the years these are some of the most important memories Charles created with his sons.

As much as she hated "killing things," Diana did nothing to stand in the way of William partaking in his royal heritage. After all, as a member of one of England's oldest and most noble families, the former Lady Diana Spencer was "blooded" at thirteen when she shot her first stag at the fourteen-thousand-acre family estate, Althorp.

It was one of the few areas in which Diana was willing to cede ground to her husband. She taught William and Harry to swim at Buckingham Palace's indoor pool ("William is more like a fish," Diana boasted) and made certain they sampled the everyday joys of modern childhood. She took them to McDonald's and her favorite, Kentucky Fried Chicken, as well as to local multiplexes, go-cart tracks, amusement parks, and street fairs.

These outings were also part of Diana's calculated, ongoing effort to expose her children to the lives of average people. Later, when they were better equipped to handle it, she would also take them to children's hospitals, homeless shelters, residences for the severely retarded, AIDS clinics, and drug rehabilitation centers. Unlike Charles and the other royals, William and Harry would, Diana promised, start their lives having "some idea of what's really going on out there."

They would also, she reasoned, be better equipped to deal with Buckingham Palace's "Men in Gray," who were already attempting to control every facet of their lives. The princes, Diana promised, "will be properly prepared. I am making sure of this. I don't want them suffering the way I did."

For the time being, William and Harry reveled in the company of each parent—as long as the other wasn't around. When they all found themselves under the same roof at Kensington Palace or Highgrove, Diana invariably locked herself in her room.

On those inevitable occasions when Charles and Diana did come face-to-face, a shouting match invariably ensued. Highgrove housekeeper Wendy Berry remembered that slamming doors and epithets screamed at the tops of royal lungs were "standard fare."

During one particularly memorable confrontation, Charles's valet, Ken Stronach, stood gape-mouthed on a second-floor landing as Diana pursued her husband from one room to another, berating him for his affair with Camilla. Finally, the Prince of Wales turned and yelled, "How dare you talk to me like that? Do you know who I am?"

"You," Diana shot back, "are a fucking animal!"

She stormed off, and Charles, red-faced with rage, hurled his riding boot across the room.

Such moments of high drama left Stronach and the rest of the household staff reeling—none more so than Jessie Webb, the plainspoken Cockney brought in to replace Ruth Wallace as nanny in July of 1990. "Those boys are going to need a lot of help," she said, "if they're not going to end up as barking mad as their dad and mum."

Things only got worse when, in September 1990, William left home for Ludgrove, an elite boarding school located thirty-five miles west of London in the Berkshire town of Wokingham. Diana made no effort to conceal that she missed her son "desperately" and was furious that Charles seemed to take it all in stride.

The public at large remained blissfully unaware of the take-no-prisoners warfare being waged between the Prince and Princess of Wales. That would begin to change in June 1991 when one of William's Ludgrove classmates was absentmindedly swinging a golf club over his head and accidentally struck the prince hard above the left eye.

Knocked cold and with blood gushing from the head wound, William was rushed to Royal Berkshire Hospital, then transferred to the Great Ormond Street Hospital in London to be examined by specialists. Worried about bone fragments, infection, and the possibility that William might have sustained brain damage, doctors wanted to operate immediately.

The surgery lasted seventy-five minutes, and Diana remained camped out until her son regained consciousness hours later.

However, Charles, who had rushed to London from Highgrove when he was told of the accident, saw no reason to stick around. Instead, he followed Camilla's advice and proceeded with plans to attend a performance of the opera *Tosca* at Covent Garden.

Diana had always believed Charles, like the rest of his family, lacked "a real soul. . . . They are cold, heartless robots. . . . There wasn't," she added, "a drop of humanity in that family before I arrived. . . . Not a single drop." Now she had the proof, and Fleet Street was happy to run with it. WHAT KIND OF DAD ARE YOU? shouted one *Sun* headline. "What sort of father," Jean Rook wrote in the *Daily Express*, "leaves the hospital before knowing the outcome for a night at the opera?"

Diana's allies quickly rallied to her side. In stark contrast to her husband's offhand response, said her friend James Gilbey, the princess had reacted to her son's injury with "horror and disbelief." Charles's actions, on the other hand, were "inexplicable."

In truth, Highgrove housekeeper Wendy Berry said Charles was "white with shock" when the call came that William had been injured. While much was made of Diana's bolting from her luncheon engagement in London and speeding to the hospital behind the wheel of her racing green Jaguar, no one reported at the time that Charles had also raced to the hospital in his blue Aston Martin sports car. Nor was it reported that, right up until William was wheeled into the operating room, both Charles and Diana had walked alongside their son's gurney, reassuring him that things would turn out fine.

No matter. Although she well knew that Charles had a close and loving relationship with his sons, Diana reveled in yet another public-relations victory over her husband. In their ongoing war to prove who was the better parent, she was clearly winning.

Crushed, Charles retreated to Highgrove and the one person

who understood him—Camilla. Mrs. Parker Bowles—known to the Prince of Wales's staff as "Mrs. P.B." (and to Diana as "the Rottweiler")—was a fixture at Highgrove whenever Diana wasn't in residence. Camilla was given a guest room, but after Charles had turned off the security system's motion detectors, she would slip into his bedroom for the night. It was the job of the prince's valet, Ken Stronach, to mess up the bed in the guest room ("but just one side") to make it appear as if she had been sleeping there.

Diana—Camilla called her Barbie—and the boys were never informed of Mrs. P.B.'s presence at Highgrove. All telltale signs—any cigarette butts the chain-smoking Camilla might have left in ashtrays, lipstick-stained glassware, the framed photo of Camilla sitting on a bench at Balmoral Castle—were all whisked away the moment Camilla departed. Much the same routine was followed at Middlewick House, the Parker Bowles family estate just fifteen minutes up the road from Highgrove—only this time Camilla's servants were told to do whatever it took to hide any traces of Charles's frequent overnight visits to Camilla's room. Since he always arrived after dusk and departed before dawn, Camilla's staff referred to Charles as "the Prince of Darkness."

According to Berry, Stronach, and others, Camilla was a calming influence. Diana, Camilla told Charles, was "a magician" when it came to manipulating the media. "She is unstable, darling. It's very sad really that she has to play these games. Pathetic."

Just two days later, William was released from Great Ormond Street Hospital. Even though it took another seven weeks for him to fully recover, William was as much concerned with his mother's well-being as she was with his. "You look so tired, Mummy," he said as they cuddled together in the backseat of their chauffeured Bentley. "Are you sure you're all right?"

William was already his mercurial mother's chief protector,

comforter, and soul mate. When Diana sank into one of her in-creasingly frequent black moods, Wills would bring a box of her favorite chocolates or announce that he had made a reservation at her favorite London restaurant, San Lorenzo. "They had," ob-served model Cindy Crawford, who had become a friend to both the princess and William, "an unspoken language."

Only a few months before his accident, during one of his par-ents' customary high-decibel quarrels at Highgrove, Diana ran upstairs and locked herself in a bathroom. As she looked down, she realized William was slipping some tissues under the door. "Mummy?" he whispered. "I hate to see you sad."

William also hated to see the effect all this bedlam was having on his little brother. "William and Harry had always leaned on each other when their parents fought," a former maid at High-grove recalled. "William was always telling Harry that mummies and daddies fought all the time, and that it didn't mean they didn't love each other."

By the time Diana and Charles grudgingly agreed to mark their tenth anniversary cruising the Mediterranean aboard Greek billionaire John Latsis's cruise-ship-size yacht, *Alexander*—a trip that was trumpeted by the Prince of Wales's handlers inside St. James's Palace as their "second honeymoon"—the marriage was irretrievably broken.

At times, said Elsa Bowker, it seemed "as if William had the weight of the world on his little shoulders. He became more quiet—far too quiet for a nine-year-old. For the first time, you could see suspicion in his eyes when he looked at people." More than anyone else, it was Diana who worried about the boy she called her "deep thinker" and "a very old soul." She told her friend Carolyn Bartholomew that she saw a great deal of herself in William. According to another friend, Richard Greene, Diana "felt that William was a male version of her. . . . She liked to say, 'We are like two peas in a pod. He feels everything too much. William is a very sensitive soul. He needs to be protected.' "

Sadly, Diana's actions in the coming months would only add to William's already crushing emotional burden. "Desperate" to make her case directly to the British people, she dictated her innermost thoughts and frustrations into a tape recorder, then had the tapes smuggled to journalist Andrew Morton through a mutual friend, Dr. James Colthurst.

While Diana plotted secretly to get out her side of the story, the marriage of Prince Andrew and Sarah Ferguson was disintegrating amidst rumors of infidelity. This was just the latest in a steady stream of criticisms aimed squarely at Diana's close friend and fellow long-suffering royal in-law. Americans may have been charmed by the decidedly down-to-earth Duchess of York, but even before she married Andrew in 1986, the press was hammering her over everything from her weight (she was cruelly dubbed the Duchess of Pork), her questionable fashion sense, and her spendthrift ways to her randy sense of humor.

Once photographs surfaced in early 1992 of Fergie living it up on the French Riviera with Texas oil heir Steve Wyatt, there seemed little recourse but for the couple to separate. Because she was still the mother of Princess Beatrice and Princess Eugenie, Fergie was not immediately cast out of the Royal Family. Months later, however, there would be new pictures—showing Fergie's "financial adviser" John Bryan sucking her toes while she sunbathed topless. This time, the Queen, who was hosting the entire family—including Fergie—at Balmoral, blasted her daughter-in-law.

"This is just unacceptable," the Queen said, shaking her head. "I mean, *really* . . ."

The ruckus over Fergie's high jinks paled in comparison to the uproar that ensued when Morton's *Diana: Her True Story* was published in the spring of 1992. Then, around the time Fergie's toe-sucking photos appeared, recordings of Diana's cell phone conversations with her friend James Gilbey were released. While Diana was mortified at the thought of people hearing her call Gilbey "Squidgy"—her pet name for him—it could scarcely compare to what lay in store for Charles.

Several months later, "Squidgygate" would be all but forgotten after tapes of a lewd cell phone chat between the Prince of Wales and Camilla Parker Bowles came to light. Most memorably, Charles expressed the desire to be reincarnated as one of Camilla's tampons:

CHARLES: Oh, God, I'd just live inside your trousers or something. It would be much easier!

CAMILLA (laughing): What are you going to turn into? A pair of knickers? Oh, you're going to come back as a pair of knickers?

CHARLES: Or, God forbid, a Tampax. Just my luck!

CAMILLA: You are a complete idiot! Oh, what a wonderful idea.

That fall, William was joined by Harry at Ludgrove while speculation raged about the future of their parents' marriage. From the moment William had arrived, Ludgrove's headmaster, Gerald Barber, had taken a fatherly interest in the prince. Now he took steps to make sure that both boys were insulated from the torrent of stories about Mummy and Papa. "Anyone visiting the school at that time would have noticed that there were no newspapers, magazines, radios, or television sets anywhere—not even in the headmaster's office," said a Ludgrove teacher. "Mr. Barber didn't want Prince William or Prince Harry to see something that might upset or concern them. None of us did."

William's personal protection officer, the curiously named Graham Craker, was also asked not to leave any publications where the boys might see them. But that didn't stop William from sneaking into Craker's room and grabbing a look at the *Sun*, the *News of the World*, or the *Daily Mail*.

While eight-year-old Harry was too young to fully understand what was going on, his precocious older brother—the one Diana called "my little old wise man"—was devastated by what he read and by what he overheard. Yet when Diana made her daily call to Ludgrove to check up on him, William was careful to put on a brave face. "I think that he was very concerned that he not add to his parents' problems," said an assistant matron at the school. "Prince William also did not want to upset Harry. He was very much the protective older brother."

Each day, William assured his mother that he and Harry were doing fine. "It is heartbreaking," Diana told Carolyn Bartholomew. "William has such a kind heart. I sometimes wonder which one of us is the adult and which one is the child."

To his credit, Charles also fretted about what effect all this was having on his sons. "I am terribly worried about how the quarreling will affect them," he told his friend and former paramour Janet Jenkins. "I want them to remember that I was not the one doing all the shouting and screaming."

Still, it was Charles, angry over what he saw as Diana's "incessant game-playing," who asked for a legal separation. In the head-master's office at Ludgrove, Diana warned her sons that a formal announcement would soon be made.

William asked point-blank if "the other lady" was to blame for the breakup.

"Well," Diana answered, "there were three of us in this marriage, and all the stories in the newspapers and on television—the two together made it very difficult. But, I still love Papa. I still love him, but we just can't live together under the same roof."

Harry sat silently, but William started crying. Then, when he had composed himself, he kissed his mother and said, "I hope you'll both be happier now."

William was not alone in his feeling of helplessness. In addition to watching the marriages of Charles and Andrew go up in flames, Granny could only watch as her beloved Windsor Castle was gutted by fire. It was the year she later proclaimed to be a true annus horribilis.

On December 9, 1992, Prime Minister John Major formally announced the separation of the Prince and Princess of Wales from the floor of the House of Commons. The statement, written by senior members of Her Majesty's staff, emphasized that the decision had "been reached amicably, and they will both continue to participate fully in the upbringing of their children. The Queen and the Duke of Edinburgh, though saddened, understand and sympathize with the difficulties that have led to this decision." Moreover, the Queen and Prince Philip hoped "the intrusions into the privacy" of Charles and Diana "may now cease. They believe that a degree of privacy and understanding is essential if Their Royal Highnesses are to provide a happy and secure upbringing for their children."

From this point on, when they weren't away at school, the boys divided their time between two enemy camps. At Kensington Palace, Diana doted shamelessly on "ma boys," as she jokingly referred to the princes in her version of an antebellum drawl, allowing them to spend hours in front of the television set, zip around the grounds on their BMX bikes, or chase each other down portrait-lined hallways and through chandeliered drawing rooms waving rubber swords. Althorp, the Spencers' baronial five-hundred-year-old ancestral estate, was equally kid-friendly. Diana's notoriously fun-loving brother—dubbed Champagne Charlie by the press—encouraged the boys to slide down Althorp's grand staircase on eighteenth-century silver tea trays fetched from the pantry.

Life with Charles was, predictably, a more staid affair. At Sandringham that first Christmas after the separation was announced, William was soon duly impressed by the abject deference shown to Granny. Not only did admirals and cabinet members and even the prime minister seem awed by her presence, but even Grandpapa—Prince Philip—was careful to always walk two steps behind his wife. "William took it all in," Diana once observed. "He always wanted to do the right thing—not to add to the turmoil around him." Soon, like the rest of the Windsor menfolk, he held back and then bowed slightly whenever Granny walked up to him.

While Diana maintained considerable respect—even affection—for "Top Lady," as she called the Queen, she also reminded William that he could trace his Spencer ancestors back nearly a thousand years, while the Windsors were "scarcely English at all." Contemptuous of their Teutonic roots—the ruling Wettins had changed their name to the more British-sounding

Windsor during World War I—Diana called her in-laws "the Germans." She matter-of-factly referred to the Corfu-born Duke of Edinburgh, a member of both the Danish and Greek royal houses, as "Stavros," while the nickname she reserved for Charles had nothing to do with his ancestry but everything to do with the hopelessness of his position. Even in the presence of William and Harry, she called middle-aged Papa "the Boy Wonder."

Not every waking moment spent with Papa's side of the family was devoted to protocol—far from it. Although Prince Philip had shown little interest in his own children when they were young, he doted on William and Harry. At Sandringham, Grandpapa took the boys shooting pheasant and grouse, while Charles took care to teach them the finer points of fly-fishing for salmon and sea trout on the river Dee at Balmoral. Although Charles still took care not to have Camilla present when the boys were visiting, Highgrove remained a sanctuary for the boys, who could ride their go-carts and their ponies away from the prying lenses of the paparazzi.

Diana, however, was determined that her sons not think of Highgrove as their base. "I want them to know Kensington Palace is their home," she stated, "and not a public building."

Perhaps. But "KP," as Diana called the imposing three-story, twenty-eight-room Georgian brick structure that had once been home to William III, was located in the heart of London. Even though it abutted 274 acres of lush city parkland, the palace afforded little privacy for William and Harry. Whenever they left the palace grounds, a small army of photographers camped at the ornate iron gates swarmed their car. Already convinced that the press was largely responsible for breaking up his parents' marriage, William now resented them even more for pushing his mother to the brink of an emotional breakdown. "Mummy cries all the time," William told one of his teachers at Ludgrove. "She says the reporters are making her life unbearable."

Diana, who now told her closest friends that she was intent on seeing her son—not Charles—crowned the next monarch, might have taken some solace in polls conducted by the *Sunday Times*, the *Daily Mail*, and other publications showing a majority of Britons wanted just that.

Diana had other reasons for wanting to make sure her son was prepared to become king. Just as she was convinced she would never become queen, the Princess of Wales heeded her astrologer's prediction that Charles would die before his mother. Unlike recent English monarchs, King William V would, Diana promised, "lead from the heart—not the head."

In the meantime, William would have to learn not only how to cope with the media, but how to use it to his advantage. Ultimately, Diana hoped that William would be able to follow the example set by another famous prince—or at least America's version of one. "I'm hoping he'll grow up to be as smart about it as John Kennedy Jr.," she said. "I want William to be able to handle things as well as John does." To accomplish this, she would have to follow in the footsteps of John's mother. "Jackie has done such a brilliant job raising Caroline and John. I want to emulate her as a mother."

Both women were shrewd in their handling of the press, certainly. But where Jackie dealt with the pressures of celebrity without ever burdening her children, Diana continued to lean heavily on William for support.

"Diana told Prince William in particular more things than most mothers would have told their children," recalled Rosa Monckton, one of her closest friends. Diana, insisted Monckton, "had no choice." Mummy wanted William to know "the truth from her about her life and the people she was seeing, and what they meant to her, rather than read a distorted, exaggerated, and frequently untrue version in the tabloid press."

On the weekends when he was home from school, William would patiently sit while Mummy used up entire boxes of tissues as she talked about her unfair treatment at the hands of the Royal Family and the Palace's Men in Gray, Papa's allegiance to Camilla, the "mad dogs" of the press who stalked Diana without letup, and her exhausting public schedule of state functions, charity events, and "walkabouts"—the endless round of hospital visits, ribbon-cuttings, unveilings, and groundbreakings that fill up the calendars of every Royal Family member.

William also got to hear all about Mummy's newfound obsession with spiritualism, including her forays into reflexology, aromatherapy, homeopathy, astrology, herbal medicine, crystals, pyramids, magnets, hypnotherapy, acupuncture, feng shui, and colonic irrigation.

Detailed descriptions of her bowel habits notwithstanding, the most disturbing—and potentially traumatizing—secrets Mummy shared with her son dealt with the men in her life. While she continued to conceal her ongoing, torrid affair with James Hewitt from William, Diana had no qualms about discussing the other men who drifted in and out of her life—and sometimes into the headlines.

"William's role was more that of alternative husband than son," Richard Greene said. "It was a heavy burden for anyone, but especially someone so young."

Diana was acutely aware of the strain she was putting on her elder son. "She was always saying William was like someone from another planet," recalled Debbie Frank, Diana's astrologer and friend. "She valued his opinion. She trusted him to know what to do."

Caroline Bartholomew could see why. Even at that age, William was "intuitive, switched on, highly perceptive . . . and kindhearted, very much like Diana."

By late 1993, William's mother was widely regarded as the globe's most high-profile humanitarian—not far behind her friend and admirer Mother Teresa. Although still unchallenged as the world's leading fashion and style icon, the princess was now just as famous for her work with AIDS patients, domestic-violence victims, cancer-stricken children, and the homeless.

William had learned much from his mother about connecting with people. "When I cup my hands around the face of someone suffering," she told him, "they are comforting me as much as I am comforting them."

With a compliant Harry in tow, William occasionally accompanied his mother on her walkabouts, smiling at strangers, shaking their hands, asking them questions, and listening intently to their answers. William was fast becoming a pro at charming the man in the street—a talent neither his father nor his grandmother possessed. According to Diana's private secretary P. D. Jephson, "it wasn't just that Prince William *seemed* to enjoy his contact with all those people lining the streets. He genuinely did."

Nevertheless, when it looked as if his mother was about to crack under the strain, William urged her to step out of the public spotlight—at least for a little while. Once again, William could point to the press—and an unscrupulous gym owner—as the cause of Mummy's misery. In November 1993, less than tasteful photos ("horrid, simply horrid") taken by a hidden camera at

Diana's gym were splashed across the front page of the *Sunday Mirror*. This time, Diana sued and won a large judgment in the form of a hefty donation to one of her favorite charities.

A few weeks later, with William's blessing, Diana choked back tears as she formally announced that she was "withdrawing from public life" so she could give her sons all "the love, care, and attention" they deserved. In truth, she was simply cutting back on her public schedule and the number of charities she would support—albeit dramatically.

For all the inherent drama in Diana's announcement, her life changed little. The time she could spend with her boys was circumscribed by their boarding school schedule and the arrangement she had with Charles to share time with them on alternate weekends. Each Sunday evening that she dropped the boys off at Ludgrove, Diana returned to KP and settled in with her customary box of tissues and "a good, long, blubbering cry."

To make matters worse, Camilla was no longer the principal focus of Diana's animosity; a new rival for her sons' affections had arrived in the form of their attractive new nanny, Alexandra "Tiggy" Legge-Bourke. Hired by Charles to be as much a companion to his sons as their caretaker, thirty-year-old Tiggy had many of the qualities that Diana despised. A boisterous, ruddy-cheeked, self-avowed tomboy, Legge-Bourke shared the Royal Family's love of fishing, hunting, hiking, and riding. She was a crack shot and could, marveled her friend Santa Palmer-Tomkinson, expertly "skin a rabbit or gut a stag."

Tiggy was far from an average servant—even by royal standards. The daughter of a merchant banker, she grew up at Glanusk Park, the family's six-thousand-acre ancestral estate in North Wales. She even graduated from the same boarding school Diana attended, the Institut Alpin Videmanette.

Perhaps because they recognized in Tiggy some of the qualities she shared with their mother—both women were young, beautiful, warm, athletic, and fun-loving—William and Harry were both smitten with her. It did not help that newspapers were now full of photos showing Tiggy and the princes roughhousing in the snow as they vacationed in the Swiss Alps or laughing on the sidelines at one of Papa's polo matches.

It did not take long for Diana to convince herself that the nanny was now in the throes of an affair with Charles. Because she was from the same social stratum as Diana, Tiggy was readily embraced by Charles's friends—many of whom she knew already. In Diana's mind, according to P. D. Jephson and others, this made her even more of a threat.

Diana peppered William with questions about Tiggy's behavior. Did Papa laugh when he was around her? Did they ever touch each other, ever hug or even kiss? Were they ever alone together? Once again, Wills was "caught in the cross fire between two people he loved," observed Richard Kay, the *Daily Mail* columnist who was one of Diana's closest confidants. "Imagine how skillful a diplomat he had to be—never taking sides, always trying to keep the peace."

William's talent for diplomacy would be sorely challenged shortly after his twelfth birthday, when Papa admitted in a June 29, 1994, BBC television interview that he had cheated on his wife. The interview, taped to promote his soon-to-released authorized biography, was intended to clear the air. But while the press and the public had been well aware of the Prince of Wales's relationship with Camilla Parker Bowles for years, actually coming clean to adultery before a national audience was an entirely different matter. "It was very rehearsed, not genuine-sounding at all," a reporter for the *Times* of London said. "It made everyone cringe. It's one thing to look the other way and pretend like we don't know it's happening, but you want the public to say, 'Sure, go right ahead, we don't mind.' Not bloody likely." Journalist Brian Hoey agreed. "In one stroke," he said, Charles had "wiped out" whatever popular support he had.

The next day commentators and columnists were questioning whether Charles now had the qualifications to become monarch, since in that capacity he would also be head of the Church of England. The *Daily Mirror* made no secret of where it stood. NOT FIT TO REIGN screamed the paper's front-page headline.

Diana could scarcely conceal her delight as she worked the crowd that evening at a gala charity event, but her taste of victory would be short-lived. That August, the spotlight shone on Diana's infidelities when it was disclosed that she had made hundreds of harassing phone calls to millionaire art dealer and married father of three Oliver Hoare. Two months later, a major bombshell exploded with the publication of Anna Pasternak's *Princess in Love*. In the book, Hewitt—whom William and Harry had always warmly regarded as something akin to a kindly uncle—recounted his scorching affair with the princess in graphic detail.

Alas, Hewitt was only one in a parade of lovers who would be trotted out in the coming months. Once she tired of Hoare, Diana moved on to rugby star Will Carling—only to have Carling's wife, Julia, a British television personality, publicly blame the princess for destroying her marriage. Then came British businessman Christopher Whalley, followed by Canadian rock star Bryan Adams and American multibillionaire Theodore ("Teddy") Forstmann.

Despite the best efforts of the Ludgrove headmaster, neither William nor Harry could be protected from the ensuing avalanche of headlines and broadcast news reports. Once again,

William, in trying to shield his brother, absorbed much of the psychological impact himself. "It was horrible for William, having to act like a little adult while the adults around him were acting like children," said Diana's friend Oonagh Toffolo. "He must have been close to the breaking point himself," Richard Greene agreed, "but he put up an awfully brave front."

Indeed. To both the casual observer and those closest to the princes, both William and Harry seemed unfazed by all the scandal and commotion. They were simply, said Toffolo, "two terribly sweet, well-mannered boys." Princess Alexandra's daughter Marina Mowatt agreed that it was "horrendous" for both little princes "having to shoulder the burden of their parents' actions."

The heaviest burden was shouldered behind closed doors, when Diana shared her innermost feelings about each paramour with William. According to her friends, each affair followed the same arc—giddy infatuation, passionate love, manic obsession, jealousy, and lastly a plunge into a black hole of depression. William, whose advice on these profound matters she actively sought, could only intently listen as Mummy poured out her heart to him.

"Can you imagine what this was teaching William about how men and women relate to each other?" asked one of the women Diana also turned to for advice. "All the cheating, the lying, the duplicity, the backstabbing—not to mention Diana's histrionics and then having it all wind up in the paper. Mind-boggling!"

Yet nothing prepared William for what Papa himself would say in the pages of *The Prince of Wales: A Biography*. In addition to claiming that his mother was aloof and uncaring and his father sadistic, Charles revealed that he had been forced by Prince Philip to marry Diana. Moreover, Charles insisted that he had never loved his wife.

"Imagine being told," Diana told her astrologer, Debbie Frank, "that your parents never loved each other." When she drove to Ludgrove to comfort the boys, William asked point-blank, "Is it true that Papa never loved you?"

Mummy reassured William and Harry that their parents did love each other in the beginning, but William was clearly not convinced. His eyes, she later said, "pierced my heart like a dagger."

The next day at Highgrove, William confronted his father. "Why, Papa?" asked William, choking back sobs. "Why did you do it?"

Notwithstanding the occasional outburst behind closed doors, to the outside world William still appeared to be a remarkably poised, outgoing, and even-tempered young gentleman. "Whatever the emotional scars being inflicted," said Richard Greene, "and they had to be pretty deep, William especially seemed to be a happy, well-adjusted kid."

He had also clearly inherited his mother's compassionate streak. After watching William interact with the homeless at the Passage day center in London, the Catholic primate of England, Cardinal Basil Hume, took Diana aside. "What an extraordinary child," he told her. "He has such dignity at such a young age."

Still, William had his decidedly undignified moments. When Diana caught William and a friend staring at a centerfold spread of Shane and Sia, *Playboy*'s busty Barbi twins, she snatched the magazine from their hands, ripped the pages in two, and gave each boy his own Barbi. "Mummy," William protested, "it was only the top halves we wanted."

Now that he was a bona fide adolescent, William also began to chafe under the control of his omnipresent bodyguards. Packing Heckler & Koch machine pistols in their shoulder holsters, William's royal protection detail virtually surrounded him whenever he left the relative security of home or school. The rest of the time, Sergeant Craker was always down the hall or in the next room—never more than a few steps away.

At Ludgrove, friends conspired to help William elude his protectors—at least so that he would have a few minutes to sneak his first cigarette or perhaps leaf through a few more copies of *Playboy*.

But when he began to vanish for up to an hour or more, Charles was asked by William's bodyguards to bring his son in line.

"I hate it, Papa," William said. "Why can't I have any time to myself? Why can't I just be treated like a normal person—just once?"

William's resentment of his minders and that he could never have anything approaching a normal life only grew in the coming years. It took a backseat, however, to his growing hatred of the press. "We only got in his way," said a member of the royal protection squad at Ludgrove whose job was to sit at the back of every class the prince attended and pretend to be invisible. "But he felt the press had destroyed his family and making his mother in particular miserable."

With Mummy and Papa looking over his shoulder, William enrolled at the world's most prestigious prep school—Eton—on September 6, 1995. History, George Orwell wrote, was "decided on the playing fields of Eton"—a nod to the school's having been educating the sons of Europe's most powerful families for 555 years.

Diana was thrilled—her father and brother had both attended Eton, and it was just a half hour's drive from Kensington Palace. Charles, who had felt alone and abandoned during his boarding-school days in Scotland, was also pleased with Eton's more congenial atmosphere. "I want William to make friends at school—something I never managed to do," he told Camilla.

Not to worry. From the start, William was taken under the wing of upperclassmen Lord Freddie Windsor, son of Prince and Princess Michael of Kent, and his cousin Nicholas Knatchbull, a grandson of the late Lord Mountbatten of Burma and like William a great-great-great-great-grandson of Queen Victoria.

No one was more pleased than Granny. From the mullioned window of her bedchamber at Windsor Castle, she could see those famous playing fields of Eton just across the Thames. Her grandson performed spectacularly on them. A natural at rugby, sculling, and of course swimming (his warm-up jacket read w.o.w., for "William of Wales"), he also proved to be a standout at a sport no other member of the Royal Family had ever tried: water polo. William also excelled scholastically, something neither his maternal grandfather nor his uncle Earl Spencer had ever done at Eton.

The most important lessons he learned over the next five years were taught outside Eton's redbrick walls. Each Sunday afternoon, William, accompanied by two armed guards, made the seven-minute stroll past Lillie Langtry's Restaurant at the Christopher Hotel, the Hogs Head Inn, Murrays of Eton, and Nutters of Savile Row, across the 190-year-old stone-and-iron arched bridge that linked the villages of Eton and Windsor, then up the hill to the castle itself.

At precisely 4:00 p.m., Granny and the Heir would sit down for tea in the Oak Drawing Room, where the Queen would actually refill the pot herself from a massive Georgian silver kettle. For the next hour they discussed everything from world politics, rap music, and the outcome of soccer matches to Harry's performance at school, the antics of TV's Mr. Bean (a royal favorite), and the newest additions to her menagerie of corgis and racehorses.

Known to his fellow Etonians simply as Will Wales, the prince still had to contend with having a security officer—one of nineteen assigned to guard him at Eton—living in a room adjacent to his at Manor House, a four-story residence hall that housed fifty boys. But now he could freely mingle with the other thirteen hundred students who darted about the campus in their Edwardian-era Mr. Chips uniform of pinstripe trousers worn with a swallowtail coat.

William was flourishing at Eton, but, ever the caretaker, he fretted about how Harry was faring alone at Ludgrove. William had, after all, always been around to soften the blow whenever a new scandal involving Mummy and Papa made headlines. Wills needn't have worried. No longer eclipsed by his overachieving older brother, the Spare—a poorer student but an even better athlete than William—relished the attention. "It wasn't that he didn't like having his brother around," one of the teachers said. "But imagine how nice it must have felt to step out of his shadow into the sunshine."

William, meantime, was developing a healthy interest in the opposite sex. Eton prohibited posters of any kind to be hung in the boys' rooms—only the occasional landscape or print expressly approved by the housemaster. But, like all of his classmates, Will made up for that by papering the inside of his locker with steamy glossies of Pamela Anderson, supermodels Christie Brinkley and Claudia Schiffer, and—of course—the Barbi twins. By way of surprising her hormone-driven son, Mummy invited her son to tea at Kensington Palace without telling him they would be joined by his favorite pinup—Cindy Crawford. William was, understandably, stunned. "He's just like me," Diana explained to the supermodel. "When he runs out of things to say, he just blushes."

William had been at Eton for a little more than a month when he attended his first dance—the infamous Toffs' Ball in London. The revels invariably got out of control, and the next day's papers were filled with pictures of bleary-eyed heirs, heiresses, and even a few titled teens stumbling out of the club drunk and, in some cases, semiclothed.

Not surprisingly, when Wills showed up with several friends and two bodyguards, he was descended upon by a horde of scantily clad teenaged girls. He was an easy target to spot. Already nearly six feet tall and broad-shouldered, with a shock of blond hair that fell over his forehead like his mother's, the young prince easily stood a full head above the other one thousand partygoers.

Their faces etched with concern, the bodyguards spent the next two hours, said one, "peeling girls off him like you were peeling a banana. Some of them held on for dear life." Later, he confessed to Diana that plenty of girls had kissed him, but that he didn't kiss back. Once again, he complained, "the cameras are everywhere."

Unfortunately, the princes were blindsided yet again—this time by Mummy. At 8:00 p.m. on Monday, November 20, 1995, William sat in his headmaster's office alone and watched as his mother spilled out her anxieties, hopes, and most intimate secrets on BBC's top-rated *Panorama* series. The unsettling interview, secretly taped with Martin Bashir over a single three-hour session at Kensington Palace, was Diana's attempt to offset the Palace's ongoing attempt to portray her as psychotic. She had to go on the offensive, she explained, to counter the idea she was "sick" and should be "put in a home of some sort."

Exhibiting remarkable control, Diana spoke of her battles with bulimia, her suicidal depression, the disintegration of her marriage, the vendetta against her perpetrated by the nefarious "Men in Gray," and how—in her opinion—Charles was unworthy of the crown.

Diana also discussed Camilla and confessed to her affair with James Hewitt. "Yes, I adored him," she said. "Yes, I was in love with him." William, crushed, returned to his room and refused to take his mother's calls for the next four days.

In the meantime, Diana realized she had made a drastic miscalculation. Although polls taken after the *Panorama* interview showed that fully three-quarters of the British people now sided with Diana, the only Briton who really counted was aghast.

Just three weeks later, the Queen wrote both Diana and Charles ordering them to get a divorce. It was a devastating blow for Diana, who now realized that she had seriously overplayed her hand.

It took three months of haggling, but on February 28, 1996, a divorce settlement was finally reached. Diana would be permitted to remain at Kensington Palace with an annual allowance of $600,000 and would share custody of William and Harry with Charles. She would also be paid a lump sum of $22.5 million in cash.

Under the terms of the agreement, however, she would have to give up one of the things she cherished most. While Diana would henceforth be known as Diana, Princess of Wales, and still hold on to her lesser titles (Duchess of Cornwall, Duchess of Rothesay, Countess of Chester, Countess of Carick, Baroness Renfrew), she would no longer be referred to as Her Royal Highness.

Seeing that his mother was clearly upset by the loss of her HRH status, William tried to cheer her up. "I don't mind what you're called," he told her. "You're still Mummy." Besides, he told her, it was only a temporary problem. He would return her to the royal fold, William promised, "when I am king."

However fraught with emotion his parents' divorce might have been, William still gamely performed his role as Mummy's confidant in matters of the heart. For the first time, Diana told Wills that she had been seeing someone for months, and that she was deeply in love with him. Best of all, she had managed to keep their affair secret.

The unlikely object of his mother's affections was Dr. Hasnat Khan, a pudgy, chain-smoking Pakistani heart surgeon. Things had started to come into focus for William, who wondered why his mother had been photographed watching a heart operation in scrubs and a surgical mask. He and Harry had also been surprised by her seemingly spur-of-the-moment decision to fly to Pakistan—twice—and that she now spent hours each evening with her nose buried in the Koran.

Diana was so smitten with "Natty" Khan that on more than one occasion, wearing a dark wig and glasses, she drove her BMW to Royal Brompton Hospital, tossed a blanket over the doctor in the backseat, and smuggled him into Kensington Palace herself. Once, when she assigned the task to her longtime butler, Paul Burrell, she greeted Khan at the drawing room door wearing a mink coat, diamond earrings—and nothing else. She took to calling him Mr. Wonderful.

At one point, Diana asked William how he felt about his mother converting to Islam if that was what was required to marry Khan. "You have to do," he replied, "what makes you happy."

Khan, however, was not quite so compliant. He jealously guarded his privacy and was terrified by the notion of having his life become fodder for the tabloids. He was also consumed by his career and "had too big an ego," said one colleague, to ever take a backseat—figuratively as well as literally—to a woman. "Not even the most famous woman in the world."

When press reports of their romance began popping up, Khan accused Diana of leaking the items and called an end to the affair. On William's advice, Diana responded by playing the field and was soon photographed in the company of opera tenor Luciano Pavarotti and real estate tycoon Christopher Whalley, among others. Soon a contrite Khan was on the phone to Diana, begging for forgiveness.

Once again, William had proven his willingness to advise his mother on the most personal issues imaginable. He had also shown that, for whatever reasons, he seemed to know what he was talking about. "William was incredibly mature for his age," Diana's hairdresser Natalie Symonds said. "All his life he had had to navigate around all the drama just for his own emotional survival. So he could see things from a very level-headed, adult perspective."

Diana's love for Khan was so all-consuming that for the first time she began to see things from Camilla's perspective. "I finally understand what it means to find that someone who is everything to you," she told Symonds. "Once you've found that kind of love, you must hold on to it—no matter what or who gets in the way."

As comfortable as he may have been giving relationship advice to his mother, William was grappling with his own newfound status as a bona fide teen idol. Magazines that carried centerfold pullouts of the prince—albeit wearing a blazer or his Eton uniform of tails and striped pants—flew off the stands. The tabloids' new nickname for the Heir: Dreamboat Willie. Not to be outdone, Diana coined one of her own: DDG, for Drop-Dead Gorgeous. "The girls," Diana boasted of her son's obvious appeal, "will go mad for him!"

In the meantime, William continued to counsel his mother—and not just on affairs of the heart. Searching for ways to raise money for Diana's favorite charities, Wills suggested that she auction off some of her old dresses. The sale, held at Christie's in New York, wound up raising $3.26 million for the AIDS Crisis Trust and the Royal Marsden Hospital's Cancer Research Fund. "It was all William's idea," she told Christie's executives. "He is brilliant . . . three million for some old frocks!"

At about the same time, Kevin Costner called to offer her the lead in his planned sequel to *The Bodyguard*—this time as a princess who falls in love with her bodyguard. Although she had been a huge fan of the original—Diana saw much of herself in the vulnerable pop superstar played by Whitney Houston—Diana hesitated at what seemed to be, on its face, a ludicrous idea.

William urged her to do the film, pointing out that Costner had assured her that both the demands on her time and the acting skills required for the part were minimal. The salary, Wills pointed out, was anything but minimal: $10 million for just a few weeks' work—all of which would go to her favorite charities. "Mummy," he told her, "*Kevin Costner*. Ten *million* dollars. You have to do it!"

Once again, Diana followed her son's advice. She called Costner and told him to proceed with the script. "I'm doing this," she told Costner, "because William thinks it's a good idea."

As eager as he was to see Mummy take her life in exciting and unexpected directions, William was upset with some of the other risks she was taking. As part of a Red Cross effort to focus attention on the dangers of unexploded land mines, Diana donned a face guard and flak jacket to take a harrowing stroll through a minefield in Angola. Although Diana was paving the way for an agreement to ban land mines that would ultimately be signed by 127 countries, William begged her not to take any more unnecessary risks. "I don't blame them," Diana said. "If something happened to me, I can't imagine what would happen to my boys."

What Diana feared most was that she was already losing William and Harry to another woman—not Camilla, but the boys' nanny-cum–"surrogate mum," Tiggy Legge-Bourke. Diana had almost succeeded in getting rid of Tiggy a year earlier when, during the Prince and Princess of Wales's annual Christmas lunch, Diana sidled up to the nanny and said, "So sorry to hear about the baby." Undone by the obvious implication that she had become pregnant by Charles and undergone an abortion, Tiggy fled in tears. Through her solicitor, Tiggy demanded that the Princess of Wales tender an official apology for her "false allegations."

Still intent on removing Tiggy from the scene, Diana would have to wait until William's confirmation at Windsor in March 1997. When the names of several Spencer relatives did not show up on the guest list prepared by Tiggy, Diana lodged a complaint with Charles. Since relations between the Prince of Wales and Diana had improved markedly following the divorce, Charles sided with his ex-wife. By April, Tiggy was no longer the boys' nanny.

William took Tiggy's departure in stride. After all, Papa still included her among the guests invited to shoot and ride at Sandringham and Balmoral. But William, who had wisely kept his adolescent crush on Tiggy a secret from his jealous mother, was moving on to girls his own age.

Fearing that their presence would spark the inevitable media mob scene, William bluntly asked both Mummy and Papa not to attend Eton's annual parents' day festivities. Instead, he used the opportunity to do his own walkabouts, introducing himself to visiting families—particularly those who had brought their attractive teenage daughters along.

"Flirting seemed to come pretty naturally to him," said the mother of an Eton classmate. "The girls were absolutely euphoric, as you can imagine."

At various points along the way, William and his fellow Etonian Edward van Cutsem ducked into a hallway and quickly jotted down for future reference the names of the girls they had met. "At this point it's all raging hormones," Diana said. "Theirs and his."

In light of these latest developments, Diana got together with the chef at Kensington Palace to come up with an appropriate way to mark William's upcoming fifteenth birthday. On June 21, 1997, the birthday boy howled with laughter when Mummy rolled out a cake decorated with the likenesses of six nude centerfolds.

On a more serious note, Diana was now giving advice to William on what to look for in a girlfriend—and a wife. Since she had none of Charles's reluctance when it came to talking to her sons about sex, Diana sat the boys down to explain the facts of life when William was ten and Harry was eight (at the time Harry fled, but William stayed). Her work with AIDS patients had made Diana acutely aware of the dangers of unprotected sex—a message she now drove home to William.

On the broader question of what to look for in a long-term relationship, Diana pointed to—of all people—Charles and Camilla. "When you find a true, deep love like that, it's a precious thing," she told William. "You've got to hold on tight to it."

Nor did it matter if the person he fell in love with was from a royal background, Diana told William. "Not important," she said. "If she is the person you truly love, then that's all that matters."

Diana knew that she was the perfect example of someone who was chosen for her family background and breeding. Lady Diana Spencer belonged to one of England's oldest and most illustrious families. Now she worried that the Machiavellian Men in Gray were already lining up European princesses and other high-born English beauties as potential matches for the future king.

"Diana's marriage was the perfect example of how disastrous it can be to put social rank above love in selecting a mate," said *Burke's Peerage* publisher Harold Brooks-Baker. "But the logic is that it's tough being a royal and that it helps if you already know the ropes. This all grows out of alliances that were forged between the royal houses of Europe. This is the way they've been doing it for a thousand years."

To be sure, Charles was sharing his thoughts on the subject with William as well. According to a senior member of the prince's staff at St. James's Palace, Charles "expected his son to sow wild oats just the way he did." But as far as getting serious about a girl, "Prince Charles felt that anyone William wanted to marry would have to be a person of substance and breeding. Not necessarily someone with a title, but of course the Queen and Prince Philip were holding out for that."

At this stage, Charles and Diana were on friendlier terms than they'd been in years—in large part because they spoke about the boys over the phone three or four times a week. But when she heard that Charles was already discussing who would or wouldn't be an appropriate match for their son, the princess became "totally exasperated," said Elsa Bowker.

"Look at Charles and me, for God's sake," Diana told Lady

Bowker. "You would think they'd have learned something from the way that turned out, wouldn't you? Catastrophe. Pure catastrophe."

At the moment, the princess's own love life wasn't faring any better. During a secret late-night rendezvous in London's Battersea Park, Diana pressed Khan to marry her. She had gone so far as to have her butler, Paul Burrell, the man she referred to as "my rock," ask a Catholic priest if he would marry them in private. She also told Khan that she wanted him to move into Kensington Palace so that William and Harry could get to know him. "I want them to know you," she told Khan, "the way I know you."

Khan was simply flabbergasted. He had already told Diana that the only way he could see them having "a normal life together" was if she moved to Pakistan. She seriously considered the idea, but was unwilling to leave William and Harry behind. "I cannot be away from my boys," she told Khan. "They need me now more than ever."

As for a secret marriage, Khan labeled the idea "ridiculous. You have obviously," he told her, "not thought about the implications." Once again, he angrily told her their affair was over and stormed off into the night.

"She was deeply upset and hurt by the breakup," Diana's close friend Rosa Monckton said. "She was very much in love with him. She hoped that they would be able to have a future together. She wanted to marry him."

Diana's tempestuous on-again, off-again relationship with Natty Khan was off again, and William once again provided a shoulder to cry on. This time, however, Diana decided not to heed her son's advice to simply bide her time. Instead, she concocted a plan to make Khan jealous—and not by merely dating someone else. If her scheme was to work, Diana told her hairdresser confidants Natalie Symonds and Tess Rock, the man she dated this time would have to be Muslim.

Enter Mohamed Al Fayed, the colorful Egyptian billionaire whose empire included the Ritz Hotel in Paris and such iconic English brands as the satirical magazine *Punch*, the Fulham Football Club, and Harrods department store. He also had a son: Dodi, a sometime movie producer (his films included the Oscar-winning *Chariots of Fire*), who had been linked with Brooke Shields, Valerie Perrine, Tina Sinatra, and Winona Ryder, among others. Diana had met him in passing a few times and seemed to remember that she found him "quite charming."

After repeatedly turning down Fayed's annual invitation to spend the holidays at his villa in St.-Tropez, Diana decided this time to accept. On July 11, 1997, William and Harry joined their mother aboard Al Fayed's sleek, white-hulled 195-foot yacht, *Jonikal*. Three days later, Dodi flew in from Paris to share a romantic candlelight supper with Diana. When the couple began throwing food at each other—"chasing each other and laughing and giggling like a couple of kids," said the yacht's chief steward, Debbie Gribble—William was overjoyed. His mother's plan to make Hasnat Khan jealous had taken an unexpected turn; her affection for Dodi seemed genuine. From the food fight forward, the Princess of Wales and her Egyptian playboy lover were inseparable.

The affair was faithfully chronicled in hundreds of newspaper stories that summer, starting with a front-page photo in the *Sunday Mirror* that showed Diana and Dodi locked in each other's arms aboard the *Jonikal*. Unlike the secretive Khan, Dodi had no compunction about letting the world know that he and Diana were in love. For a woman whose insecurities were legion ("I want to be wanted"), the obvious pride Dodi took in their relationship was enormously reassuring. "She wanted the person to abandon *everything* for her," Lady Bowker said. "Prince William knew that she needed this special kind of man in her life."

Even after William and Harry traveled to Balmoral to spend the rest of the summer with the Royal Family, Mummy was constantly phoning—first from London, where she and Dodi spent time together at his sprawling Park Lane apartment, and later from the *Jonikal* as they cruised from Nice to Sardinia. Each time, Diana chatted amiably with Harry for a few minutes before consulting with William on the progress of her newest romance.

"She ran everything by William that even remotely affected him," Rosa Monckton said. "She valued his judgment." He was telling Mummy now that he was happy for her. "As long as you're happy, Mummy," Wills said, "that's the important thing."

For the moment, Diana no longer intended to marry anyone. "I need it," she told her friend Annabel Goldsmith, "like a bad rash on my face." But she was in the throes of an affair that she described with one word: "bliss." Said her friend Richard Kay, "Diana was as happy as I have ever known her. For the first time in years, all was well with her world."

Yet even as she dined with Dodi in the Imperial Suite at the Ritz in Paris on August 30, 1997, Diana's thoughts never strayed far from her boys. In just two weeks, Harry would be turning thirteen, and Diana—wary of the paparazzi gathering outside the hotel—had asked a Ritz staffer to locate the Sony PlayStation he had asked for.

William was thinking about Harry, too. Over the phone from Balmoral, he told his mother that he had been ordered by Buckingham Palace to pose alone for photographers at Eton. William worried that his little brother, a struggling student who was going to have to repeat a year at Ludgrove before joining his brother at Eton, might feel slighted.

In his customary caretaker role, William was again thinking of ways to spare someone else's feelings. Diana was flying back to London the next day, and she would ask Papa to intervene with the Palace so that Harry could be included in some way.

"William is so kind," she had told her clairvoyant friend Rita Rogers a few hours earlier. Rogers, who had warned Dodi not go to Paris because she had had a vision of him facing danger in a tunnel there, pleaded with Diana to return to London. "Don't worry, Rita. I'm going home tomorrow," Diana said. "I'm looking forward to seeing my boys."

I pity any woman who marries into this family.

—*Diana*

3

One year later

"Do you see him?" the redhead asked excitedly as she whipped out her compact and checked her makeup one last time. "Well, do you?" The girls of Marlborough College, gathered along a fence, stood on tiptoe and craned their necks waiting for the field hockey players to come into view. There was polite applause as the home team, clad in Marlborough's distinctive black-and-red-striped uniforms, made its way onto the field. In a strange but understandable departure from the norm, the Marlborough girls cheered when the blue-and-tan-clad Eton players made their entrance. Even in a crowd of improbably tall players, one stood out.

"It's *him*," several voices squealed in unison. "Isn't he *gorgeous*?" Ever since he was greeted by thousands of teenage girls screaming, "William, William, William," during a March 1998 visit to Vancouver, the prince had become accustomed to causing pandemonium wherever he went. This afternoon, he chose not to react to the shrieks and giggles wafting from the sidelines.

One of the girls stood off to the side and slightly apart from the rest, watching as William—who had a knack for taking charge whatever the sport—conferred with his teammates. It was the first time Kate Middleton had ever laid eyes on the future king, and she carefully studied his every move on the field. Ostensibly, she was there as the captain of the girls' hockey team, and for the primary purpose of rooting for her fellow Marlburians.

"Kate was so cool and calm," a classmate remembered. "She was excited about it, but not hysterical like everybody else." There was, however, a fleeting moment between them. "I think they locked eyes for a few seconds, but he didn't actually wait around to talk with anyone, really. His bodyguards were there, and right after the game he was whisked off with the rest of his team." As for Kate, "she didn't," said the classmate, "seem as besotted as the rest of us standing there."

In truth, Kate had long harbored a crush on the handsome prince. While other girls decorated their rooms with photos of soccer players and rock stars, Miss Middleton's dormitory room was dominated by a color photograph affixed to the wall directly above her bed of the Heir in boots and tight-fitting jeans. (The snapshot, taken of William and his father standing beside a stream at Balmoral, originally included both princes; Kate simply cut Harry out of the picture.) She devoured every newspaper and magazine article about William and kept track of his schedule on the Internet. "A lot of girls said, 'Oooh, I'm definitely marrying Prince William,' " one of her classmates recalled, "and maybe some of them really meant it. But you got the feeling that Kate *really* meant it."

Kate's position along the fence that day—just a little removed from the rest of the pack—may not have been entirely accidental.

As a student of royal affairs of the heart, she paid close attention to the way another commoner like herself had won the heart of an heir to the British throne.

Kate had read that Camilla Parker Bowles first met Prince Charles while watching a polo match at Windsor in 1971. Standing slightly apart from the rest of the crowd, Camilla shouted, "That's a fine animal, sir! I thought you played wonderfully well." This was enough to attract Charles's attention—the beginning of an enduring relationship that would, after triggering a series of events that rocked the monarchy, ultimately lead to marriage. (Camilla, who is related to Edward VII's mistress Alice Keppel, used a more daring line for their second encounter: "My great-grandmother and your great-great-grandfather were lovers. So how about it?")

Although Kate hoped to introduce herself to William that afternoon, it was unlikely that she would ever shout anything at a member of the Royal Family. "Kate is far too dignified and proper for anything like that," one of her college friends later mused. "She probably thought that would just turn him off, and I think she was right."

After the field hockey match, Kate returned to her room at Elmhurst, the Victorian-era mansion that served as one of the school's main residence halls for women. Although an upstart compared to Eton—Marlborough was founded in 1843 for the sons of Anglican clergymen—the school was built alongside the river Kennet on a chalky, Druid-built hillock called the Marlborough Mound. A moat-ringed Norman castle also occupied the spot at one point, presumably built to protect the remains of the person who, according to legend, was buried here: Merlin.

For the most part, the campus is composed of stone and brick buildings representing a variety of traditional architectural styles from Georgian and Victorian to faux-Tudor. At the school's center stands a Gothic-style chapel famous for its stained-glass windows by William Morris, the nineteenth-century poet, socialist, and designer regarded by many as the founder of the Arts and Crafts Movement.

Over the years, Marlborough numbered among its distinguished and varied alumni the actor James Mason, globe-circling sailor Sir Francis Chichester, and English poet laureate Sir John Betjeman, as well as pop singer Chris ("The Lady in Red") de Burgh and the notorious Russian spy Anthony Blunt. After going coed in 1968, however, the school began to shed its musty old-boy reputation. Now boasting its own observatory, trout ponds, an Olympic-size swimming pool, playing fields, and tennis courts, Marlborough courts both the cream of Britain's aristocracy and the offspring of the newly wealthy.

Kate fit solidly into the latter category. While she suddenly found herself surrounded by viscounts, ladies, earls, and even the son of a duke who could trace his family back to one of Henry VIII's six wives, her own family owed its fortune to paper hats and piñatas.

Michael and Carole Middleton could not have foreseen the life that awaited their then five-year-old daughter when they started Party Pieces, a company specializing in children's party supplies, in 1987. From the beginning, Kate had her special role to play in the family business. She modeled tiaras, tyke-size plastic jewelry, and princess gowns before they were packed up and shipped to customers.

"I remember Kate in her sparkly princess dress and little rhinestone crown, watching Princess Diana on the television and imitating her," a neighbor remembers. "Of course, all the little girls wanted to be Diana."

Before anyone had ever heard of Lady Diana Spencer, Kate's mother was one of the millions of young women growing up in the 1960s who dreamt of marrying the Prince of Wales. As a teenager, Carole Goldsmith—like Diana and the young Camilla Shand—hung a photo of the then dashing Prince Charles on her bedroom wall alongside posters of the Beatles and Mick Jagger.

Nothing in Carole's gritty family background would remotely have hinted at a future royal connection. Kate's maternal grandmother, born Dorothy Harrison, traced her roots back to the coal fields of County Durham in northeastern England, where Carole's forebears risked injury and death working hundreds of feet below ground under Dickensian conditions. Along the way, many of Kate's ancestors fell victim to diseases that went virtually unchecked among the working poor—cholera and influenza among them.

Meanwhile, things weren't going so well on the other side of the family, either. Kate's great-great-great-grandfather Edward Glassborow was arrested for public drunkenness in 1881 and thrown into London's infamous Holloway Prison, his head shaved, feet and hands manacled. None of which would have sat too well with his father, Kate's great-great-great-great-grandfather Thomas Glassborow, who as one of the city's more aggressive constables arrested scores of petty criminals who wound up being shipped to penal colonies in Australia. Later, the ranks of the men on the Middleton side would be seriously thinned by World War I; of that generation, four out of seven male cousins were killed in battle.

Kate's family history yielded a few bright spots, however. On her father's branch of the family tree, Kate was related to *Peter*

Rabbit creator Beatrix Potter, as well the legendary stage actress Dame Ellen Terry, actor Sir John Gielgud, and even Madonna's ex-husband, film director Guy Ritchie. There was also a tenuous if fascinating connection to aristocracy. Both the Middletons and the Spencers are direct descendants of seventeenth-century English statesman Sir Thomas Fairfax, making Kate and Prince William fifteenth cousins.

There were also ancestors who had managed to amass a considerable fortune. Kate's paternal great-great-great-grandfather Frank Lupton built William Lupton & Company into a major textile manufacturer and on his death in 1884 left an estate that would have been equivalent to more than $50 million today.

The Lupton-Middleton fortune had all but evaporated by the time Kate's father was born in 1949. Ironically, the drive to succeed would come not from the comparatively well-to-do Middletons, but from the scrappy women who raised Carole. Left alone to raise six children in a condemned flat after the death of her husband, Kate's great-grandmother Edith Goldsmith supported her brood working at a pickle factory. Standing just five feet tall and weighing under ninety pounds, Edith was a chain-smoker and a drinker—every night she sent one of her children to the local pub to fill up her jug with ale. She was also a strict disciplinarian, and not above, in the words of Kate's great-aunt Alice, taking "the odd swipe at her kids herself."

Edith instilled in her children the will to survive. But it was her daughter-in-law Dorothy Harrison—Kate's grandmother—whose own unbridled ambition would set the tone for future generations of Middleton women.

From the moment she married Edith's son Ronald in a Church

of England ceremony in the west London suburb of Southall, Dorothy made it clear that she intended to leave her hardscrabble childhood far behind. She demanded the best of everything, even when the couple was living with Edith and struggling to make ends meet. "She was a snob—always thought she was one cut above everybody else," said her niece Ann Terry. Dorothy, said her cousin Pat Charman, behaved as if she "was too good for the rest of us."

To finance her expensive tastes, Dorothy pushed Ronald, a carpenter and housepainter, to the limit. "He was henpecked," Pat Charman said. "Dorothy wanted more and more money so she could impress people, and that meant he had to work harder and harder. But she ruled the roost."

The Goldsmiths were still merely scraping by when Carole was born in January 1955. But that did not keep Dorothy from buying a huge and expensive Silver Cross pram to impress the neighbors. Nor did Dorothy, slender and always stylishly turned out, ever skimp on her own wardrobe. To the rest of the family, she was now Lady Dorothy.

Carole was eleven and her brother, Gary, just one when the family moved into a comfortable three-bedroom home on Kingsbridge Road in the more upscale community of Norwood Green in the London borough of Ealing. According to Ann Terry, Carole followed her mother's lead. "Carole loved to dress up and play her pop music and dance around the room," Terry said. "She was a very feminine, sweet young girl and very well behaved." Brother Gary, on the other hand, was a holy terror. "He was always breaking things, finding ways to get into mischief. He had a wild streak."

Once ensconced in what she now considered a passably upper-middle-class home, Dorothy showed up at the town's annual Village Day on the green. She then invited the wives of the town's more prosperous citizens to tea, insinuating herself even more into the social fabric of the town. "Dorothy had this need to be respected, to be looked up to," said one of her cousins. "She was very insecure and she could go absolutely mad if she thought she was being made fun of. She passed that on to Carole."

Social airs aside, the Goldsmiths could not afford to send their children to expensive prep schools or help them pay for college. No matter. Carole had long had her sights set on embarking on a glamorous career that would not require a degree. Not long after graduating from high school in 1974, she began training to become a British Airlines stewardess.

A decade later, Princess Diana dressed up in a Virgin Airlines flight attendant's uniform, grabbed the microphone as her flight passed over Windsor Castle on its approach to Heathrow airport, and announced to the startled passengers, "If you look out the window to your right now, you'll see Granny's place." But Diana had not yet turned thirteen when Carole Goldsmith joined the ranks of British Airways flight attendants.

At a time when air travel was still primarily for the affluent and *comfort* was the operative word, British Airlines and other carriers pulled out the stops to attract fliers. Many wide-bodied planes such as the Boeing 747 and the DC-10 featured lounge areas on board, some complete with a pianist playing background music on a baby grand. British Airlines, like its competitors, recruited only the most capable, charming, and attractive women to don the airline's distinctive dark blue uniform. In her blazer, knee-length skirt, and Jackie Kennedy pillbox hat, Carole more than fit the bill.

Even Dorothy Goldsmith was impressed. Not only did Carole's job offer decent pay and opportunities for exotic foreign travel, it also put her in proximity to the wealthy and powerful. It was hard to imagine, Dorothy told her niece, a better or faster way to find a rich husband.

"There were a lot of us who were looking for rich husbands," admitted a coworker. "What's wrong with that? Carole was no exception. She paid more attention to the attractive men in first class, whether they were wearing a wedding ring or not."

Michael Middleton wasn't exactly rich. But as a British Airways dispatcher who basically ran operations on the ground, he was entitled to wear a captain's uniform and, more important, collect the same pay.

Like his father, Peter, who had served in the Royal Air Force during World War II and later became a flight instructor for British European Airlines, Michael joined BEA with the intention of becoming a pilot. After six months of flight school, he decided he wasn't aviator material and opted instead to work on terra firma. When BOAC merged with BEA to form British Airways in 1974, Michael stayed on with the new airline. "He always assumed he would follow in his father's footsteps," Carole explained. "Flying just wasn't for him."

That down-to-earth quality was what most appealed to Carole, who had spent no small amount of time fending off advances from womanizing pilots and unruly passengers. Michael was, with the exception of a couple of boys she had gone to dances with in school, Carole's first serious romance. That he was six years her junior added to his appeal. "He was very grown-up but he still had this marvelous boyish quality," she explained. "And of course was so good-looking. Love at first sight, yes—absolutely!"

Michael and Carole dated for three years before finally deciding to move in together—first sharing a tiny flat in a gritty neighborhood west of Heathrow before buying a modest brick house in the picturesque hamlet of Bradfield Southend. Nearly a year later, on June 21, 1980, they wed at the twelfth-century Church of St. James the Less in Buckinghamshire. The ceremony, from which the bride and groom departed in a horse-drawn carriage, was regal by Goldsmith standards.

Dorothy was thrilled at the union—so much so that, out of twenty or thirty Goldsmith relatives, she invited only the two she felt were presentable.

Carole was an active participant in the decision to exclude 90 percent of her family from the wedding. "Carole is a smart girl," said a cousin who was not invited. "She was marrying up, into a family with money and connections. She didn't want anyone around to embarrass her, or to remind her that she's from working-class stock."

A year later, Carole and Michael joined 750 million people from around the world who were glued to their television sets as Lady Diana Spencer wed Prince Charles at St. Paul's Cathedral. Carole was particularly impressed with Diana's wedding dress, an ivory taffeta and antique-lace gown designed by trendy British designers David and Elizabeth Emanuel.

Like everyone else watching that day, the Middletons viewed the royal wedding as nothing short of perfection. Diana was now the most glittering jewel in the Windsor crown. Only a handful of people in St. Paul's that day knew the truth—that Charles still loved Camilla and was only marrying Diana to produce an heir. Sadly, Diana was one of them. When she discovered bracelet Charles had had specially made for Camilla, Diana considered calling the wedding off. "Well, bad luck," ters replied, "your face is on the tea towels so you're too late to chicken out."

Blissfully unaware that the royal marriage was doomed from the start, Carole viewed the trappings of aristocracy with no small amount of envy. "Carole was always very aware of the difference between affluence and wealth," a Goldsmith cousin said. "She was a lot like her mum in that way. She wanted the finest things, and she knew it took money—money that she didn't have."

Although they could not know it at the time, the Middletons took their biggest step toward the top rung of the social ladder on January 9, 1982. That afternoon, Caroline gave birth to blue-eyed Catherine Elizabeth Middleton at the Royal Berkshire Hospital in Reading.

On June 20, Carole wore a Laura Ashley dress and Michael a navy blue Hardy Amies suit to Catherine's christening at St. Andrews in Bradfield, a fourteenth-century red stone church that more closely resembled a turreted Norman castle than a place of worship. The next day, Mum and Dad celebrated their second wedding anniversary—and, along with the rest of the nation, the birth of Prince William.

Catherine—she would not be called Kate until she was well into her teens—was joined by a sister, Philippa (Pippa), in 1983, and by brother James four years later. Quitting her job to devote herself full-time to her family, Carole dove headlong into mummyhood. She drove her children to the local play group at nearby St. Peter's Church, where mothers could sit in a circle trading village gossip while keeping a watchful eye on their toddlers.

As soon as they were old enough, Carole enrolled Kate and Pippa in St. Peter's Preschool. Catherine's mother quickly became one of the school's most reliable volunteers. "Carole wasn't afraid to get her hands dirty," one of the other mothers recalled. "She took the children's hands and escorted them to the loo if they needed to go, or she'd help line them up and march them out to the playground. After class, she was always right in there cleaning up. Carole was kind of a whirlwind."

She had also already begun to exhibit a special talent that would transform the Middletons' lives. Since her circle of friends consisted almost entirely of young mothers, Carole found herself constantly preparing little gift bags for children to take away from parties. These colorfully packaged, homemade goodie bags—each filled with trinkets, toys, games, and candy—quickly became the talk of tiny Bradfield.

Not that Carole was the only mother who was forced to spend time and money on these bags. "Carole was fed up," the Middletons' cleaning lady, Yvonne Cowdrey, remembered, "and she realized other mums must feel the same." Seizing the opportunity, she offered to make up the bags for the other mothers—for a price.

Catherine's fifth birthday and the birth of James a few months later seemed to mark a turning point. In the summer of 1987, Carole rented a storage space a few miles from her house and launched Party Pieces, a mail-order business designed to, she explained in her prospectus, "inspire other mothers to create magical parties at home and to make party organizing a little easier."

Soon Party Pieces was selling paper plates, party hats, noisemakers, cupcakes, invitations, lanterns, costumes, balloons, streamers, glitter, games—essentially anything anyone could possibly need to throw a children's party. To promote Mummy's line of merchandise, Catherine and Pippa both posed for ads and flyers.

Since the Middletons were their own best advertisement, they pulled out the stops for their own children's parties. "They always had the very best," a neighbor said, "with the top treats and latest gadgets—floating lanterns and, when they were the thing, indoor fireworks."

Carole was right: the demand was there. Soon thousands of orders flowed in, making Party Pieces an instant success. Before long, Michael quit his job to join the family firm.

By the time Kate turned seven, the Middletons could afford to spend the $20,000 a year it took to send her to St. Andrew's school in nearby Pangbourne. Consisting of a massive Victorian mansion surrounded by fifty-four acres of woodlands, lawns, and playing fields, St. Andrew's was, Carole said, "the kind of school I dreamt of going to but could never afford."

Kate flourished there, academically and athletically. Always taller than the rest of the children her age, she was a standout at volleyball, basketball, tennis, hockey, swimming, and track and field (she set a school record for the high jump that stood for years).

"She was the kind of girl you'd have a crush on," a classmate said. "She wasn't particularly beautiful, but she was always the tallest, which had a certain impact."

While parents and students alike described her as quiet and reserved, Kate did not hesitate to take to the stage in several student productions. Kate danced in *The Nutcracker*, recited poetry by Alfred, Lord Tennyson, and sang the lead in *Rats!*—a musical based on the Pied Piper of Hamelin.

In 1992, when William was coping with his parents' unraveling marriage, ten-year-old Kate was singing "I Could Have Danced All Night" as Eliza Doolittle in the St. Andrew's production of

My Fair Lady. "Kate was enchanting," said her Henry Higgins, Andrew Alexander. "She played the role with passion and a steely conviction." When the curtain came down for the last time, precocious Kate asked Alexander if he wanted to go to the movies with her. Suddenly flustered ("flushed . . . and tongue-tied"), Alexander turned her down. Even at ten, he said, Kate was "so mature at the time" that he found her "intimidating."

Another classmate, Kingsley Glover, also remembered an embarrassing encounter with Kate. Although she was a day student who rarely stayed overnight at the school, on one of those occasions a breeze parted his robe—the only thing he had on. (While it made him "cringe" at the time, Glover later joked, "The future queen of England has seen my crown jewels.")

Kate's final performance at St. Andrew's, captured on video, seemed especially prescient. Playing the female lead in John Latimer's Victorian melodrama *Murder in the Red Barn*, Kate, wearing a flowing white gown and ribbons in her hair, is told by a fortune-teller that she will meet "a handsome man, a rich gentleman."

"It is all I have ever hoped for," Kate replies in the video. "Will he fall in love with me?"

"Indeed he will."

"And marry me?"

"And marry you," the fortune-teller answers.

"Will he take me away from here?" Kate asks.

"Yes, to London."

"Oh," Kate replies, holding her hands to her chest, "how my heart flutters."

Later, the love of her life, who is named William, gets down on one knee and proposes marriage. "Yes, it's all I've ever longed for," Kate replies. "Yes, oh yes, dear William!"

Kate's parents were in the audience that evening, just as they were at every one of their children's recitals and sporting events. "Michael and Carole Middleton were very involved parents," one of Kate's teachers said. "Not pushy, but they certainly wanted their children to do their best, to succeed in everything they did. Winning was obviously very important to them, and they passed that along to Kate especially."

Not that the Middletons didn't have their hands full. Convinced that the embryonic Internet might extend the reach of their business, Carole set up a Party Pieces website in 1992 and shrewdly registered the name. Demand exploded, and in 1995 Party Pieces relocated to larger quarters in the neighboring town of Ashampstead Common, Berkshire.

Eventually, thirty employees would be spread out among the four farm buildings—including a two-hundred-year-old barn and a hayloft that had been converted into a warehouse—that made up the Party Pieces world headquarters. The business was now grossing an estimated $3 million annually, and the Middletons decided that they could afford to buy their dream home.

In the summer of 1995 they bought Oak Acre, a stately Tudor-style manor house in Chapel Row, not far from the Party Pieces complex. Adjacent to the privately owned Bucklebury Estate on the banks of the river Pang, Oak Acre boasted six bedrooms, five fireplaces, a solarium, and brick walls covered in wisteria—all concealed behind neatly trimmed hedges. "Hardly anyone even knows," real estate agent Dudley Singleton said, "that the house is even there."

Bucklebury and the surrounding villages with names such as Burnt Hill and Tutt's Clump are a Wodehousian vision—all narrow country lanes, stone-walled cottages, quaint tea shops, and the occasional pub. For their part, the Middletons partook fully in village life, never missing a country fair or a carnival fund-raiser. This interest in what Prince Charles often wistfully referred to as "time-honored country pursuits" did not extend to hunting, however—and definitely not to foxhunting. "Kate and her parents loved to be around livestock and animals of all kinds," one of their Bucklebury neighbors said, "but they were completely against killing creatures simply for sport. I remember Kate saying she thought it was cruel and quite sickening."

Like Princess Diana, Kate was willing to overlook William's interest in "killing things" as part and parcel of his Windsor heritage. When the eleven-year-old prince horrified animal-rights activists by shooting six rabbits in two hours at Balmoral, Kate suggested to her school friends, "The Queen must have made him do it."

In 1994, William triggered protests yet again when he led his first pheasant shoot at Balmoral, bagging fifteen of the birds before lunch. Not long after, he pleaded with Diana not to accept the presidency of the Royal Society for the Prevention of Cruelty to Animals. "You can't do that," he said. "Every time I kill anything, they will blame you."

Admiring her Prince Charming from afar, Kate could only speculate that William was merely being put through his royal paces. "It's all part of his training to be king," she reasoned. "He's too kind a person to enjoy shooting animals."

At the same time newspapers were trumpeting the arrival of Prince William at Eton in September 1995, Kate enrolled at Downe House, an exclusive all-girls boarding school that started out in the family home of Charles Darwin but had since taken over the Cloisters in the nearby town of Cold Ash. Until World

War I, the Cloisters housed a strict and mysterious religious order known as the School of Silence.

For Kate, who had always gone to coeducational schools, the next several months spent in an all-female environment were the unhappiest of her young life. On her own for the first time, she quickly grew homesick. Nor did it help that, in the schools' cliquish environment, Kate found it difficult to fit in. "She was a very sweet, friendly girl—not a mean bone in her body," a former teacher said. "Unfortunately, there were girls there whose parents had spoiled them rotten, and they didn't know what to make of a girl like Kate. So they just set out to make her miserable."

Singled out by the most notorious bullies in the school, Kate soon had to deal with being shoved and kicked on the playing field and tripped in the hallways. Her books and school supplies mysteriously disappeared. Most disturbingly, Kate became the target of malicious gossip.

The bullying took its toll, and by early 1996 Kate's parents decided to pull her out of Downe House. Starting at Marlborough in April of that year, Kate was once again an outsider; the other students had gotten to know each other over the previous eight months.

Kate was quickly taken under the wing of student Jessica Hay, who helped the new arrival unpack, gave her a quick tour of the campus, then ate dinner with her in the main dining hall. It was then that Kate might have reconsidered her desire to be educated in a coed environment. A group of boys at a nearby table glared intently at the newcomer in their midst, laughing and elbowing each other as they each jotted something down on a napkin.

"And what are they doing?" Kate asked her new friend.

"Oh, they do that with every new girl," Hay told her. "You know, rating us one to ten."

The boys then held up their napkins in unison. No one had rated Kate above a 2.

Kate was still suffering from her earlier exposure to bullying. She was also intimidated by students who had the social pedigree she lacked. Skinny, awkward, and more withdrawn than she had been before, the girl who once enjoyed singing before an audience now spent endless hours holed up in her room studying. "She didn't really have much to do with the rest of us at first," Hay said. "She wasn't being rude or mean. She just felt homesick."

"Kate had very little confidence," said another friend and classmate, Gemma Williamson. "She changed, but it took some time."

Even after sister Pippa joined her in the fall of 1997, Kate remained standoffish. It was another full year before Kate emerged from her shell.

Over the summer of 1998, Kate, with Mum's help, set out to transform herself. She combed out her lush chestnut hair and started wearing makeup—though sparingly.

"It happened quite suddenly," Williamson said of Kate's return that fall. Kate "came back after the long summer break the following year an absolute beauty." This was despite that she remained one of the school's more conservative dressers. "Most of the girls at school would dress quite tartily to attract the boys, but not Kate," Williamson said. "Kate never wore particularly fashionable or revealing clothes"—just jeans and sweaters "with discreet pearl earrings and lots of bangles." She hardly even wore any makeup." Apparently no embellishment was needed. "Everything looked good on her," Williamson said, "because she had such a perfect body."

Now that she was a bona fide 10 out of 10, Kate attracted plenty of male attention. "She is very good-looking," Hay said of her leggy, dark-maned chum, "and a lot of the boys liked her. But it used to go over her head. She wasn't really interested and she had very high morals."

Williamson agreed, "Kate wasn't one for the random snog [kiss]. She didn't need a guy to be happy." Indeed, Williamson insisted that Kate was "quite old-fashioned . . . she wanted to save herself for someone special."

Kate did indulge in the rare "snog," random or not, during her time at Marlborough. Bowing to peer pressure, she succumbed to school lothario Charlie Von Mol's overtures and ducked out with him for a necking session. Then there was math wiz Willem Marx, who would later attend Oxford, learn Arabic, and wind up as a journalist in Iraq. None of these apparently amounted to much. "She never lost her virginity at school," Hay said pointedly. "In fact, she only had two or three snogs."

This natural reticence also applied to partying. Whenever the other girls smuggled liquor or marijuana into school, Kate declined to participate. She did, however, agree to stand guard while her friends drank themselves into oblivion. "She was always the one you could trust to do the absolutely right thing," Hay said. "She was always very levelheaded. . . . I never once saw her drunk."

Apparently Kate didn't need to be inebriated to engage in a strange pastime that would earn her one of the school's most original nicknames. The rooms shared by Kate and Jessica Hay faced the boys' boardinghouse. "Every night we took turns to show our bare bums to the guys to see if they could guess who they were." But where Jessica quickly tired of literally hanging her backside out the second-story window, Kate "got kind of addicted to it," Hay admitted. "We must have done it ninety times." Kate's addiction to mooning earned her the moniker Middlebum.

It was apparently not the only less-than-decorous stunt Kate liked to pull. Noting that Miss Middleton harbored a secret "obsession with her tits," one classmate wrote in the school yearbook that Kate "is often found squinting down her top screaming: 'They're growing!' "

Well-liked by both sexes, Kate remembered how she felt being the outsider and went out of her way to welcome new students. "She was the most kindhearted woman," Williamson said. "There are always cliques at school, but she would have time for absolutely everyone. That's what made her special."

That and the mooning, of course—and her frequently voiced desire to marry Prince William. Over the year since Diana's stunningly tragic death, Kate had made a careful study of everything the Heir was up to. "She read absolutely everything about him," Hay said. "She was besotted."

In fact, when Hay, Williamson, and her other friends sat around talking about the boys they "fancied," Kate would have none of it. "I don't like any of them," she would reply. "They're all a bit of rough. There's no one quite like William. . . . I bet he's really kind. You can just tell by looking at him." Soon, the other girls were calling Kate "Princess-in-Waiting."

Kate could base this conviction at least in part on what she learned about William from her friend. For three years beginning in 1998, Jessica Hay was the on-again, off-again girlfriend of William's Eton mentor and cousin Nicholas Knatchbull. While being shown around Eton, Hay first met Wills. "He was shyer than I ever thought," she told Kate. "I got the feeling he wasn't used to normal girls being around him."

Later, during a pheasant shoot at Broadlands, Hay also met the Queen, Prince Philip, Charles, and Harry. Early one morning

Hay walked down the hall to the bathroom, only to encounter William walking out in a "pink, fluffy bathrobe" that had obviously been left behind by his room's previous female occupant and was the only robe available for him to wear. "When he saw me, he was so embarrassed at what he had on, he exclaimed, 'Bugger!' and dashed back to his room."

Jessica also talked about William's smoking habit, and about his "wicked" sense of humor. During a cigarette break at Broadlands, Hay, Knatchbull, and William spread out on the grass. "Better be careful," said the prince, pointing to Hay's short skirt, "there are paparazzi hiding in the bushes. You don't want them taking photos of your knickers."

Through Hay, Kate was also exposed to some surprising inside information involving Prince Harry. On a chilly Saturday afternoon in the fall of 1998, Hays, Knatchbull, and fourteen-year-old Harry ducked inside a viaduct behind Eton's soccer field to sneak a smoke. When Harry asked for a cigarette, Knatchbull pulled out a huge joint, lit it up, and handed it to the Spare. "Harry only had one puff and went really red," Hay recalled. "I think he felt embarrassed."

Did William know about it? Kate asked. "No, no," Hay said. "If he'd known Nick was like that, he wouldn't have let Harry hang out with him."

Hay shared another observation with Kate that made her wonder aloud about Harry's true place in the House of Windsor. "I noticed how close William and his father were, always standing or sitting close, chatting across the table, checking that each other was okay," Hay said. "But Prince Charles didn't seem as close to Harry at all." When the families came down to breakfast, William and Charles arrived together, but Harry would arrive alone fifteen minutes later and be basically ignored. "Harry looked a bit out of place," Hay added, "and I felt sorry for him."

Kate and her fellow students were all aware of the speculation that Harry might actually be the love child of Diana and James Hewitt. Now that he was getting older, the resemblance between Harry and the princess's riding instructor was striking. "I wonder if it's true," Kate said. "Poor Harry."

Poor William, as well. Even as Kate dreamt of her prince from the comfort of her dorm room at Marlborough, Wills juggled a number of challenges that would have stymied even the most seasoned diplomat. Just nine months after his mother's death, Wills arranged to meet Camilla Parker Bowles for the first time. The "surprise" meeting—William dropped in on Charles and Camilla at St. James's Palace on the way to the movies—left Charles's mistress of twenty-six years, in her words, "trembling like a leaf. I really need," she added after William left for the theater, "a vodka and tonic."

William quickly discovered that he liked Mrs. P. B. Sixteen months older than Charles and anything but a raving beauty, Camilla bore scant resemblance to Diana. An unrepentant chain-smoker, she had little interest in fashion and preferred traipsing through muddy fields in her Wellingtons to attending galas or openings in London. Camilla had a talent for self-deprecation and was as uncomplicated and unquestioning as Diana had been insecure and self-absorbed.

Precisely because she was so unlike their mother, William and Harry both warmed to Camilla. "If she had resembled their mother in the slightest way," said a friend of Charles's, "they would have seen her as someone trying to replace their mum."

William's motivation was clear: after living his entire life engulfed in the storm that was his parents' marriage, he wanted peace. "Camilla makes their father happy," Harold Brooks-Baker said. "That's all that counts at the moment."

Unfortunately, in the eyes of Diana's friends, that William had even met Camilla was nothing less than an outright betrayal of her memory. Having such a meeting take place less than a year after Diana's death was, said her friend Richard Kay, "astonishingly insensitive."

Unbeknownst to William and Harry, many of their mother's friends were actually being barred from contact with the princes. "I am told," Diana's longtime friend Roberto Devorik said, "they are unavailable." Their free time was now largely devoted to polo, shooting, and foxhunting—all those pursuits for which the Windsor men were famous. "They've been," said Richard Greene, "completely Windsorized."

William was soon engaged in another pursuit for which the Windsor men were equally famous. In July 1998, Charles, his sons, and a handful of friends boarded the *Alexander*—the same lavishly appointed yacht (five swimming pools, a ballroom, movie theater, helipad, gold plumbing fixtures) on which the prince and princess took their ill-fated "second honeymoon" cruise to celebrate their tenth anniversary. This time, Charles's chums Patty and Charles Palmer-Tomkinson were on the passenger list along with their twenty-seven-year-old daughter, Tara.

An early crush of Wills's, Tara was a self-described free spirit who took no small degree of pleasure in embarrassing the prince. Once he arrived, she thrust her hand down the front of his pants—the same "greeting" she had used when they were children. She also had the habit of randomly reaching over and fidgeting with his zipper.

At another point during the trip, William, who had just turned sixteen, came upon Tara sunbathing topside. "Come on then," she said, stripping off her bikini top, "have a proper look!" William ran off, humiliated.

Tara's contact with the Royal Family was put on hold when she later admitted to being a cocaine addict. But she found newspaper stories about her snorting coke in the bathrooms of aristocrats less objectionable than rumors she had given herself to William as a birthday present. "I'm a cocaine addict," she protested, "not a pedophile."

Neither of Diana's children were ever particularly shy; before 340 invited guests at Papa's fiftieth birthday, William and Harry did a send-up of the final scene in *The Full Monty*, stripping off their shirts and unbuttoning their pants to "You Sexy Thing" by the group Hot Chocolate. Although Tara may have come on a little strong, William was beginning to relish his newfound sex-symbol status.

His love of sports and the outdoor life notwithstanding, William was soon making his first forays into London's frenzied nightclub scene. In addition to his ever-present armed body-guards, William was accompanied on these after-hours expeditions by Camilla's hard-partying children, Tom and Laura Parker Bowles.

At clubs such as Chinawhite, K-Bar, Foxtrot Oscar, and Crazy Larry's, William chatted amiably with the young ladies who approached him and in some cases took their numbers. The next morning, a lucky girl would be asked to join him for tea at York House, the residence he shared with his father and brother inside St. James's Palace. Before a young woman was actually invited to the palace, however, she had to go through an extensive background check.

By the time a young lady actually arrived at York House, "they were pretty intimidated," recalled a former member of St. James's household staff. "It was all very innocent when he began asking girls up—tea and a little harmless teenage flirting."

William's first real crush was actually on a more mature woman—Camilla's niece Emma, who at twenty-four was eight years his senior. A blond, willowy former model, aspiring journalist, and race-car aficionado, Emma conceded she was "immensely fond" of the young prince. But if he took her affection as anything other than sisterly, she insisted, he was mistaken. St. James's Palace was eager to get out that message. Since Camilla might eventually become William's stepmother, any romance with Emma would have appeared unseemly at best.

William's infatuation with Emma soon ended, but not before her behavior and that of Camilla's own son would call into question their fitness to keep company with the impressionable young prince. Battling an addiction to alcohol, Emma spent thirty-five days at the same Arizona clinic where Tara Palmer-Tomkinson was treated for cocaine abuse.

Tom was a much larger problem. Arrested in 1995 for possessing the drug ecstasy as well as marijuana, Tom now admitted to snorting cocaine in the same establishments where he was seen with William. That confession resulted in a cascade of revelations concerning Camilla's son, most memorably his participation in a "fetish party" wearing full dominatrix gear. Tom's ensemble consisted of a black plastic dress, fishnet stockings, stiletto heels, and a whip.

Charles barred Tom from seeing either William or Harry until he overcame his cocaine problem, but it soon became clear that William's circle abounded with drug abusers. Izzy Winkler, another beauty who had befriended William, also admitted to using cocaine, as did Wills's cousin and fellow Etonian Lord Frederick (Freddie) Windsor, son of Prince and Princess Michael of Kent. Nicky Knatchbull, who had already introduced Harry to pot, was soon pulled over and arrested for narcotics possession along with two teenage passengers whose socks were stuffed with drugs. Knatchbull spent three months in rehab only to return within the year.

Back at Marlborough, Kate read about William's tarnished circle of friends and was, said a classmate, "deeply concerned. She was a huge admirer of Princess Diana—we all loved her—and the idea of Diana's son becoming just another aristo druggie really disturbed her."

But Kate had faith in William's innate common sense. "I don't think he would take drugs," she told her sister, Pippa. "He cares too much about Harry, and he wouldn't want to upset his father or the Queen."

Wills's secret admirer was reassured by front-page photos of the prince at the christening of Konstantine Alexios, grandson of King Constantine of Greece and William's godson. With his left arm in a sling—the result of a rugby accident—William gingerly dabbed holy water on the infant's head.

In July 1999, however, Kate was less pleased to learn that one of her Marlborough classmates had been invited to accompany Wills on the Wales family's annual cruise aboard the *Alexander.* Devonshire beauty Emilia (Mili) d'Erlanger was the niece of the tenth Viscount Exmouth and through her family had ties to both the Spencers and the Windsors.

Equally well connected were two other young ladies Wills invited along: sixteen-year-old Mary Forestier-Walker and Davina Duckworth-Chad, twenty-one. The lushly beautiful, wild-haired Davina, a distant cousin of Diana's whose two-thousand-acre family estate was just down the road from Sandringham, had made headlines of her own. After posing in a rubber dress to promote an Internet site, she was promptly dubbed "the Deb on the Web."

D'Erlanger, Duckworth-Chad, and Forestier-Walker had unseen competition from a young woman who had been on *Alexander* just prior to their departure and left a signed glossy photo of herself for the prince. From that point on, William exchanged a series of sizzling e-mails with Lauren Bush, a model, granddaughter of former U.S. president George H. W. Bush, and niece of future president George W. Bush.

It was not Wills's only cyber-romance with a beautiful, high-profile American that year. When Britney Spears was told he had taped a poster of her on his wall at Eton, she began an e-mail correspondence that one of his chums described as "naughty." When her concert schedule made it impossible for Spears to accept Wills's invitation to be his date for the millennium party he was planning to usher in the twenty-first century—an extravaganza he liked to call "The Willenium"—she suggested they get together in London on Valentine's Day. But after their plans were leaked to the press, St. James's Palace issued a swift denial. Careful to never actually deny that he was corresponding with Spears, William vaguely objected to the "nonsense put out by PR companies" and complained of being "exploited."

As the new millennium approached, Kate made plans to quietly celebrate with her family at home in Bucklebury. The prince had something else in mind. Turning down Papa's offer to use

Highgrove for his Willenium celebration, William scaled back his plans considerably. Instead of a public event, he got together with friends at a cramped, decaying village hall near Sandringham and wound up "very seriously, seriously drunk." Two days later on a flight to Wales, he told a British Airways flight attendant that he was still suffering from a hangover.

William recovered at the chic Swiss ski resort Crans-Montana. There he drank only lemonade and danced the night away with a twenty-two-year-old barmaid, Annaliese Asbjornsen. Surprised that William had "no inhibitions," Asbjornsen recalled that he "was thrusting his hips, gyrating . . . he knew all the moves." Three hours later, during the song "Closer Than Close," William pulled her to him, wrapped his arms around her waist, and whispered in her ear, "You're gorgeous." Then, as Wills's bodyguards pretended to look the other way, they began kissing. The next night, it was nineteen-year-old cocktail waitress Lydia Truglio's turn. "He's a beautiful young man," she sighed.

Increasingly, William's desire to spread his wings put him in direct conflict with the men assigned to protect him. He chafed at the constant presence of his security detail—not because he felt uncomfortable being watched, but because it might intimidate the young women he was approaching. "God, I look over a girl's shoulder, and there they are, just *standing* there," Wills griped to Freddie Windsor. "It's so terrible, never to be left alone."

At times, however, William was grateful that the men were there to protect him—not only from harm, but from scandal. At one popular nightspot, William and a nearly naked blonde were sharing an intimate moment when one of his royal protection officers spotted a security camera recording the entire episode. Taking a deep breath, the bodyguard stepped in to halt the proceedings and seize the tape.

"Willmania" was in full force on June 21, 2000, when the world's most famous young man—and most eligible bachelor—turned eighteen. Several Commonwealth countries issued stamps commemorating the event, and William's official coat of arms was unveiled. At his insistence, Diana's Spencer insignia—three red scallop shells that had been erased by Charles after the divorce—was restored to the design.

"It's wonderful that he is paying tribute to his mother like that," Kate told a classmate. "It shows he's still his own man." She was also impressed that William was bucking tradition by insisting he not be called Your Royal Highness or Sir—the two forms of address required by royal protocol now that he was turning eighteen. He wanted to be addressed as "William—just William."

Kate was less thrilled to read what Wills had to say about his dating habits in a carefully controlled birthday interview with veteran royal correspondent Peter Archer. How did William decide if a girl might be someone he'd like to know? "Trying to explain how," he answered, "might be counterproductive." In the meantime, he stressed, "I like to keep my private life private."

Increasingly, he sought to keep his private life private at his rooms in York House, where two women in particular—Mili d'Erlanger and Nicholas Knatchbull's younger sister Alexandra—were frequent guests. Having apparently bested her competition aboard the *Alexander*, Mili was soon invited to meet Prince Charles on at least two occasions. When news of this reached Kate and her Marlborough classmates, she seemed shaken. "She's very sweet and reserved," a mutual friend of both girls said, "so it's hard to tell what she's thinking, really. But she always turned very quiet when people starting talking about Mili and Prince William."

Mili had stiff competition in the stunningly attractive Alexandra Knatchbull, a favorite godchild of Princess Diana's. Alexandra was also the niece of Amanda Knatchbull, who turned down Charles's first marriage proposal twenty-three years earlier. According to one of Alexandra's closest friends, she and William were "completely potty for each other. She was desperately in love, I can tell you that!"

For Will and Kate, however, thoughts of love took a backseat to their A-levels, the equivalent under the British system of the SAT and final exams combined. Both had already distinguished themselves as athletes: he shattered several Eton records and ranked among the top one hundred swimmers his age in the fifty-meter freestyle; her record in the high jump would stand for years. Both were leaders: she was chosen as a school prefect despite having joined Marlborough a year behind everyone else; he joined the school leadership society called Pop and as a member of Eton's cadet force was awarded its Sword of Honor.

Neither took any of this for granted—and that included getting the grades and scores that would earn them entrance into a top university. While Kate pored over her books in her room at Marlborough, Wills dug in at Eton for a marathon study session.

The decision to devote himself entirely to studying, on June 21, 2000, proved just how disciplined—and headstrong—the Heir could be. Not only was Queen Elizabeth hosting William's official birthday party at Windsor Castle that day, but she was also marking four other milestone birthdays occurring in 2000. Princess Margaret was turning seventy, Princess Anne fifty, Prince Andrew forty, and the Queen Mother one hundred.

Everyone—including the Queen Mother and even the heretofore exiled Duchess of York—attended. Not William. Although he was just a brief stroll from the castle, the guest of honor remained at Eton, cramming until dawn.

The extra effort paid off for both Wills and Kate. She graduated with an A average—good enough to guarantee her admission to virtually any major university in the UK. William, whose grades had always placed him in the top 10 percent of his class, did equally well—although it was hard to imagine that any institution of higher learning would have had the temerity to turn him down. "He wants to earn it," Nicky Knatchbull explained. "He doesn't want to have everything handed to him when other people have to work for it. He has too much pride for that."

Since the Spencers claimed Oxford as their alma mater and Papa went to Cambridge, those two universities were out. "I'm not going to do what everyone expects me to do," Wills declared. "I will decide what's best for me."

He *was* inclined to take the advice of one person. The Queen had mentioned in passing during one of their Windsor teas that with the rise in Scottish nationalism, he might consider a school in Scotland. Given his love of Balmoral—and that neither Diana's relatives nor the Windsor men had lobbied for it—the idea of a Scottish university appealed to him.

It also helped that William's housemaster at Eton, Andrew Gailey, had attended St. Andrews University and offered to give him a guided tour of the campus. Even though it boasted a student body of six thousand, Scotland's leading university felt more like a small college—thanks in part to the town of St. Andrews itself.

Famous as the birthplace of golf, St. Andrews was a drizzly, fog-shrouded, gray-to-the-marrow outpost jutting into the North Sea some seventy-five miles north of Edinburgh. Dotted with drab tourist hotels, moss-covered ruins, and tacky souvenir shops, St. Andrews has only a few nondescript restaurants and a single movie theater—The New Picture. The town offers next to nothing by way of entertainment—with one notable exception: the narrow cobblestone streets of St. Andrews are lined with twenty-two pubs (more per square mile than any other Scottish municipality), making it number one among UK party schools. According to one student, drinking—not golf—is really the number one sport at "St. Randy's." Added another underclassman, Crispin Dyer, "Here there's really nothing to do *except* get lashed."

Binge drinking at St. Randy's was not merely the province of the martini-worshipping James Bond Society or, at the other end of the social scale, the stout-guzzling Dead Parrot Society. The annual Student Run was a time-honored tradition during which "freshers" (freshmen) chugalugged beer at each of five pubs. They stumbled from one establishment to the other, pausing only to urinate through the mail slots of the few unfortunate homeowners who forgot to nail them shut. Female students, expecting to be rendered comatose by the evening's revels, often scrawled the names of their residences on their forearms so they could eventually be helped home.

Unfortunately for those suffering from hangovers, St. Andrews was also close to the Royal Air Force Base at Leuchars. Several times a day, Tornado fighters shrieked across the sky on their way to and from maneuvers over the sparsely populated Scottish Highlands.

For William, the chance to experience college life far from London—and in a school not forced upon him by his father or his Spencer relatives—was immensely appealing. So, too, was St. Randy's awe-inspiring reputation for rowdiness.

Kate viewed things differently. Since neither of her parents had graduated from college, they were eager to see their daughter attend a university with a marquee name—Oxford, Cambridge, or possibly the University of Edinburgh. Since she intended to major in art history, Kate was leaning toward the school that had the strongest art curriculum: Edinburgh. Carole and Michael Middleton encouraged this choice; both of Kate's siblings wound up going to Edinburgh.

"There was never any doubt that Kate was going to Edinburgh," said a fellow Marlburian. "She visited Edinburgh with her mum and came back raving about it." Kate applied and was accepted, much to the delight of both Michael and Carole Middleton. Then she began making plans for her "gap year"—the time off after high school customarily used to broaden a student's horizons before entering college. Like thousands of other art students, she chose to spend her gap year in the birthplace of the Italian renaissance: Florence.

Carole Middleton, along with thousands of other young women and their parents, soon had a change of heart about her daughter's college plans. When St. James's Palace announced that the Heir would be attending St. Andrews in the fall of 2001, a seismic shift occurred in the number of applications submitted to the college—a 44 percent increase over the previous year. Nine-tenths of those additional last-minute applications were from women.

Carole moved quickly. She had learned that Mili d'Erlanger now planned to attend St. Andrews, putting her in proximity to William. There was no reason, Carole told her daughter, for Kate not to be right there on campus with her old Marlborough friend—and the prince. Moreover, they had made contacts in the area through both their days in the airline industry and their rapidly growing mail-order company—now billing itself as the largest of its kind in Britain. When it came time to make housing choices, Carole suggested there would be ways to get even closer to the prince.

Kate was not convinced. In early September 2000, she departed for Florence, still intent on attending Edinburgh the following year. Along with thirteen others, Kate had signed up for a three-month course in Italian at the British Institute. But she was really there to experience all that the city of the Medicis had to offer—from Michelangelo's *David* and Botticelli's *Birth of Venus* to the Ponte Vecchio and the tile-domed Duomo.

Sharing a flat over a trattoria with three other girls, Kate walked each morning to her classes at the British Institute in the Palazzo Strozzino. The rest of her time was spent exploring the city's sculpture-lined squares, narrow streets, museums, cafés, and bars. As for which university she was attending the following year, she made it clear that she had no intention of attending St. Andrews merely because Prince William would be there. "She hadn't confirmed where she was going," said a fellow student at the British Institute. "She certainly wasn't going to St. Andrews at that point."

While mothers around the world scurried to get their daughters into St. Andrews, William had eluded the press and flown secretly to the tiny Central American nation of Belize. There, in jungles teeming with poisonous snakes and scorpions, William indulged his appetite for action and adventure training with a unit of the Welsh guards.

From Belize, he went directly to Rodrigues Island, in the middle of the Indian Ocean. Taking part in the Royal Geographical Society's marine observation program, Wills scuba dived and snorkled in search of specimens for the society's Shoals of Capricorn Project. He also fished, swam, and played soccer with the local children—all under the alias Brian Woods. Michelette Eduard, one of the housekeepers at the spare, tin-roofed inn where he had been staying, was shocked to learn the true identity of Mr. Woods. "I was serving him breakfast every morning," she said, "and had no idea who he was."

Still ignoring her mother's request that she consider switching from Edinburgh to St. Andrews, Kate focused her attention on her Italian studies—and a fellow Marlborough alumnus named Harry. Tall, dark-haired, and rich, Harry was among a select few enrolled in the costly John Hall Pre-University Course that immersed students in Italian culture as they traveled from Venice to Florence and then Rome.

Sex, drugs, and alcohol were all part and parcel of the student scene in Florence at the time, and several of Kate's peers indulged fully in all three. "Kate was very interested in a guy, Harry, and they went to clubs together and you saw them together quite a lot," a fellow student recalled. "But he messed her around quite a bit and strung her along." After a few weeks, Harry moved on to Rome, leaving Kate "a little disappointed but not distraught."

If Kate did ever get emotional, she never let anyone see it. "She liked to be in control of herself," observed Jessica Hay. "She wasn't a bore, and she didn't judge other people. She liked to have fun, but she didn't want to do anything foolish."

This extended to the number one pastime among British students abroad: drinking. Kate realized early on that her capacity for alcohol was limited. "Kate would like a glass of wine—and always had a few with dinner," a fellow student said. "She would get giggly and silly after a few glasses, so then she would stop. She was never interested in getting really drunk." Drug-taking was also rampant among her fellow students, but Kate "wouldn't be judgmental—in fact, she was quite interested in what they did to you. It was simply that she did not want to try them. I never saw her smoke, either."

Another Marlburian studying in Florence agreed that Kate "didn't like getting out of control, but this doesn't mean she wasn't sociable. She would mingle and she loved to dance." At a bacchanalian soiree thrown by students from Johns Hopkins University, for example, Kate nursed one glass of wine the entire evening. "It was quite a drunken affair . . . clearly it was most people's intention to get hammered, but not Kate's."

Then something occurred that revived Kate's dormant feelings for the prince. On September 29, she was among a group of British students gathered in a Florentine café watching William give his first hastily called televised press conference. Diana's senior aide P. D. Jephson, had just published *Shadows of a Princess*, a tell-all book that was making headlines on both sides of the Atlantic. Among other things, Jephson described Diana as an unstable, narcissistic, deceitful, and shrewdly manipulative neurotic. The Princess of Wales, he wrote, seamlessly blended a "radiant smile with a knife between the shoulder blades."

For the first time the prince, standing outside Highgrove with his father by his side, felt compelled to fight back. William told reporters he was "horrified" when he read excerpts of the book in the *Sunday Times* of London. "Of course, Harry and I are both quite upset about it—that our mother's trust has been betrayed and that even now she is still being exploited."

What Wills had to say was not nearly so interesting as the way he said it. Dressed in jeans and a Burberry crewneck, he looked—

and sounded—every inch the confident, self-assured heir to his mother's charisma. The press embargo that had been in force since his mother's death (and that was now about to be lifted) had worked so well that this marked the first time that the world had actually heard him speak.

Hearing Will's voice for the first time—clipped, upper-class, slightly adenoidal but at the same time seductively soothing—Kate sat with her fellow female gap-year students in gape-mouthed awe. "My God, that voice!" she said. "Isn't he sexy?"

Kate was also impressed that Wills was standing up for his younger brother. "We all thought it was wonderful how protective William was of Harry," said a Columbia University student who had gotten to know Kate in Florence. "But Kate—she was actually Catherine at the time—was maybe a little more enthusiastic about Prince William than the rest of us. She kept saying, 'He's mine, you know.' Joking, of course, since she'd never even met him."

The press conference also gave William the chance to announce where he intended to spend his gap year. Rumors had been rampant among the expatriates crammed into such Florentine cafés as the Antico Caffé del Moro, Le Logge, and the Gran Caffé San Marco that the prince, also probably an art history major, might soon land in their midst.

Instead, after his father had rejected William's original plan to play with an Argentine polo team as "too elitist," the Heir decided to head for the remote Chilean region of Patagonia. So, while Kate was sipping espresso and strolling along the banks of the Arno, William was scouring toilets, painting houses, and chopping wood in the tiny Chilean coastal village of Tortel. As part of Operation Raleigh, William was helping to rebuild Tortel and at the same time working shoulder to shoulder with juvenile offenders, recovering drug addicts, and homeless teens enlisted through a nonprofit program called At-Risk.

Once again, the Palace public-relations machine went into overdrive, showcasing the young prince's compassionate streak. Soon papers around the world were carrying photographs of William sawing lumber, scrubbing floors, and playing with local children. They had their desired effect, particularly on Kate. She promptly clipped the color photos out of *HELLO!* magazine and taped them to the wall of her room.

In early November, Kate's parents dropped in on their daughter in Florence. They stayed just a few blocks away at the opulent Grand Hotel, where they invited Kate and several of her new friends—British and Italian—for a drink. Later, they mingled with the younger crowd at a couple of local hangouts.

Michael, like his daughter, impressed everyone as charming and soft-spoken, almost to the point of being self-effacing. Carole, on the other hand, was anything but shy and retiring. Chain-smoking, gregarious, and always impeccably dressed, Mrs. Middleton "came across as nice but flashy," said a student. "Kate was never one who sought the limelight. Her mother was very different."

Carole took advantage of their time together to once gain press her daughter on the subject of St. Andrews. Kate countered that perhaps Pippa, who many regarded as the more attractive of the two Middleton sisters, could be enlisted to attend St. Andrews when she graduated from Marlborough in two years.

By Christmas of 2000, Kate finally caved in to her mother's incessant demands. She agreed to enroll at St. Andrews the following fall—but not before starting up a brief romance with an Oxford-bound student named Ian Henry. Each had signed up to serve as a crew member aboard different yachts sailing The Solent, a strait of the English Channel between the coast of Hampshire and the Isle of Wight. They met on the dock in Southampton and, over several weeks, wound up sailing together.

That summer, Kate and Henry went sailing again—this time in the Caribbean. "I would call her bubbly, outgoing, and down-to-earth," Henry said, neither admitting nor denying that their relationship was serious. "She is a fun girl."

Fun girls managed to find William—and vice versa—even while living in a tent city in the wilds of Patagonia. "There were lots of little romances," At-Risk volunteer Diane Tucker said of William's experience in Chile. Once again, royal protection officers reportedly tried not to invade their charge's privacy whenever a female coworker—and, on one occasion, two—spent the night in his tent.

Apparently not everyone was aware of Wills's fast-growing reputation as, in the words of one male volunteer, a "one-man wrecking crew among the girls." After downing a few glasses of wine around the campfire one evening, nineteen-year-old Claire Flood inexplicably asked the prince, "Are you a virgin?" Shocked, William did not respond. Instead, Flood said, "He just turned red!"

If his confidence was shaken, that was scarcely evident to another At-Risk volunteer, Kevin Mullen. Mullen, a recovering heroin addict, was mildly amused when William began "dirty-dancing with a lot of girls and making a spectacle of himself." But when Wills grabbed Mullen's girlfriend, Sasha Hashim, and started grinding his pelvis into hers, Mullen began screaming expletives at the prince. Fortunately for Mullen, Wills's bodyguards were ready to pounce but didn't. Before they could draw their weapons, a contrite Wills backed down. "He understood how hotheaded Kevin could be," Hashim said. "I was really embarrassed. . . . Will was a gentleman about the whole thing."

The dirty-dancing incident notwithstanding, William's security detail had found guarding the prince was a much simpler task away from civilization. Returning with the prince to England in late December, they now began drawing up plans for how to keep him safe at St. Andrews.

Of special concern was the Real IRA, the IRA splinter group that had set off a bomb in 1998 killing twenty-eight people in the tiny Ulster village of Omagh. Over the Internet, Real IRA operatives were trading detailed information about security measures being planned for William at St. Andrews, as well as providing a map that showed places where assassins might position themselves within "extremely accurate range" of Prince William. A group of Scottish separatists were even more to the point. "Anyone," wrote one of their leaders in an e-mail, "could shoot the fucker any time they wanted."

With the approval of Prime Minister Tony Blair, Britain's domestic intelligence agency, MI5, combed the rooms William was set to occupy at St. Andrews. They found electronic devices everywhere—devices that had actually been planted by the overzealous royal protection squad.

William was livid and threatened not to attend university at all if a total lack of privacy was the price he was being asked to pay. Remembering the humiliation he experienced after his phone conversations with Camilla became public, Papa did not have to be convinced. At Charles's insistence, all listening devices were removed.

Still, Wills wondered if he would be able to have anything approaching a normal love life in college. "What girl is going to want to spend five minutes with me," he asked Nicky Knatchbull, "if they think everything we do or say to each other is going to wind up in *News of the World?*"

In the months ahead, William and Harry, who was again happy to step out of his brother's shadow now that Wills was leaving Eton, had several important decisions to make. First and foremost was deciding among various proposals for a monument to their mother. The Queen had nixed the boldest of these—renaming Heathrow after Diana—leaving the boys to choose between several designs for statues and fountains.

On July 1, 2000, the $3 million Princess Diana Playground was opened within sight of Kensington Palace. Now William was eager to see something more ambitious. In the spring of 2001 the two young princes gave the go-ahead to a memorial fountain along the Diana Memorial Walkway winding from Kensington Palace to Westminster Abbey. Along the walkway were seventy plaques bearing an English rose—a nod to Elton John's lyric honoring his friend Diana, "Good-bye, England's Rose."

The Men in Gray had plenty for Wills to do now that he was back in London. Among other things, he was coaxed into attending the tenth anniversary of the Press Complaints Commission—a gesture of gratitude for keeping the tabloids at bay in the years since his mother's death.

Papa also seized the opportunity to ease Camilla into the royal fold and gain her at least a modicum of public acceptance. For the first time, Charles's still much reviled mistress attended the same function as the Prince of Wales and Prince William, although she was careful not to actually be seen alongside them. The Queen's rule that William not be photographed with the woman who destroyed his parents' marriage remained in full force. "There was nothing the Queen could do about her son," a courtier observed, "but she did not want anything to tarnish William."

Unwilling to spend the balance of his gap year being used as a pawn in the battle over Camilla, Wills headed off to another foreign adventure. In mid-March he arrived at the fifty-five-thousand-acre Lewa Conservancy, an African wildlife preserve on the Laikipia Plateau stretching from the Great Rift Valley to the slopes of Mount Kenya. The Lewa Conservancy was the world's largest rhino sanctuary.

For the next four months, William dug trenches, repaired fences, and lived under conditions that were even worse than those he experienced in Chile. On the preserve, he coped with hyenas, vipers, and—worst of all—plumbing facilities that consisted of a hole in the ground and a bucket for bathing.

None of this stood in the way of William's whirlwind romance with nineteen-year-old Jessica "Jecca" Craig, the stunningly attractive, ash-blond daughter of sanctuary owner Ian Craig. The Craig family started the Lewa Conservancy in 1922, and the Craigs were so immersed in East Africa and its customs that Jecca's older brother was named Batian, after one of Mount Kenya's highest peaks.

Over the four months of their working side by side, the relationship deepened to the point where William admitted to another sanctuary volunteer that she was "the most wonderful girl I've ever known." Educated at Pembroke House, a boarding school near the Kenyan village of Gilgil in the Great Rift Valley, Jecca "always had a lot of admirers—hardly surprising for a slim, sporty blonde," a Pembroke House schoolmate said. "Jecca is very striking indeed and it makes sense that William would be attracted to her. She's a lovely, down-to-earth girl."

Shortly before leaving for home in mid-July, William and Jecca left their compound and drove at breakneck speed toward the foot of Mount Kenya. Wills's royal protection officers followed right behind, squinting through the clouds of white-yellow dust churned up by the couple's Land Rover.

Once at their destination, William and Jecca gazed up through the acacia trees at the jagged, mist-shrouded peak. The prince's bodyguards, meantime, hung back, trying as always to keep a discreet distance. William pulled Jecca toward him and they kissed. Then, to the astonishment of his bodyguards, he got down on one knee.

"Jecca," William asked solemnly, "will you marry me?"

Why would anyone want to go out with *me*?
　　　　　—William

There's no one quite like William, is there?
　　　　　—Kate

I'm only going to university. It's not like I'm getting married,
although that's what it feels like sometimes.
　　　　　—William

4

When I first met Kate, I knew there was something special about her. I knew there was something I wanted to explore there. . . .

—*William*

"Bugger!" William said as his father steered their racing-green Vauxhaul Estate onto the North Street approach to St. Andrews and past a crowd of four thousand fans straining against police barricades. Charles was so startled that he misjudged the angle into the narrow archway beneath the St. Andrews medieval clock tower. Embarrassed, he backed up and tried again.

Both princes managed a wan smile for the screaming, camera-clicking mob—although Charles later confessed that at that moment he was genuinely frightened that the local police on hand might not be able to handle things. "I almost," he said, "turned around and fled."

Clad in the usual student uniform of jeans and a navy blue sweater, William emerged from the car and strode confidently toward the cheering bystanders. Already accustomed to working a crowd, he shook a few hands, made some small talk, and moved on. "He touched my hand," said one of the lucky few women he stopped to chat with. "Wait till I tell my sister!"

Kate hung toward the back of the crowd, fascinated and a little excited to be part of all the commotion, but also a little embarrassed to be there at all. "I think most thought it was a bit uncool to be seen waiting for him," said organic-chemistry student Erin Bedard. "That's why we were hiding at the back like twelve-year-olds. But it probably will be the last time we see him, even though we study here." Fellow student Allie Giddings, an American, surveyed the pandemonium. "I feel," she sighed, "kind of sorry for the dude."

No one was feeling sorrier for "the dude" than Kate. She later told friends that, as she watched Wills do his gentlemanly best to connect with his subjects, she could see "sadness in his eyes. I think he just wants to be left alone to have a normal college life, but I suppose that's impossible."

William devoutly hoped that was not the case. In another carefully circumscribed interview granted in exchange for being left alone by the press, he asked to be "treated like any other student." Reading the interview back in Bucklebury, Carole Middleton paid close attention to what William said about the prince's taste in friends. He bristled at the implication that he would seek out only people of his own class. "It's about their character and who they are and whether we get on," he said, adding somewhat tentatively, "I just hope I meet people I get on with."

One of the few people he felt he could share his innermost feelings with was forty-six-hundred miles away in the wilds of East Africa. Although their secret "engagement" ceremony at the foot of Mt. Kenya two months earlier had been nothing more than a teenage lark, Wills and Jecca Craig had continued their close relationship via e-mail. It remained to be seen, he told her in one, if he would ever find any girl at St. Andrews "as brilliant as you."

Following his brief walkabout that first day, Wills stepped onto the broad, manicured lawns of the St. Andrews quadrangle, trailed by his security detail. He gingerly sidestepped a memorial stone bearing the initials *PH*, for Patrick Hamilton. The first Protestant martyr in Scotland, Hamilton was burned at the stake on the grounds of the university. According to St. Andrews superstition, anyone who stepped on the stone would fail to earn his degree.

As he walked toward his rooms at St. Salvator's residence hall, Wills might have hoped for a little peace. During the two months leading up to his arrival at St. Andrews, it had been, as Richard Kay put it, "one hammer blow after another."

Over the years, several of William's closest friends and even a few relatives had grappled with substance abuse. Wills and his father had been blissfully unaware of Harry's first exposure to pot at the age of fourteen. But after he was caught in July smoking a joint behind a toolshed at the Rattlebone Inn, a four-hundred-year-old pub not far from Highgrove, it quickly became clear that Harry, now sixteen, might be headed for a drug problem of his own.

Somehow managing to keep the incident out of the papers—at least for the moment—Papa consulted with Wills before sending Harry to spend a day talking to recovering heroin and cocaine addicts at South London's Featherstone Lodge Rehabilitation Centre. The experience left Harry shaken, but not enough to sober him up. Within weeks he was drinking himself into oblivion on a near-nightly basis. Soon Harry, who was now passing out or throwing up in some of London's most fashionable nightspots, would earn a new nickname from his friends: the Sponge.

In time the press got wind of Harry's visit to Featherstone and the marijuana use that triggered it. The sordid details of Harry's drunken escapades and his pot smoking would shock the nation and leave Wills feeling he was somehow responsible. "Harry always depended on his mother for guidance," Diana's brother Earl Spencer said, "and on William." With William away on his gap-year adventures, Harry was left to his own devices. Diana and William, Spencer said, would "never have let things get out of hand the way Charles did."

The brothers were not prepared for the arrest of their mother's trusted butler, Paul Burrell, formally charged that August with pilfering 342 items worth an estimated $7.7 million from Diana's Kensington Palace apartments. The case would drag on for two years, pushing Burrell to the brink of bankruptcy and suicide. Only then, on the eve of Burrell's court testimony, did the Queen rescue the butler by suddenly recalling a meeting at which Burrell had told her he was setting aside some of the princess's belongings for "safekeeping."

At that same meeting, the Queen took Burrell into her confidence—if only fleetingly. "Be careful, Paul," she warned him. "There are powers at work in this country about which we have no knowledge." Burrell recalled that the Queen "fixed me with her eye and made sure I knew she was being deadly serious. I had no idea who she was talking about. . . . But she was clearly warning me to be vigilant."

Before it was all over, the Burrell Affair would unleash a series of scandalous revelations that rocked the House of Windsor. Chief among these was an accusation by former Kensington Palace footman and valet George Smith that he had been raped by one of Prince Charles's senior manservants—and that Smith had witnessed a similar incident involving another male servant and an unnamed member of the Royal Family. Moreover, there were hints at a royal cover-up; Charles had, it was reported, paid for the alleged rapist's lawyers to the tune of nearly $200,000. The matter would eventually be dropped, but the headlines generated (I WAS RAPED BY CHARLES'S MANSERVANT, PANIC GRIPS THE PALACE) left everyone—especially the hypersensitive William—shaken.

The September 11 terrorist attacks on the World Trade Center and the Pentagon put everything in perspective. While Kate and her family gathered in their living room to watch the BBC's live coverage of the unfolding events, members of the Royal Family were glued to their television screens at Balmoral. The Queen, who had been alerted to the attacks by her private secretary, Robin Janvrin, was visibly moved. For the first time, William saw tears well up in Granny's eyes. Later, the Queen could manage only a few words to describe her reaction. She was, she said, "watching developments in growing disbelief and total shock."

William was equally upset. "They are a very stoic bunch, the Royal Family," a member of the household staff observed. "But not this time." Harry "could not sit down—he just jumped out of his chair and stood there, with his fists clenched. I remember Prince William with his head in his hands when the towers collapsed—not crying, but very shaken. He kept saying, 'Oh, my God, oh, my God.' "

Wills and Harry had long shared their mother's affection for America; at the time of her death, she was in the market for a beach house in Malibu where they could all get away from the English press. Now, beyond the formal statements of support issued by the Queen on behalf of the British people, William in particular was determined to express solidarity with the Americans in his own way. He suggested that for a time only patriotic American music be played during the daily Changing of the Guard ceremonies at Buckingham Palace.

Spurred on by her grandson, the Queen did her part. During a memorial at St. Paul's Cathedral, she stood up and became the first British monarch in history to sing "The Star-Spangled Banner." Since the Queen does not even sing "God Save the Queen," it was a major show of royal support from Granny. "The way William took charge to tell America, 'We're with you,' " said Harold Brooks-Baker, "was inspiring."

After such a tumultuous summer, William was eager to start his new life at St. Andrews. Home for him now was a single fifteen-by-fifteen-foot room at St. Salvator's for which the average student paid nearly $4,000 a year. Built in 1930, "Sallies" was a brooding, vine-covered Gothic-style monolith that overlooked the North Sea. Although William strictly obeyed house rules against lighting candles or joss sticks, he would not be required to ask the house warden for permission to stay out all night. With his bodyguards staying in a room adjacent to his, the prince's whereabouts would never be in question.

At the same time, Kate was moving into her own fifteen-by-fifteen-foot room at St. Salvator's, but on a different, girls-only floor. For Kate, who had been forced to adapt after switching schools when she was younger, adjusting to her new environment was relatively easy. She had known several of her St. Andrews classmates—perhaps most notably Mili d'Erlanger—at Marlborough. Another Sallies resident, Virginia "Ginny" Fraser, had known Kate even longer, since the time they were both students at Downe House. Carole was pleased that her daughter was in such impressive company; Fraser's father was Lloyd's underwriter Lord Strathalmond.

From the beginning, William was made painfully aware that his was not likely to be a normal college experience. Sticking to their agreement with St. James's Palace to give the prince his privacy, camera crews that had been filming his arrival that first day departed that evening.

Everyone's but Prince Edward's. Wills's uncle had dispatched a camera crew from his fledgling TV documentary unit to shadow the royal fresher during his first few days at St. Andrews. Both William and his father were, said a Palace spokesman, "incandescent with rage" over this treachery perpetrated by none other than a member of the Royal Family. After a blistering dressing down by his big brother, Edward called a halt to the project.

Determined at first not to draw undue attention to himself, Wills declined invitations to join any student clubs or organizations. Instead, he concentrated on his studies and tried to stick to a schedule that would leave him little time for socializing: up at 5:30 a.m. so he could jog under cover of darkness, shower and dress, then off to his first lecture of the day in the Buchanan Building. (At William's request, his bodyguards waited for him at Marmaris, a tiny Middle Eastern restaurant down the street that specialized in shish kebab.) Every Friday was dedicated exclusively to his tutorial group, a cluster of a half dozen students who went over the previous week's lessons.

William's concerted effort to remain detached did not go unnoticed. "He never smiles back," said one female student in his geography class. "No eye contact. Strictly business. It must be very hard, really, to know that people are watching you and you mustn't let them *know* that you know."

Nevertheless, within days of arriving at St. Andrews, William decided to break the ice with his fellow students by asking them up to his room for a drink. To his tight circle of college friends, which already included Fergus Boyd and fellow Etonian Oliver Chadwyck-Healey, William added Jules Knight, the son of a Sussex banker, a comely brunette named Carly Massy-Birch . . . and Kate.

"Kate and Carly are both very beautiful, very smart girls," said an eyewitness to this first meeting. "But they were a little intimidated at first, just like the rest of us. We all got a little giggly—Kate as well—before going up to his floor. But Will puts one at ease right away."

"We all played it extremely cool, of course," said Knight, who met both William and Kate while waiting outside the Buchanan Building for their first lecture to start. An actor and singer, Knight would later join with three friends to form the classical-pop group Blake. "But there was something unsaid, an electricity in the air, and it would be churlish to pretend it did not exist. Being English, William's presence was almost completely ignored in terms of conversation, but everyone was thinking the same thing: 'This *is* exciting!' "

William was always aware of the impact he had on people. He was, after all, not only destined to be king, but he was the eldest son of the most famous woman of the twentieth century. Add to that his physical presence—blond, handsome, six foot three—and, Kate told a classmate, "he takes your breath away."

When Kate first met William at St. Salvator's, she later recalled, "I turned bright red and sort of scuttled off, feeling very shy about meeting him." But before long Wills, said a mutual friend, "spilled a drink on himself, swore as he dabbed it up, and instantly made himself look like a real human being, which he is."

Kate's reaction to the fumbling prince? "She laughed, of course. That's the idea. Will can be clumsy, actually, but most of the time it's really just an act. Otherwise, people would just keep gawping at him."

William was smitten from the beginning—not with Kate, however, but with Kate's friend Carly Massy-Birch. An aspiring actress, Massy-Birch was the daughter of a Devon farmer, and perhaps because William had done work on a Devon farm during his gap year, the two clicked instantly. Before long, Carly told her parents about the handsome young man she was dating. When she left home for St. Andrews, Hugh Massy-Birch had jokingly cautioned his daughter not to bother bringing a boy home unless his family had a household staff that included a groundsman and a gamekeeper. "Oh, don't worry, Dad," she told him. "His family has those."

For the next seven weeks, William and Carly were inseparable. "They were lovers, yes," said Carly's mother, Mimi Massy-Birch. "William had only been with one girl before, I think. . . ." The first girl he had "been with," suggested the mother of Wills's first college lover, was either Jecca Craig or a girl who lived not far from Highgrove, Arabella Musgrave. "He is such a good, good guy—he *really* is," Mimi Massy-Birch continued. "So down-to-earth. Very kind, very shy."

The business of dating a prince was anything but down-to-earth, however. On several occasions, Carly would be picked up by one of William's bodyguards and driven to a pub. Then she walked through the establishment and out the back door, where a second car was waiting to whisk her off to yet another location, where the prince was waiting for her.

The drama proved too much for Carly. According to her mother, Carly "got so fed up and bored with it. It was too much for her, really." Seven weeks into the affair, Carly confided to her parents that she had had enough. "I just can't live like this," she told them. "Constantly being chased by the wretched paparazzi, the constant attention—it's all William has ever known, but it's too much for me. In late November the relationship ended as quickly as it began. Carly waxed philosophical about the breakup. "William is brilliant," Carly told her mother. "But I think we were only meant to be great friends."

William, still avoiding events for first-year students such as Raisin Weekend (which includes yet another pub crawl, a costume party, and an alcohol-fueled "foam party"), stayed largely out of sight. Occasionally he would drop in at P.M.'s diner on Union Street and order the house speciality—Southern-fried chicken. At other times, he would order Chinese takeout from Ruby's on Market Street or indulge his love of candy at Burns Sweets Shop.

To get around St. Andrews, he drove either his white VW Golf or the 125 cc Kawasaki motorcycle his father gave him (he later acquired a Yamaha 600 off-road bike as well). For security purposes, he varied the routes he took, although in such a tiny town the options were limited. One day he might cut across an alleyway named Butts Wynd heading toward Union Street, and the next simply stay the length of a street called The Scores.

Even though his royal protection officers trailed behind in a Land Rover, Wills could maintain some anonymity on his motorcycles because he wore a helmet. "I look right at them and they can't see my face," he told his friend Hamish Barne. "It's wonderful!"

With a nod to the country he now found himself in, William tried his hand—or rather his feet—at some traditional Scottish dances, such as the Highland fling and the occasional reel. "I am hopeless at it," he said, "but I do enjoy it. I do throw my arms dangerously around and girls fly across the dance floor." For the moment, he drew the line at wearing kilts—something his father and grandfather did in public quite a lot. "I haven't got into it yet," he said. "It's a bit drafty."

As much as he loved Scotland, as soon as the weekend arrived, Wills was eager to escape. "Weekends at St. Andrews," he complained to the British Press Association's Peter Archer, "are not particularly vibrant." During his first year there, he would spend a scant seven weekends on campus. Instead, he preferred to jump in his VW and make the ninety-minute drive south to Edinburgh. "I imagine my father would go absolutely bananas if he saw me driving," Wills said, "blaring music out the windows."

There were also forays north to Balmoral, where the Queen had set aside a three-bedroom bungalow for the exclusive use of the Heir and the Spare, and south to London for club-hopping with old friends. William, however, felt most at home at Highgrove. There he could also indulge in his favorite pastime at the nearby Beaufort Polo Club, squaring off against Harry. Invariably, one or the other prince wound up being pitched off his horse headfirst, only to pop back up, dust himself off, and remount.

William had other reasons for wanting to spend weekends at Highgrove rather than St. Andrews. While playing at the Beaufort Polo Club, several months earlier, he'd met Arabella Musgrave, whose father, Major Nicholas Musgrave, managed the rival Cirencester Park Polo Club. Unaware of Jecca Craig, there were those who touted "Bella" Musgrave as Wills's first love. That is why, a Musgrave family friend said, the prince was "taken by complete surprise" when Bella broke with him just before he left for St. Andrews. "She was worried that he had a roving eye. . . . From what I understand, he took the breakup quite hard."

So hard that he made several trips back to Gloucestershire for the express purpose of winning her back. Although they could be seen talking at Tunnel House, a favorite hangout of Wills's near Highgrove, it was not to be. Certainly Bella's concerns were valid; at the same time he was trying to woo her back, Wills was dating Carly Massy-Birch back at St. Andrews. He was also exchanging e-mails with Jecca Craig and, when the spirit moved him, snogging with various females he encountered while clubbing in London and Edinburgh.

Just as important, Bella would later concede, was that she was being "suffocated" by all the attention. "I hated," she said, "being famous for going out with William."

While William was between girlfriends, Kate was happily involved with a darkly handsome, six-foot-two-inch-tall senior named Rupert Finch. Oddly enough, Rupert's father, John, managed to earn a substantial enough living as a tenant farmer on Norfolk land owned by Diana's brother, Earl Spencer. To supplement the family's income, Rupert's mother, Prudence, gave riding lessons.

Despite Carole Middleton's constant inquiries about Prince William, Kate was "head over heels" about Finch, said a friend from her days at Marlborough College. A star player on St. Andrews's cricket squad, he had been picked to head up the team when it toured South Africa. "Rupert was gorgeous and sporty, like Kate—and very funny," Kate's friend said. "They came from similar backgrounds and liked the same things. Prince William was friendly, but I think she felt being with Rupert was a little more . . . realistic."

Through Kate, Finch also became acquainted with William, who scrupulously avoided coming between the two. However, since they were both art history majors, Wills did begin to lean more heavily on Kate for advice. "She is a very levelheaded girl," he told one of his friends. "She doesn't try and tell me what she thinks I should do. I like that. I am so tired of people telling me what they think I should do."

Wills's having to bail out of St. Andrews every weekend and drive for hours just to see friends and family was fast taking its toll. "It's easy to feel cut off," observed his Eton chum David Walston, "if you're not around the few people you can really count on."

William, said another Etonian, was "desperately unhappy with the choice he'd made. He knew St. Andrews was not going to be terribly exciting, but he hadn't expected it to be the most drab place on earth, which it is."

That Christmas, feeling isolated and—despite his new friends—very much alone, William begged his father to let him transfer to another school. But the political ramifications were too great. William's mere presence at St. Andrews had already served to tamp down the more extreme factions in the Scottish nationalist movement. During one of their teas at Windsor Castle, the Queen had gone so far as to thank her grandson for helping her forge stronger ties between Scotland and the Crown. To leave now, he was told by Charles's advisers Mark Bolland and Sir Stephen Lamport, would send entirely the wrong signal. It would also, said a courtier, make the future king of England look "like a whinger [whiner]."

Charles asked his son to stick it out for one more year—"for Granny." Still not entirely convinced that he should remain at St. Andrews, William turned to his friend Kate for guidance. Even as he was harboring doubts about his choice of St. Andrews, Kate, too, was having second thoughts. She consulted her parents, confiding in them that William might consider leaving as well.

Taking an approach similar to Charles's with William, Michael and Carole Middleton urged their daughter give it at least another year. Once back at St. Andrews that January, Wills and Kate made a pact to try to make a go of it for at least another year. "If we feel then like we do now," she said, "I'm leaving with you!"

It was just the pep talk Wills needed. "I don't think I was homesick," he said of his early "wobbles" concerning St. Andrews. "I was more daunted."

No sooner had the new semester begun than William suffered personal losses in which the entire nation shared. In February, the Queen's only sibling, the notoriously high-living Princess Margaret, succumbed to a variety of health problems at the age of seventy-one. Seven weeks later, William, Harry, and Charles were skiing in Switzerland when they received word that William's indomitable great-grandmother, the Queen Mother, had died at 101.

Ever since she and her husband, King George VI, chose to stay in London and brave Nazi bombs during World War II, the Queen Mum had been the most beloved member of the Royal Family. To William she was "Great Gran," a kindred spirit who loved Balmoral, off-color jokes, and gin and tonics. Wills told Kate about how the Queen Mum loved to imitate Ali G, the faux rapper created by Sacha Baron Cohen of *Borat* fame, and what she said when he told her he had decided to attend St. Andrews: "If there are any good parties, invite me down."

Now Kate watched her friend from a distance as he joined his relatives and more than sixty heads of state for the Queen Mother's funeral service at Westminster Abbey. "My father is completely undone by this," William said. Indeed, Charles admitted, "Somehow, I never thought her death would come. She seemed gloriously unstoppable, and ever since I was a child, I adored her."

For the first time, Kate was getting an inside look at how William's personal life was tethered to history. According to friends, it both frightened and fascinated her. "Watching Prince William have to deal with such pressure," Peter Archer said, "and to do it so graciously, had to have greatly impressed her."

Digging in for another semester at St. Andrews, Wills and Kate—who was still very much involved with Rupert Finch—made a concerted effort to involve themselves in student life. In response to the campus's all-male Kate Kennedy Club—an organization so notoriously chauvinistic that William turned down an early invitation to join—Kate started a club of her own. The rival, all-female Lumsden Club was named for prominent nineteenth-century women's educator Louisa Lumsden. Its purpose: to raise money for charity, although, as was the case with most such fundraising efforts on campus, the Lumsden Club's approach consisted largely of hosting events such as the Pimm's Party and the Red-Hot Martini cocktail party.

Spurred on by Kate's involvement in her all-women's club, William changed his mind and became a member of the ostensibly woman-hating Kate Kennedy Club. "Maybe I can change things," he told her halfheartedly. Wills's new commitment to campus also meant that he was no longer dashing home every Friday afternoon to cross mallets with his father and his brother on the polo field. Instead, the prince stayed to compete in weekend soccer and rugby leagues. He also captained the school's water polo team, and water-skied and surfed in the North Sea.

Since he was now living where the sport was invented, Wills was even persuaded to take up golf. But first, William had to suppress the still vivid memory of being struck in the head by a nine iron at the age of eight—a mishap that left a visible dent above his left eye. Before he took his first swing, it was pointed out to the future king that Mary, Queen of Scots, had also played the course at St. Andrews. After her husband, Lord Darnley, was murdered in 1567, the Scottish Queen celebrated by taking to the links.

Kate had one last inhibition of her own to conquer. At William's urging, she agreed to participate in the university's annual Don't Walk charity fashion show sponsored by Yves Saint Laurent. Before the show got under way, all eyes were on one audience member; Wills had plunked down two hundred pounds for a front-row seat. When Kate loped down the runway wearing a transparent lace sheath over a bandeau bra and black bikini bottoms, the prince led the applause. Whoops and cheers went up later when she returned to the catwalk wearing a white lace bra and white lace panties—this time accompanied by Wills's old Eton chum Fergus Boyd in black boxer briefs. "We were all wowed," Jules Knight recalled. "Here was this reserved girl we knew up onstage, looking like a smoldering temptress."

Understandably, designer Charlotte Todd was "over the moon" when Kate appeared wearing her lingerie on the catwalk "because she has got a fabulous figure and looked absolutely brilliant in it." It didn't hurt that Prince William seemed to appreciate how the transparent sheath and barely there bra and panties looked as well. "It was a side to her we didn't know existed," Knight said, "and it was a turning point in people's perception of her. Everyone took note, including Will."

Rupert Finch, now heavily into preparations to take the St. Andrews cricket squad to South Africa, also made time to catch his girlfriend prance down the runway in her sexy underthings. But as Kate's first year at St. Andrews wound down, Finch was preparing to graduate and had even lined up a trainee position with the prestigious London law firm of Mills & Reeve. Kate was, she later said, "happy to see Rupert get on with his life."

So was William. When he learned that Finch was no longer in

the picture, he told their mutual pal Fergus Boyd, "Then I think I'll have a go." The prince's first step toward having a "go" was asking if Kate would join him and Boyd in sharing an apartment off-campus—a move designed to free them all from the constraints of dormitory living at Sallies. Kate hesitated at first; she told her mother that it felt "awkward" being the only girl in the equation. Carole Middleton apparently found the proposed arrangement anything but awkward. Prince William and Boyd were longtime friends and could certainly be trusted. She urged her daughter to accept their invitation—without delay.

Despite the tight rental market, Wills was able to pull some royal strings and arrange to rent a four-bedroom flat on the ground floor of a Georgian-style town house in the middle of St. Andrews's exclusive Old Town district. Each would pitch in $165 a month for his or her own room, the fourth being set aside for Wills's security detail and of course paid for by the Crown.

Wills and Kate brushed off the inevitable headlines (WILLIAM AND HIS UNDIE-GRADUATE FRIEND KATE TO SHARE A STUDENT FLAT in the *Mail on Sunday*, WILLIAM SHACKS UP WITH STUNNING UNDIES MODEL in the *Sun*) by maintaining that she already had a boyfriend. Besides, Boyd and their other pals insisted, William and Kate were merely "mates."

For the time being at least, Kate and William headed off in separate directions for the summer holiday. Intent on earning some pocket money of her own, she took a job serving drinks at $8 an hour for a British catering firm called Snatch. "Kate's a superb barmaid," Snatch owner Rory Laing said. "She's a pretty girl, so she takes home plenty in tips."

While Kate worked as a barmaid that June, William joined his family in celebrating Granny's fiftieth year on the throne. Kicking off the Golden Jubilee festivities was a classical concert, followed two days later by a "Party at the Palace" pop concert held in the Buckingham Palace gardens. William sat between his father and the Queen, clapping and singing along with Phil Collins, Tom Jones, Elton John, Tony Bennett, and Paul McCartney.

A few weeks later, on what would have been her forty-first birthday, William and Harry visited their mother's grave at Althorp. It was something, Earl Spencer was quick to point out, that in the five years since her death neither Charles nor the Queen had ever done—"not a single time."

From Kate's new vantage point as a barmaid, William's other life seemed distant indeed. "Sometimes I can't believe the Will I know and Prince William are the same person," she told her sister. She kept her cell phone on vibrate so as not to disturb patrons when serving drinks, but when she checked and recognized Wills's number, it all seemed "surreal" to her.

Still, they kept in touch throughout the summer, chatting over the phone nearly every day. In August, Kate called after reading about a bizarre attempt on the prince's life. When she asked him about a twenty-two-year-old Montana woman who had been arrested for trying to send a cyanide-laced bottle of Coke to William in the mail, he merely laughed it off. "If my paella didn't kill me," he joked, "nothing will."

Kate was falling hard for her prince, and according to one of her Snatch coworkers, "you could see her face light up every time he called. She was walking on air." A number of patrons and one or two Snatch staffers asked Kate out during the summer, but she declined. That summer of 2002, she only went out for the occasional drink with female friends or in a group. "Kate's a sweet, unassuming kind of girl," Jules Knight said. "She felt something for Will straightaway, and he was all in for her, completely."

Perhaps. But whatever Kate's feelings for him, that summer

William was very much living the life of a playboy prince. The three girls who famously cruised with him aboard the "royal love boat" *Alexander*—Mary Forestier-Walker, Davina Duckworth-Chad, and St. Andrews pal Mili d'Erlanger—were still in the picture, spotted snuggling up to Wills at some of the hotter night-spots in London. Natalie "Nats" Hicks-Lobbeke, an army officer's daughter and a student at Bristol University, soon joined their ranks.

Before long another attractive St. Andrews student was added to the royal mix—Olivia Bleasdale, daughter of a Royal Artillery officer—as well as a stunning blonde with a name that was tongue-twisting even by royal standards: Lady Isabella Anstruther-Gough-Calthorpe.

Just down the road from Highgrove at the Beaufort Polo Club, William was having an up-close-and-personal relationship with club employee Amanda Bush—Tigger or just plain Tig to her friends, after Winnie-the-Pooh's bouncy sidekick. Always cheering him on from the sidelines, Tigger pretended to be flustered when, after one match, he suddenly stripped off his sweat-soaked shirt. She then knelt down and helped him pull off his riding boots.

Their relationship was not confined to daylight hours; Wills and Tig were seen at local hangouts such as the Wild Duck, holding hands and whispering into each other's ears. "She's a very natural-type girl, and he responds to that," a Beaufort staffer said. "She'll creep up on him and poke him in the ribs, then he'll tickle her, and when they think no one is watching, they'll sneak a kiss."

Such dalliances aside, the greatest threat to William's image that summer came from his consumption of alcohol. "There was a lot of drinking going on," Jules Knight said. "It was part of the social culture. It was nonstop." Several times a week, the Heir could be spotted, red-faced and bleary-eyed, trying to sneak out of a London club. One of the more embarrassing episodes occurred at a party at a friend's castle in Suffolk. Around 3:00 a.m., a clearly inebriated William peeled down to a pair of swim trunks and took a dip in the castle moat. Emerging from the filthy water, he strolled across the dance floor, wrapped a baby blue feather boa around his neck, and began doing a striptease. Apparently not satisfied that the drunken prince looked silly enough, a pretty brunette wrapped a pink boa around his waist as he danced.

William's summer of fun came to an abrupt end with the publication in September of yet another Diana tell-all—this time by a man he once regarded as a father figure. As children, William and Harry were both deeply fond of their bluff, ruddy-cheeked personal protection officer, Ken Wharfe. An accomplished amateur opera singer who sometimes burst into song without warning, the outgoing Wharfe also kept the princess and her sons entertained by tap-dancing around Kensington Palace. Soon Charles and Diana both worried that the boys were becoming too attached to Wharfe and had him reassigned as the princess's exclusive personal bodyguard—a move that nevertheless meant that he would still be a presence in the boys' lives.

In the pages of *Diana: Closely Guarded Secret*, Wharfe joined the chorus of former employees who painted a picture of the princess as calculating, neurotic, and reckless. Among the more tawdry revelations: that she thought nothing of waltzing about him in the nude, and that she had a name for the vibrator that she always carried in her purse: *le gadget*.

An angry Prince Charles called for Scotland Yard chief Sir John Stevens to take legal action against the retired Wharfe. Meanwhile the Queen, said her private secretary Robin Janvrin, "is very perturbed. She is extremely worried about the effect all this will have on her grandsons."

Scandalous headlines about their mother were nothing new, of course. And after James Hewitt, Paul Burrell, and Patrick Jephson, it could hardly have come as a surprise when another trusted adviser and friend decided to cash in. "The princes are accustomed to seeing the people they once trusted sell them out," said a friend of the princess. "They grew up in an atmosphere thick with betrayal."

Nonetheless, it all seemed to be having a cumulative effect. According to Wills's close friend Guy Pelly and others, William turned to Kate for comfort. Over the phone, Wills told her that he was concerned about his brother, that he worried the stress might push Harry back in the direction of drug abuse. "Kate always offered a sympathetic ear," Jules Knight said. "She is very compassionate, very kind." According to another acquaintance, Kate offered something "none of the other girls had. Take a close look at Kate. There is a serenity about her, a kind of calm. It's hard to put your finger on it, but so many of these other beautiful girls don't know when to shut up and listen, and she did."

Wills and Kate wasted no time rekindling their romance once they returned to St. Andrews. Within days of moving in together that September of 2002, their relationship was, said one housemate, "no longer platonic."

Unlike some of the other women Wills had dated, Kate quickly adjusted to the bodyguards shadowing their every move. Understanding that these serious-looking men packing equally serious firearms had an important job to do, she went out of her way to befriend them. "She is a delightful girl," said one. "Very down-to-earth, very considerate. She says hello and treats you like a person, never acting like you're not there."

Invisibility, in fact, was what Will's bodyguards were aiming for. The Close Protection Team, as the prince's security detail was sometimes called, was "incredibly discreet," Knight said. "There was the odd amusing time when Will would be in a bar, and we'd all play 'Spot the Bodyguard,' trying to figure out who they were. Of course, he knew who they were, and we got to know them, too. But part of their effectiveness was that they were unremarkable-looking people wearing nondescript clothes." On one early outing, for example, Knight was on his way to the restroom when he saw three men at the bar, all drinking Coke. "They were leaning forward with their arms on the table," Knight said, "and with the outline of the handguns in their pockets inadvertently visible." It was a sight, he added, "you quickly got used to if you were a friend of Will's."

For the most part, William and his roommates stuck close to home. They continued to rely heavily on take-out food, from Ruby's and now Pizza Express, and prepared their own meals two or three times a week. William was, by his own admission, "absolutely useless" in the kitchen, despite having taken cooking classes at Eton. Fortunately, both of his roommates had mastered several basic chicken, pasta, and curry dishes so that they could dine at home. "I've got some very good cooks in my house," he told a reporter during another Palace-arranged interview. "I cook quite regularly for them and they cook for me . . . but I obviously make out better in the end."

Trying to make up for his lack of proficiency in the kitchen, William took it upon himself to do much of the food shopping at local supermarkets such as Safeway and Tesco (bodyguards stationing themselves inconspicuously at each end of the aisle he was shopping in). Supermarket shopping would prove to be therapeutic. "I do all my own shopping," he mused. "I enjoy the shopping, actually. I get very carried away, you know, just food shopping. I buy lots of things and then go back to the house and see the fridge is full of all the stuff I've just bought."

In the interest of fairness, the rest of the household chores were divided up equally among William and his roommates—an arrangement that quickly unraveled. "We got on very well," he said, "but of course it just broke down into complete chaos." In the end, "we just attended to things in the usual haphazard way."

Evenings at home were usually spent listening to R&B or rock on the stereo, and occasionally playing chess—a game William learned during his gap year abroad—with Boyd and Kate. "It was quite a cozy setup."

William and Kate could scarcely have been described as homebodies during this period. "I'm not a party animal, despite what some people might think," Wills insisted. "But I like to go out sometimes like anyone else."

William and Kate were frequent customers at such student hangouts as Broons, the Gin House, the West Port Bar, and the bistro bar inside the Byre Theatre. Their favorite haunt was Ma Bells, a cramped, brightly lit, ground-floor pub at the St. Andrews Golf Hotel. Sometimes referred to as Yeah-Yeah Bells because of the number of tony London "yeah-yeah" girls who frequented it, Ma Bells looked more like a local's rumpus room than a royal sanctuary. The walls were knotty pine, the decor was canary yellow, and narrow windows overlooked a parking lot to the sea beyond.

In addition to the golf games that seemed to run continuously on overhead TV screens, Ma Bell's offered video games and a karaoke machine. In addition to the *Full Monty* karaoke routine he had perfected with Harry, William was not above offering impromptu renditions of Gloria Gaynor's "I Will Survive" or any number of songs by the Bee Gees. On the rare occasions when she'd had more than two or three drinks, Kate sometimes joined him at the microphone. "There really aren't many places he can go where they don't make a fuss over him," one of their friends said. "When he finds a restaurant or a club where he won't get mauled, he tends to stick to it."

St. Andrews itself functioned as one big club for the press-wary prince. "St. Andrews University has the feeling of one big private house party," their friend Jules Knight observed, "because it is so cosseted. . . . We were all in a safe bubble at St. Andrews. There was no intrusion. Kate and Will could go for a drink and hold hands and no one batted an eyelid. They genuinely had deep feelings for one another. Nothing was staged about their relationship." Nor were they, in Knight's words, "showy in their affection for one another. But the odd comment here and there, and the odd smile or touch, was enough to know that they were very, very fond of one another."

The "bubble" allowed the prince to move about town freely, with or without Kate or his friends. "I do all my own shopping," he reiterated. "I go out, get takeaway, rent videos, go to the cinema, just basically anything I want to, really."

What Wills, Kate, and their small coterie of friends shared, said Knight, was "a sense of fun. We were all there for the same reasons. We just wanted a laugh and a life experience."

At the end of his first year, Will had managed a B-plus average—enough for Papa to reward him with a $32,000 gold-inlaid hunting rifle. But Wills's friends hardly thought of him as the bookish type. "Will and I weren't known for being studious," said Knight, who recalled that they were often so bored during lectures—"We quickly regretted signing up for a course called Moral Philosophy"—that they spent the time playing noughts-

and-crosses (tic-tac-toe). "Every now and then, when I spotted a particularly weird headline involving Will," Knight said, "I would cut it out, and halfway through a lecture I'd pass it to him." The two students would then spend the rest of the lecture trying to control their laughter.

Even in the quiet confines of St. Andrews came periodic reminders of William's global fame. Knight recalled standing on a quiet street having a chat with Will one morning when a bus loaded with Japanese tourists pulled up. "A girl got out and ran in our direction, screaming like a banshee, camera in hand," Knight said. "We both noticed, smiled, and quickly walked off in different directions before she could get to us."

Such encounters with adoring fans were few and far between. For the most part, Knight said, Wills and his friends led a fairly "carefree existence. . . . We bonded over our love of dinner parties, heavy drinking, and staying in lovely big houses for parties on weekends."

More often than not, the "lovely big houses" were castles owned by William's friends or the royal palaces that would someday be his. Knight, like everyone else in William's circle, had learned to live with the constant presence of the royal bodyguards. But few people were aware of the new precautions in the wake of 9/11 to protect the Queen's family. Now Windsor Castle and Buckingham Palace boasted "panic rooms" encased in eighteen-inch-thick, fire-retardant steel shells designed to withstand a direct strike by a light aircraft or a protracted artillery attack.

Even at St. Andrews, there were constant reminders of William's status as a royal target. It didn't help that the prince and most of his friends were smokers, and that they were constantly setting off smoke detectors. When the smoke detector went off at one party William was hosting at this flat, he switched off the power to stop it and inadvertently disabled the security cameras. William's bodyguards swarmed the house with their guns drawn and kicked down the door, sending his guests scrambling for cover.

Setting off smoke detectors was a constant problem for William—even when he stepped outside for a cigarette. "When I used to go up on the roof for a smoke," Knight said, "I would accidentally trip the security sensors, and two minutes later police would be looking up asking, 'Are you all right?' "

William's smoking wasn't the only problem. At Ma Bells, while Kate nursed a single drink, her prince could polish off ten pints of hard cider in three hours. "Wills managed to stay on his feet at the end," bartender Nick Philpott said. "He seemed to be able to take the drink easily. He is very polite even when he gets tanked up."

Unlike other royals who seldom if ever paid for anything, William made a point of buying rounds of drinks for the house. "He was always generous, sometimes walking in the pub with a tray of twenty shots for everybody," said Knight. "But he wasn't flashy. He didn't make a great big deal out of it. It wasn't in his character. He was just a young guy who wanted to have fun." That often entailed showing up at afterparties with his own bottle of Jack Daniel's or becoming an enthusiastic participant in the drinking games for which St. Andrews was famous.

Fortunately for the prince, he was never tempted to get behind the wheel after a night of drinking; his security detail was always waiting outside ready to drive him home and, if need be, carry him up to bed. "There was no way he was going to drive drunk," said one friend. "Not after what happened to his mother."

More often than not, it was Will who provided safe transportation home for his tipsy friends. Several times Knight and his pals would be exiting a bar when William would drive by and offer them a lift. "This," Knight said, "would then provoke a worried phone call from the Land Rover with the blacked-out windows that always followed Will's car." It was the prince's bodyguards "wanting to know who those drunken idiots were opening his car door." According to Knight, William took such intrusions "in stride. He was polite and respectful to his bodyguards, but he wanted to be able to live as much as possible like a normal person—and he was the boss."

At times, however, Wills's antics came close to having deadly consequences. Early one morning when they were staggering home drunk from a bar near Wills's flat, Wills noticed a bulge in Knight's jacket. "What's that?" he asked, reaching into Knight's pocket and pulling out a lethal-looking pellet pistol. Laughing, the prince started to wave the pistol in the air.

Instantly, two bodyguards emerged from the shadows—again with their weapons drawn—and, Knight said in a masterpiece of understatement, "gave me a look of great alarm." Realizing that his good friend was in imminent danger of being shot, Wills shrugged, threw the gun on the ground, and kept walking.

Such potentially deadly episodes aside, Wills was, said Knight, "the most down-to-earth chum a person could have. I'm tempted to call him normal, but even he would admit that he's not." At yet another raucous bash, this one a costume party at Badminton House, the magnificent Palladian estate of the Duke of Beaufort where the game of badminton was popularized in the nineteenth century, William came dressed as a milkman—one of the characters in the card game Happy Families.

Initially, William, ever sensitive to the feelings of others, took Knight aside to criticize the way Knight handled his breakup with his girlfriend, an American named Meghann. "He knew

Meghann and was upset that I had upset her," Knight said. "But then I explained it from my side and we cleared the air. We then proceeded to get quite drunk."

While Guy Pelly and Harry, who were also at the party, amused themselves by leaping into the topiary and bouncing back, Wills and Knight went swimming in the historic estate's ornate formal fountain. "We were soaking wet," Knight said, "running up and down the lawns of Badminton and jumping into the warm water." William and Knight then took turns "climbing to the top of the statue in the center of the fountain and diving in." There was, Knight conceded, "something rather *Brideshead* about the whole night."

At the end of the evening, a dozen inebriated partygoers crammed into the back of the SUV driven by William's protection officers. They were then deposited one by one at their respective homes until only Wills and Knight were left. "I obviously had too much to drink," Knight recalled, "so Will just said, 'Come back to my place and stay in the spare room.'" They were dropped off at the back of Highgrove and climbed up the rear stairs.

The two fell fast asleep in their respective rooms, only to be rousted awake two hours later by Harry returning from the party at 4:00 a.m.

When it came time to leave around noon, a "massively hungover" Knight made his way down the corridor to Wills's room, knocked, and quietly opened the door. "It was completely dark," he recalled, "and I said his name and then sat on his bed and woke him with a few prods. He asked me if I wanted to stay and watch football." When Knight politely declined, Wills called the police detail permanently stationed at Highgrove's main gate to alert them to Knight's departure. As he left the prince's room,

Knight encountered a man who appeared to be wearing evening attire. "Would you," asked the butler, "like any breakfast, sir?" It was all, Knight reflected, "completely surreal."

As the school year got under way in earnest, Carole and Michael Middleton remained unsure of the exact nature of their daughter's relationship with William. Kate had promised William that—for the time being, at least—she would tell no one. That included her parents and her sister, Pippa, who, said a Middleton cousin, was "a delightful girl but not the sort of person who could be expected to keep a secret like that."

Carole, however, suspected that her daughter and the prince were more than just roommates. That November of 2002 the Middletons purchased a stucco-walled, two-bedroom flat on a quiet street in Chelsea. If William was going to spend weekends in London, at Highgrove, Sandringham, and Windsor, then Kate would need a London base of operations. The price of the Middletons' new pied-à-terre: $2 million.

Days later, Kate was invited along with five other girls and nine boys to a shooting party at Sandringham. Wills's pals stayed put at Wood Farm, a six-bedroom "cottage" on the estate grounds, while Papa was at the main house playing host to the Queen of Denmark. As eager as Kate and the others may have been to meet the Prince of Wales, his royal obligations took precedence.

For William, considered the best marksman in the Windsor family, the shooting party gave him a chance to show off his skills to his new circle of college friends. For Kate, whose exposure to firearms and hunting had been limited, it was a test of her ability to adapt to the ways of the royal family.

"Miss Middleton did quite well," said one of the beaters who was hired to flush out game. "She's not a bad shot, it turns out. She bagged four or five grouse one morning—not at all bad for a beginner." By comparison, Wills could be expected to shoot several dozen birds in a single outing.

By the time they returned to St. Andrews, newspapers were filled with stories about Wills's weekend shooting party, and the inevitable snickering about who slept with whom. In addition to the usual onslaught of unflattering stories about his mother, Harry's pot smoking, and the ongoing soap opera starring Charles and Camilla, the press was now taking aim squarely at William's receding hairline.

On any given day, Wills could expect another newspaper or magazine photo of his thinning pate accompanied by a headline like ONE DAY WILL WILL BE AN HEIR WITHOUT HAIR or WILLIAM GOING BALD—LIKE FATHER, LIKE SON. Even with Kate to turn to for comfort, it was all taking its toll.

"He pretends he's not affected," Peter Archer said, "but of course he is—deeply so. There's a very big worry that if William keeps repressing these things in this way, it will just keep building up. . . . Something has to give."

Something gave. As Charles and William galloped toward Highgrove on the way back from a fox hunt, photographer Clive Postlethwaite was waiting for the royal party. "Prince Charles went by first, and then William saw me and just went mad. He rode towards me with his eyes wide and his teeth showing."

"Fucking piss off!" William yelled as he headed straight for the terrified photographer. Postlethwaite kept from being trampled by dropping his camera and diving headfirst into a ditch.

"I was shaken," Postlethwaite said, "and just about managed to shout, 'Steady on, Wills.' "

William may periodically have yielded to the pressure, but Kate continued to do what she did best: provide some degree of serenity in his life. "Kate is beautiful, sweet, and she likes to have fun,"

Will's friend Guy Pelly said. "She's also very calm and cool, which Will needs."

To unwind, Kate and Wills sometimes headed to Edinburgh to party with friends. One of their favorite restaurants there was Oloroso, a sleek glass-enclosed penthouse owned and operated by Tony Singh, the talented Sikh chef who for years ran the galley aboard the royal yacht *Britannia*. From there, they might head to Opal's VIP lounge for Red Passions, a thick, layered red-and-yellow concoction of champagne, Campari, and peach schnapps.

The couple also made forays into London, where Camilla was in the midst of redecorating Clarence House, the stately mansion inside the walls of St. James's Palace that had been home to the Queen Mother and was now the official residence of the Prince of Wales and his family. The cost of Camilla's ambitious redesign of the royal apartments: a whopping $10 million.

For the time being, Wills refrained from inviting Kate to Clarence House in hopes of throwing off the press. "They'll jump all over her," he said, "if she comes to the palace." Instead, they hit his favorite clubs and then departed separately, meeting up later at her Chelsea apartment.

It was one thing to be asked to accompany Wills on club-hopping excursions in London and Edinburgh. It was quite another to be invited to Balmoral, which William's great-great-great-great-grandmother Queen Victoria called "this dear Paradise." By all accounts, Kate was the first girl Wills ever brought to Balmoral—in large part because, said Archer, "he must have known how much she would love it."

The baronial granite mansion built by Victoria and her husband, Prince Albert, on the banks of Scotland's river Dee was the spot where William and Harry learned of their mother's death. But it was also where they rode, fished, and hunted amidst some of the most spectacular scenery anywhere. There were purple savannas of heather, dark pine forest, and groves of birches that glistened in the sun.

After his grandmother's death, Charles and Camilla had been given Birkhall, the Queen Mum's fourteen-bedroom residence at Balmoral on the banks of the river Muick. William and Kate preferred the seclusion of a smaller bungalow set aside for Diana's children by the Queen. As Kate stood on the riverbank angling for salmon, trout, and pike, it quickly became clear to one member of the Balmoral staff that she seemed "perfectly at home here. Princess Diana looked like she could hardly wait to leave when she came, but Miss Middleton is a perfect fit. We said to ourselves, 'The Queen is going to like this one.'"

During her first visit to Balmoral, Kate jumped one significant hurdle. She met Charles and, said one of his senior aides, "impressed the Prince of Wales immediately with her unassuming grace. She is clearly a country girl, which is a huge advantage when trying to impress the Royal Family."

Kate celebrated her twenty-first birthday that January 2003 with a small family party at home in Bucklebury. Halfway through the festivities, two Land Rovers pulled up Oak Acre's gravel drive and a lone figure knocked on the door. William had slipped quietly out of London, and now he was meeting Kate's dazed but not entirely surprised parents for the first time. "I wouldn't," he told them, "have missed the chance to sing 'Happy Birthday' to Kate for the world."

Even at St. Andrews, only a handful of students knew that William and Kate were in the throes of a deepening love affair. Protected by their tight circle of friends, the couple refrained from most public displays of affection—with the exception of holding hands at Ma Bells and being seen together in the produce section at Safeway.

That began to change in the spring, when as a member of the less-than-savory Kate Kennedy Club, Wills invited his Kate to the club's annual May Ball. The event was held at Kinkel Farm in the Fife, and while everyone else danced, the prince and his lady never left each other's side.

With speculation concerning the real nature of their relationship revving up again, Michael Middleton stepped forward to "categorically confirm that they are no more than good friends. There are two boys and two girls sharing the flat at university," he insisted. "They are together all the time because they're the best of pals. . . . But there is nothing more to it than that. We are very amused at the thought of being in-laws to Prince William, but I don't think it is going to happen."

Not long after, Kate cheered William on from the sidelines as he played rugby for the West Port Bar against a team fielded by the rival Gin House. After the game, they stretched out on the grass together and gazed up at the clouds—a quietly idyllic scene that was captured by paparazzi hunkered down in the bushes not fifty feet away.

With their second year at St. Andrews behind them, William and Kate focused on planning what would be the royal bash of the year. Wills's twenty-first birthday party at Windsor Castle. After listening to him rave for two years about his gap-year experiences in Africa—Wills was so affected by the experience that he was now learning Swahili—Kate suggested a theme based on one of her favorite films: *Out of Africa*.

The Queen consulted with Robin Janvrin and other senior advisers before giving a green light to Wills's African theme, with one important stipulation: his three hundred guests had to agree to refrain from any references to race, the British Empire, or colonialism when choosing their costumes. "The last thing your grandmother wants," Charles reportedly told William, "is an international incident."

The birthday boy showed up at the party in something akin to his birthday suit: a black-and-yellow-striped loincloth and nothing else. Harry, Earl Spencer, Prince Andrew, and Prince Philip all donned safari garb. Papa opted for a billowing caftan, while Camilla's multicolored tribal outfit was topped with a red-feathered headdress.

William's cousins Princess Beatrice and Princess Eugenie wore skimpy leopard-print minidresses—a popular choice among younger women at the party. Bush pilots, pharaohs, Foreign Legionnaires, animal characters from *The Lion King*, and witch doctors rounded out the rest of the guest list. But none were more impressive than Her Majesty, attired as the Queen of Swaziland in a white sheath, white African headdress, and a white fur wrap.

At a cost of more than $800,000, monkeys swung on vines overhead, elephant rides around the castle grounds were offered to guests, and revelers danced to the music of the Botswanan band Shakarrimba. At one point, Wills leaped onstage and joined in on the African drums.

No one seemed to take notice when a beat-up white van decorated with balloons pulled up to the castle gates and disgorged a contingent of William's friends from St. Andrews—Kate among them. The birthday boy's girlfriend wore a ragged animal-print dress that, on closer inspection, was the match to William's Tarzan loincloth.

The rest of the partygoers, it seemed, were buzzing about another striking young woman who never left Wills's side. With Kate's consent, Wills had invited Jecca Craig as his guest of honor. No sooner did the press get wind of the invitation than they speculated that the prince and his old flame had rekindled their romance. (Reporters were unaware that William had also invited Carly Massy-Birch, the young St. Andrews student who had broken off their affair because she couldn't stand being pursued by the paparazzi. Massy-Birch came dressed, she said, as a "jungle queen.")

Intent on setting the record straight—and perpetuating the myth that Wills was unattached—Charles took the unprecedented step of issuing a public denial "that there is or ever has been any romantic liaison between Prince William and Jessica Craig." Complicating matters was that Jecca was still technically engaged to shipping heir Henry Ropner, although they had broken up and reconciled several times over the previous few months. At the last minute Ropner, who had intentionally been left off the guest list, was sent an invitation—which he promptly accepted.

Jecca Craig was not the problem. As long as they kept their relationship secret, William and Kate were convinced they could continue to lead something approaching normal lives at St. Andrews. Toward that end, Wills went out of his way during his official twenty-first birthday interview to state unequivocally that he was unattached.

"There's been a lot of speculation about every single girl I'm with," he said, "and it actually does quite irritate me after a while, more so because it's a complete pain for the girls. These poor girls, whom I've either just met or are friends of mine, suddenly get thrown into the limelight and their parents get rung up and so on. I think it's a little unfair on them, really. I'm used to it, because it happens quite a lot now. But it's very difficult for them and I don't like that at all."

Of course, William was really concerned about only one girl, and he hinted at his concern for her welfare when he described how he played the dating game. "If I fancy a girl and she fancies me back, which is rare," he said coyly, "I ask her out. But at the same time, I don't want to put them in an awkward situation, because a lot of people don't understand what comes with knowing me, for one—and secondly, if they were my girlfriend, the excitement it would probably cause."

Excitement of a different sort occurred shortly before midnight when William thanked everyone for coming. Halfway through Wills's speech, a cross-dressing Osama bin Laden—beard, turban, strapless pink satin evening gown, red high-heeled pumps—grabbed the microphone out of his hand and began singing.

Kate, watching from the edge of the crowd, assumed the man in the bizarre outfit was fun-loving Prince Harry. So did the Queen. It would be a full minute before security guards pulled self-styled "comedy terrorist" Aaron Barschak off the stage—but not before Barschak grabbed Wills and kissed him on both cheeks.

It was the thirteenth major breach in royal security since Her Majesty woke up to an intruder sitting on the edge of her bed at Buckingham Palace in 1982. There were break-ins into Prince Charles's private quarters, the nude paraglider who landed on the roof of Buckingham Palace in 1994, and the day Princess Anne answered her bedroom door only to greet a tourist asking for directions to Victoria Station.

Charles and the Queen were outraged, and the ensuing investigation prompted Scotland Yard chief Sir John Stevens to apologize to William for the "appalling breach of security." The party crasher could not have agreed more. "It was unbelievably simple," Barschak said. "I'm amazed I got in. . . . I was carrying a bulging rucksack. I could have anything in it." Incredibly, videotape showed a security officer actually giving Barschak directions to the party.

William took it all in stride, laughing off the incident and partying until 4:00 a.m. The next day, he was back in the saddle at the Beaufort Polo Club, this time riding his birthday gift from the Prince of Wales: a new $165,000 Argentine pony.

Polo was not the only thing Wills had on his mind that summer. There would be more hurtful stories about Mummy and Papa, including James Hewitt's attempt to sell sixty-four handwritten love notes from Diana—including the one in which she referred to his penis as "my friend"—for $16.5 million. "It just never stops," Wills told Kate and Guy Pelly as they walked past a kiosk plastered with more scandalous headlines. "It never stops."

His own dark moods aside, Wills worried about his little brother—the only person who fully understood what he was feeling. Harry had graduated from Eton with a D in geography—the lowest mark of any student—but he had shown leadership qualities as head of the school's Combined Cadet Corps and was runner-up to receive the coveted Sword of Honor won by Wills several years earlier. Since Sandhurst Academy would not accept cadets under the age of twenty, eighteen-year-old Harry planned to make the best of a twenty-four-month gap year before starting his military career in earnest.

In the meantime, the Heir was determined to cheer up the Spare. With Kate's blessing, William and Harry went to the twenty-fourth-birthday party of sports broadcaster Natalie Pinkham at Purple, one of the most popular clubs in London.

Well before the evening drew to a close, Harry was openly fondling the birthday girl's breasts. A very drunk William, in the meantime, was sprawled out on a banquette, his arms wrapped around several buxom blondes.

The dynamic duo returned to Purple a few nights later, this time to celebrate Harry's imminent departure for Australia and a three-month gig herding cattle and mending fences on a ranch in the outback. Anticipating his twenty-two-hour flight the next morning, Harry stayed sober. William, on the other hand, danced wildly onstage with a succession of women before collapsing at his table in a drunken stupor. Wills's bodyguards had to pick him up and, said eyewitness Sue Thompson, "literally carry him off."

The scene would be repeated over the next several weeks, particularly when Purple had one of its "Dirty Disco" nights. Before long, several of the women William groped and kissed on these evenings began talking to the newspapers.

"William has too much of a roving eye to settle down," twenty-nine-year-old Purple patron Solange Jacobs said after being told William reportedly had a girlfriend named Kate Middleton. Jacobs was among several women who danced, drank, and snogged with William one night. "The way he acted with me, he didn't seem to be in love with anyone else. He also chatted with a dancer and eyed up a girl in the VIP area. You wouldn't have guessed he was seeing Kate. Wills looked very much on the prowl. Kate better watch out if she doesn't want to be made a fool of."

William was not above using his being a royal as a come-on. He took Jacobs's phone number with the promise that he would call her and invite her to his palace. At no time, apparently, did he ever mention that he had a girlfriend. "I wish Kate the best of luck," Jacobs said. "She might need it."

Carole Middleton was not amused at the stories she was reading. Nevertheless, she called Kate to reassure her that William's behavior constituted little more than "harmless flirting."

Kate wasn't so sure. Both of his parents had cheated, and the Windsor men had a long history of womanizing. "I believe William loves me and would never do anything to intentionally hurt me," Kate said. "But it's that family . . ."

With that in mind, Kate took her mother's advice and began spending more time at the Middletons' flat in Chelsea. "If anyone is going to have fun with him," she chided Will's drinking buddy Guy Pelly, "it's going to be me."

The next time William appeared at Purple or Boujis or Chinawhite or the Sofa So Bar or any of his other favorite London hangouts, Kate was nestled at his side. "Miss Middleton is a very smart girl," Camilla told her son Tom after learning that Kate was now keeping a watchful eye on William. "Yes, a *very* smart girl."

———————

Frankly, life's too short.
   —*William, when asked if he ever worried about becoming king*

Why should he worry? He will be brilliant.
                    —*Kate*

I have to put up with this because it's the world I was born into. But why should Kate?
   —*William, on the paparazzi's relentless pursuit of Kate*

———————

5

By the time he arrived at Ninewells Hospital in Dundee, just north of St. Andrews, William was doubled over and clutching his stomach in pain. His face was sheet-white. Unlike Charles, the country's most celebrated complainer, William had a stoic streak, especially when it came to physical pain. He shrugged off the cramps for two days—until Kate, sensing that this was more than just a run-of-the-mill stomachache, insisted he seek immediate medical attention.

It was a good thing she did. Blood tests revealed that William, who had just returned in late October from a month in Africa—two days of which were spent white-water rafting down the Nile—was suffering from bilharzia, a parasitic ailment that can lead to paralysis, seizures, liver damage, even death. Indeed, bilharzia kills more than twenty thousand people each year.

Doctors promptly prescribed praziquantel, a veterinary antiparasitic drug that is also given to humans, and Wills was soon on the road to recovery. Kate might have been excused for seeing the prince's illness as some form of divine retribution. He had, after all, gone to Africa to spend some quality time with Jecca Craig and her family—not three months after Jecca's controversial appearance at his twenty-first-birthday party. At the time of his departure, Kate, who was well aware of William's affection for the Craigs and rightly believed that his romance with Jecca was in the past—wisely chose not to object. When Wills initially arrived back in Scotland looking sun-burnished and happy, Kate welcomed him home with open arms.

With Kate looking after him in St. Andrews, William was cured by late December—just as Michael Burgess, coroner to the Queen, announced that he would finally be opening his own formal inquest into the death of Diana. Scotland Yard investigators would ultimately take a mind-numbing four years to arrive at the same conclusion that had been reached days after the accident: Diana was the victim of a drunk-driving accident. In doing so, they had to have witnesses, detectives, forensics experts, conspiracy theorists, and armchair experts of every stripe dredge up the tragically gruesome details almost daily. "Every time," Wills said, "it's like taking a little piece of me."

Around the same time, Andrew Morton released the secret recordings made by Diana that were the basis of his 1991 book, *Diana: Her True Story*; Diana's voice coach, Peter Settelen, released videotapes in which she shared the most intimate details of her life with Charles; and, worst of all, photos of Diana snapped immediately after her fatal crash were shown on U.S. television. The photos had left the boys feeling "deeply upset" as well as "shocked and sickened."

Kate was coping with losses of her own that fall. Carole's father Ronald Goldsmith, who had been driven by his wife Dorothy to earn enough money to make the family at least appear respectable, died of heart disease at seventy-two. Kate had been especially close to her grandfather, who was as kind, good-natured, and pleasant as Dorothy was driven and pretentious.

To complicate matters as they began their third year at St. Andrews, Wills and Kate were adjusting to a new living arrangement. With their erstwhile roommate Fergus Boyd in tow, they took up residence at Balgove House, a roomy, fuchsia-covered farmhouse on the outskirts of town.

William, in particular, had been eagerly anticipating the move. "Most people tend to move houses, and that was always my intention," he explained. "In my third year, I have fewer lectures and have to spend less time in the university, and so I thought, 'How about moving somewhere different?' I do think I am a country boy at heart. I love the buzz of towns and going out with friends and sitting with them drinking and whatever—it's fun. But, at the same time, I like space and freedom."

Providing space and freedom for the prince and his friends would cost British taxpayers in excess of $2.5 million—most of that spent on installing bulletproof windows, panic rooms, new security cameras and surveillance devices, and of course a beefed-up force of armed guards stationed in a separate building right next door. With memories of the twenty-first-birthday party gate-crasher still fresh in everyone's mind, such precautions only seemed prudent. "At least now," Will cracked to his guards, "Osama bin Laden impersonators don't stand a chance!"

While Kate and Wills pulled on sweaters to fend off the autumn chill, Harry was in Africa on a mission of mercy. Accompanied by a documentary film crew, Harry journeyed to the South African enclave of Lesotho to help build a clinic for AIDS-infected orphans. "I believe I've got a lot of my mother in me, basically," he said as he cradled an HIV-positive infant in his arms, "and I just think she'd want us to do this—me and my brother."

Before he settled down to building bridges and digging ditches in Lesotho, Harry stopped off to see an old friend in Cape Town,

South Africa. The Spare had gotten to know blond, tanned, and gorgeous Chelsy Davy years earlier, when she was a student at Cheltenham Ladies' College not far from Highgrove. Ever since she'd returned to study art at Cape Town University, Harry'd started telling friends that he was afraid he had let "someone really special slip through my fingers."

Despite her exotic background—her father was a wealthy safari-park owner and her mother a former Miss Rhodesia—Zimbabwe-born Chelsy was as free-spirited and outdoorsy as she was lushly beautiful. Before long, she would play Fergie to Kate's Diana—with a few crucial differences. The two young women soon became fast friends and mutual pillars of support, giggling and whispering to each other on the sidelines about their potential royal in-laws. Both also proved to be masters of discretion.

On the snow-covered slopes of Klosters in March 2004, Wills and Kate let their cloak of secrecy slip, if only for a passing moment. Although the couple brought four chums along to join Papa on his annual Swiss ski vacation, they felt free to share a lift chair, and once they reached the top, they warmly embraced.

Unfortunately, paparazzi captured the touching scene of Wills and Kate cozying up on slopes, and the next morning the photographs ran on the front page of the *Sun*. When Wills's friend Guy Pelly, who was among those invited on the trip to Klosters, showed Wills the pictures, he exploded. "Fuck!" he shouted within earshot of other skiers. "They have no right. We have an agreement!"

Charles was equally furious. He had been assured that the official interviews and photo opportunities provided the press were enough to keep the paparazzi at bay during Wills's college years. The Prince of Wales swiftly instructed his office at St. James's Palace not only to officially condemn the *Sun* for publishing the shots, but to ban the paper's photographers from any planned photo ops of both William and Harry.

Now more wary than ever of being caught in a tender moment, Wills and Kate seldom strayed from their farmhouse digs. Once again, William returned to the rugby field in April to play for his favorite pub, the West Port Bar. Only this time, there was no lazing with his girlfriend on the grass during breaks in the action. Kate stayed away until after the game, when she showed up at Ma Bells to console him for yet another loss to the Gin House.

Now when someone suspicious-looking showed up, their friends nonchalantly ringed the couple to form a human shield. Behind this wall of improbably tall young Englishmen and their girl-friends, Kate felt free to sit on Wills's lap and, for the first time in a public place, actually kiss. Now Wills and Kate had pet names for each other: she was Kat, or sometimes Kitten—later to be re-placed by Babykins. He was and would remain Big Willy. It was no coincidence that *willy* is the standard British colloquialism for the male sex organ.

They used the same ruse at the May Ball and a couple of weeks later when they showed up at a costume party dressed as Rhett Butler and Scarlett O'Hara. "Will wore a mustache and looked very dashing," a partygoer recalled, "and Kate was swanning about saying, 'Fiddle-dee-dee.' I was hoping he'd say, 'Frankly, my dear, I don't give a damn,' but I doubt if he really knew that much about *Gone with the Wind* to begin with."

Early that June, Kate was at the farmhouse in St. Andrews packing up for the summer and William was away on a geography field trip in Norway when his father called to say that his grand-mother had passed away. Wills dropped the phone and nearly col-lapsed before he understood that Diana's mother—and not the Queen—had died of Parkinson's disease at the age of sixty-eight.

William and Harry, who was still doing his gap-year service in Lesotho, immediately flew back to the United Kingdom for the funeral of "Gran Fran," Frances Shand Kydd. Even though she had been estranged from her daughter and never had quite the presence in the boys' lives that the Queen did, Gran Fran frequently visited them when they were growing up in Kensington Palace. Diana recognized the bond in her will when she made Shand Kydd the guardian of her sons in the event something happened to both her and to Charles.

A visibly shaken William stood up at Gran Fran's funeral, his voice trembling slightly as he read a passage from the New Testament. After the all-Spencer service, from which the rest of the Royal Family was specifically excluded, William was surprised to learn that Gran Fran had left him and his brother $1 million each—this in addition to the roughly $10 million they each inherited from Diana on her death.

Shand Kydd did not live to see the Queen pay fulsome tribute to Diana at the July 6, 2004, dedication of the Diana Fountain in Hyde Park. Both William and Harry fought back tears as the Queen recalled how England "came to terms with the loss, united by an extraordinary sense of shock, grief, and sadness."

Kate realized how much the memorial meant to William, but she also knew her presence at so public an event would be monumentally distracting. Not that she even had the option of attending the ceremonies—the Queen controlled the guest list.

No longer willing to appear insensitive when it came to her late daughter-in-law, the Queen had ordered Charles and the boys to be there. The Spencers, after all, had already announced their intention to attend en masse. William and Harry were not the only Windsors who were told they had to attend solo; Camilla, for obvious reasons, was asked to stay home.

During a photo session in 1987 with Spain's royal family, Diana tried to steady a squirming William. Meanwhile, Kate (seen here at around age seven in a school photo) enjoyed dressing up as a princess during her childhood in the tiny Berkshire hamlet of Bucklebury. Soon, she would tack a poster of the young prince on her bedroom wall.

1

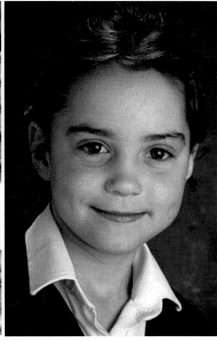

2

3

4

Along with the rest of a grieving world, Kate was transfixed as William, fifteen, walked behind Diana's coffin with his grandfather Prince Philip, his uncle Earl Spencer, Harry, and Prince Charles. Years later, Kate would do the transfixing when she modeled underwear at St. Andrews University. Below, Wills and his fellow university students cool off in the chilly waters of the North Sea.

6

Kate and her mother Carole, a former stewardess who made a fortune selling children's party supplies, watch William in action at the Beaufort Polo Club near Highgrove.

Tongues started wagging when both William and his African flame Jecca Craig showed up at the wedding of his pal Edward van Cutsem in June 2005—sans Kate. To prove she wasn't threatened, Kate took to wearing Jecca's trademark cowboy hat.

7

8

9

10

Granny beamed with pride when William and Kate, his roommate of three years, graduated from St. Andrews University on June 23, 2005.

11

12

Sporting the new military buzz
cut he acquired at Sandhurst,
William was for the first time
openly affectionate with Kate
during an Eton "old boys" field
game in March 2006. Kate made
a solo splash later that spring
at London's Lancaster Hotel,
when she wore a striking BCBG
Max Azria gown to the Boodles
Boxing Ball.

13

William and Kate lazed on the deck of their borrowed yacht while vacationing on Ibiza in 2006. Their host, Kate's uncle Gary Goldsmith, would soon be embroiled in a major sex and drugs scandal.

Although he was barred from fighting in Afghanistan as Harry did, "Will Wales" secretly took part in exercises on Cyprus in late 2006.

A few weeks later, Kate—
flanked by her father Michael
and mom Carole—attended
William's Sandhurst graduation.
The prince tried to keep
a straight face as Granny
reviewed the troops.

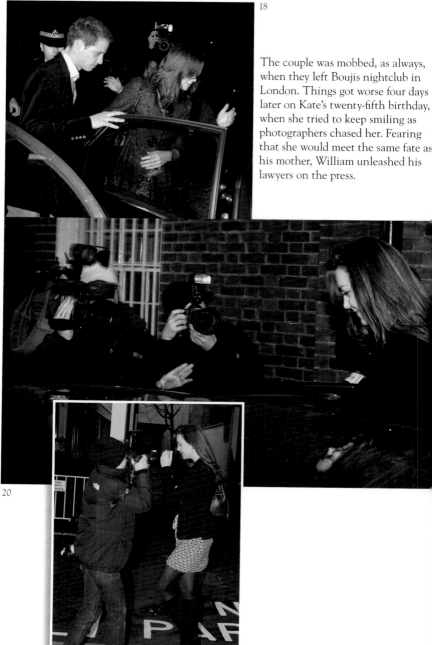

The couple was mobbed, as always, when they left Boujis nightclub in London. Things got worse four days later on Kate's twenty-fifth birthday, when she tried to keep smiling as photographers chased her. Fearing that she would meet the same fate as his mother, William unleashed his lawyers on the press.

20

19

Convinced that Kate would soon become Mrs. William Wales, Woolworths began selling souvenir wedding merchandise in early 2007.

At a rugby match that February their love seemed stronger than ever.

On the ski slopes
that March.

Six days after
they were
photographed
kissing in
Switzerland, the
couple seemed
oddly tense
at the annual
Cheltenham
Festival horse
race. This
was the last
photograph taken
of them together
before their
shocking split in
April 2007.

Alone now and without police protection, Kate was still stalked by the paparazzi. The day the split became public, she packed up personal items and carried them home to her parents' house in a cardboard box.

Far from looking defeated, Kate hit the London social scene with a vengeance—often with her sister Pippa. She even trained to cross the English Channel with the Sisterhood, an all-female rowing team. Kate, not surprisingly, steered the boat.

27

During the star-packed tenth anniversary memorial Concert for
Diana at Wembley Stadium, Kate (at right, next to her blazer-clad
brother James) looked over from her discreet third row seat to check
on Wills. The public was unaware that the couple, later shown
leaving a London club, were already back together.

31   32

At the Cheltenham Festival horse race, where only a year before she and Wills were grim on the verge of their breakup, Kate returned to cheer for the winning horse.

Training to become an RAF helicopter pilot, Wills got into trouble for buzzing the Middletons' house, Highgrove, and Windsor Castle—and for taking joyrides at the taxpayers expense. All was forgiven by the time Kate saw Wills get his wing from his father Prince Charles.

34

35

36

37

38

Already on several best dressed lists, Kate created another stir wearing a shocking pink gown to the Boodles Boxing Ball. Much to the delight of Harry, Kate, and Camilla, it was the Heir's turn to make a fashion statement with Papa during Wills's investiture into the Order of the Garter at Windsor Castle.

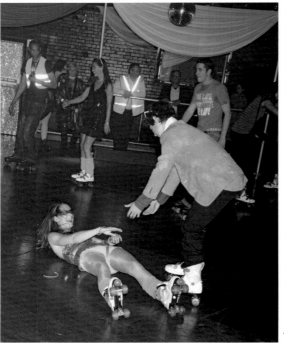

Even before she took a spectacular spill on the rink, Kate was the star attraction the Day-Glo Midnight Rolle Disco, an event in London to raise money for a new ward Children's Hospital in Oxfor Kate laughed it off as she wa helped to her feet by event organizer Sam Waley-Cohen

Kate was more than willing to maintain a low profile. She was not, however, thrilled with the notion of Wills returning to Jecca Craig's Kenyan game preserve for the third summer in a row. If William did not want to encourage speculation about his relationship with Kate, then why, she asked, would he want to fan the flames of gossip concerning his relationship with Jecca?

"She felt threatened and humiliated," said one their closest friends at St. Andrews. "It was one thing to never be publicly acknowledged, but quite another to have someone else bandied about in the press as the woman in his life. She knew that would happen all over again if he went to see Jecca Craig."

At first, Wills stood his ground. Like his father, he took offense at anyone's giving him an order—with the exception of the Queen, of course. "Do you know who I am?" Wills demanded, repeating the uncharacteristically imperious line that, according to Diana and several others, Charles used many times over the years. "No one tells me what to do. I do what I want." Besides, William insisted yet again that he no longer had romantic feelings for Jecca—she was only a great friend who had once opened his eyes to the wonders of Africa.

For two weeks, the battle raged on. At one point Wills and Kate were seen arguing on a street corner when the prince suddenly jumped on his motorcycle and zoomed off, the royal protection officers in their Land Rover scrambling to keep up. On another occasion, they sat in his parked VW Golf outside Ma Bells, screaming at each other before Kate stormed off alone.

Eventually, Kate won what the press was now calling the "Battle of the Babes"—in part because Papa and the Palace agreed with her argument. No matter how many denials were issued, Jecca would once again be thrust into the spotlight as Wills's presumed girlfriend. "You mustn't put her through that, William," Charles reportedly said. "It isn't fair to Jecca."

Or to Kate. Wills now faced the challenge of proving to her once and for all that she was the only woman in his life. Instead of heading for Africa alone, he took Kate on their first summer vacation together—to the Eden-like island of Rodrigues, due east of Mauritius in the Indian Ocean. It was here, during his gap year, that Wills did field work for the Royal Geographical Society's Marine Observation Program. He had fallen in love with Rodrigues's glistening white sand beaches, lush tropical forests, and crystalline waters—now he wanted to share it all with Kate.

Their days were spent motorbiking through the hilly countryside or scuba diving and snorkeling among the island's luxuriant coral reefs. Evenings were devoted to joining their friends at the island's cabana bar for glasses of Sex on the Beach—a libation consisting of cranberry juice, grapefruit juice, peach schnapps, and vodka—and Wills's customary stint singing disco tunes on the karaoke machine.

After she returned to the UK, however, Kate soon learned that Jecca wasn't the only "other woman" who could still set tongues wagging. An American attending Edinburgh University, Anna Sloan—yet another comely blonde—actually turned down a date with Wills shortly after they met in September 2001. But weeks later her millionaire father, champion steeplechase rider George Sloan, was killed when his shotgun went off as he climbed a fence on his 350-acre farm outside Nashville. Wills and Anna quickly bonded over the shared loss of a parent, something that—in the beginning, at least—Kate understood and accepted.

With plenty of time left before school resumed in September, William decided to accept Anna's long-standing invitation to visit her in Tennessee. In early August, William arrived at the

Sloan farm with three gangling chums and five beefy bodyguards. Once again fearing that as a couple Wills and Kate would be relentlessly pursued by the press, the prince's real girlfriend stayed home in Bucklebury.

The experience lasted for only a week, but it afforded William a rare glimpse at life the way it is lived by most Americans his age. He relaxed by the pool, shared a bucket of popcorn at the local multiplex, checked out the action at the local mall, and knocked back a few at several Nashville honky-tonks.

What made the experience even more special was his ability to move about unrecognized. "Every so often," he said, "I see someone's eyes sort of get big, and then that 'Oh, no, it's not him. . . . What on earth would he be doing here?' look."

Will and his posse wolfed down pancakes, waffles, and scrambled eggs and bacon at the Country Boy diner, then headed off to shop at the CoolSprings Galleria Mall. At Abercrombie & Fitch, Wills almost went undetected until his rowdy friends started acting up. "I didn't even realize who he was," one of the clerks said, "until a couple of his friends with English accents wanted the clothes off the mannequins, and I told them no. They were really cute. All the women wanted to wait on them."

A half hour later, tittering female shoppers swarmed the counter as Wills paid $69.50 for a pair of jeans. "See," one of his friends said to the prince as they left the store, "we can't take you anywhere."

That evening, the prince was among a party of fifteen at Sperry's, a pricey Nashville restaurant with an English motif. Focusing on his filet mignon cordon bleu wrapped in bacon (the restaurant later named the dish after him), William pretended not to notice as patrons nonchalantly ambled by his table for a glimpse of the future king. "There was a constant stream of people," waitress

LuAnn Reid said, "going to the bathroom so they could walk by him. People were phoning their daughters and granddaughters so they could come in and see him."

None of which seemed to bother William or his friends, who consumed drinks and a dozen bottles of wine—nearly one for each person at the table. "They were really laid-back," the manager said, "and they were laughing and cutting up and having fun." After splitting the check, William, said Reid, left a "generous" tip.

William continued "cutting up" back on the Sloan farm, where he had stocked up on alcohol purchased from Puckett's Grocery store. When William and his friends bought several cases of beer, store owner Billy Raynor took notice. "Are you sure," he asked William, "you're going to drink all that?"

Wills just laughed. "Oh, we'll be all right," he replied, deflecting the question by pointing out that he and a young clerk behind the counter were wearing the same checked shirt. "Oh, yes," one of Wills's British pals chimed in, "we'll be just *fine*."

Thanks to the efforts of his American hosts, Tennessee William managed to fly under the radar throughout his entire visit. Only after he left did the press get wind of his presence in the heart of America. Feeling more free to be himself than he had in years, the prince "acted up" enough for his Yankee friends to bestow a new title on him: the Duke of Hazard.

As Kate might easily have guessed, William's Nashville escapade served only to revive rumors that the prince was back on the prowl. To make it all up to her, Wills bundled Kate off to Balmoral for a cozy weekend together. Since Papa and Camilla were also there at the time, Big Willy was also sending his Babykins the unmistakable message that he took their relationship seriously. Wills had never before asked a girl to spend time with his family there.

He wanted to squeeze in one more adventure before they returned to St. Andrews, however. Once again Wills took off for a Mediterranean cruise, only this time with an all-male passenger list. The crew, however, was made up entirely of women. "Kate was speechless," said a member of their St. Andrews set. "He saw nothing wrong with it, of course. But she was definitely humiliated. It was getting harder and harder for her to read him."

No sooner had William returned from his boys-only cruise than two old flames—Jecca Craig and "Deb on the Web" Davina Duckworth-Chad—were back in the picture. In September, the prince and Jecca both attended Davina's wedding to Tom Barber, the son of a baronet. Kate was, yet again, excluded from the guest list.

Another high-society wedding just two months later—this time between Lady Tamara Grosvenor and his old chum Edward van Cutsem—threw the rumor mill into overdrive when Jecca and Wills showed up again, sans Kate. The Queen and Prince Philip were there, and since Wills and Harry served as ushers, it was expected that William would invite a guest. Kate's absence was soon touted as proof positive that their royal romance was on shaky ground.

William and Kate weren't the only couple for whom the van Cutsem–Grosvenor wedding was problematic. As the groom's godfather, Prince Charles had fully intended to be there—until he was informed that he and his mistress would have to sit in separate pews and arrive and depart in separate cars. Incensed, Charles and Camilla not only boycotted the ceremony, they started planning one of their own.

The last fall in St. Andrews, Kate and William had once again tried to insulate themselves from the outside world at their farmhouse on the outskirts of town. More than anyone, she realized that her prince was coping with so much more than a heavy course load—at her suggestion, he had changed his major from art to geography—and interminable gossip about their love life.

In addition to the strains between the Queen and Charles over Camilla and the ongoing investigation into Diana's death, Harry was becoming more of a concern to William with each passing tabloid headline. Distracted and depressed by the Palace wars over his longtime mistress, Charles had essentially abdicated parenting duties to his elder son, who checked on Harry every day by phone and e-mail.

In October, former Eton teacher Sarah Forsythe accused Harry of cheating two years earlier on his final art exam. A special panel hearing the case somehow confirmed Forsythe's accusations but at the same time cleared Prince Harry of any wrongdoing. Harry reacted, as he so often did when he felt he had let down the family, by going on a bender.

As he left the London nightclub Pangea around 3:30 a.m., Harry screamed obscenities before grabbing photographer Chris Uncle's camera and striking him with it. Even after he saw that Uncle's lower lip was bleeding, Harry, still spewing four-letter words, had to be restrained by his bodyguards.

William was concerned about his brother's wild streak, but Wills told Kate that he was also immensely proud of him. The following spring, Harry was scheduled to start his military education at Sandhurst, which would put him a year ahead of Wills at the academy.

From their earliest days together, William had shared his dreams for a career in the military with Kate, and she encouraged him to pursue them. But she told one girlfriend that she wasn't "overjoyed" at the prospect of her man fighting alongside British soldiers in Iraq. "He would be a target, I'm afraid, and that does frighten me."

As heir, Wills knew that Charles and the Queen—not to mention the omnipotent Men in Gray—would resist any attempts to send him into combat. "The last thing I want," Wills told the British Press Association in an interview marking his last year at St. Andrews, "is to be mollycoddled or wrapped up in cotton wool, because if I was to join the army, I'd want to go where my men went and I'd want to do what they did. I would not want to be kept back for being precious or whatever, that's the last thing I'd want. . . . It's the most humiliating thing."

Humiliation was something Kate knew quite a lot about. For most of their romance, she had been forced to remain invisible while Wills was linked in the press to a bevy of beauties on both sides of the Atlantic.

Privately, however, Kate was making important inroads. Still a clear favorite of Charles's, she was among a small group at Highgrove on November 14 celebrating his fifty-sixth birthday. While an invitation to join the entire Royal Family for Christmas at Sandringham would have to wait, Wills rushed back to Kate's side in Bucklebury on December 26. At one of the Middletons' favorite local hangouts, the Yew Tree pub, Wills and Kate toasted the New Year.

In the meantime, William had confided in Kate that his father was finally going to pop the question to Camilla and had asked his sons for their blessing. They gave it, which came as no surprise to Kate. "William and Harry are quite fond of Camilla," Kate said after informing a friend that Charles had sealed the deal with an eight-carat emerald-cut diamond ring that had belonged to the

Queen Mother. "They've always just wanted Prince Charles to be happy, and she makes him happy."

Oddly enough, the feeling was far from mutual. As early as 2004, Camilla made it clear to Charles that she felt William should wait to marry an aristocrat—ideally someone from another royal house. She did not feel, from what she knew of the Middletons' working-class roots, that Kate would be up to the sacrifices demanded of a royal wife. As for Camilla's own commoner status, Mrs. P.B. had always believed that as the great-granddaughter of King Edward VII's mistress Alice Keppel, she was in a category all her own.

"Camilla smiled, as she always does, and was very pleasant to Miss Middleton in front of Prince William," a member of the staff at Highgrove said. Camilla, however, "went out of her way whenever Charles said how much he liked Kate to say something catty about her." At the time, Camilla was overheard describing Kate as "pretty, but rather dim."

Unaware of Camilla's early attempts to undercut Kate, William excitedly shared details of his father's secret wedding plans with his girlfriend. Those plans would actually remain secret for six weeks, primarily because the country was distracted by yet another royal scandal.

Once again, Harry was in the crosshairs. This time, he showed up with his brother at a costume party wearing a Nazi uniform, complete with swastika armband. William, who wore a lion costume, helped Harry picked out his Third Reich attire. Both princes were so happy with their outfits and so oblivious to the firestorm that Harry's uniform would ignite that they unhesitatingly allowed snapshots to be taken.

The next day, the *Sun* ran a front-page shot of Harry in his German getup with the headline HARRY THE NAZI. Within hours, he was denounced by the Israeli foreign minister, several Jewish and World War II veterans groups, Holocaust survivors, and several members of Britain's Parliament. "Appalling," "shameful," and "grotesque" were just a few of the adjective used by dignitaries, politicians, religious leaders, and commentators to describe Harry's latest gaffe.

Most disturbing, perhaps, was Harry's lack of knowledge about fascism and the significant role his own family had played in fighting it. Harry had only a vague idea who Adolf Hitler was, but it did not end there. William had obviously shared Harry's cluelessness and even continued to defend Harry's costume to friends even after Clarence House had issued an apology on his behalf.

By contrast Kate and the Middletons were shocked when they saw the pictures. But Kate sympathized with William for all that he was going through. "His mother was right," she told a former St. Andrews roommate. "No one else in his family feels things as intensely as he does. I'm worried about him."

Kate was, in many ways, becoming the one true constant in his life. "I can rely on her totally," he told Guy Pelly. "She is completely there for me. I've never had anyone in my life like Kate."

Kate was, to be sure, naturally protective toward her prince. Newspaper columnist Katie Nicholl got a glimpse of what typically occurred when she was dining at a restaurant in Mayfair called Automat. Kate came in, scoped the place out, and located a booth in the back where William could sit so his back would be to the rest of the diners. Once Kate had the seating all arranged, she motioned for William to enter with his old crush Arabella Musgrave and her new brewery-heir boyfriend James Tollemache. "I just thought, 'Gosh,' " recalled Nicholl, " 'I don't think I've ever met another twenty-four-year-old who would have done such a thing.' "

In late January 2005, Kate and Wills hied away to Balmoral for another long weekend together. A few weeks later, they rented a chalet with three other couples at Verbier in the Swiss Alps. For the most part they only ventured out with their group, still not quite ready to advertise their love. When they sat together in a corner at the Farm, a well-known nightclub in Verbier, they held hands under the table and occasionally nuzzled each other when they thought no one was looking. "Their eyes were always sort of scanning the room to make sure no one would see them," one of the bartenders said. "They looked a little wary."

On March 29, 2005, they joined Harry and a dozen friends at the Sugar Hut in Fulham, a church that had been converted to one of London's hottest clubs. While Harry and the others sprawled out on divans and drank themselves into a stupor, Wills and Kate tried to maintain some degree of decorum. Shortly before 2:00 a.m., they left the club separately—Wills with his intoxicated brother, who had to be helped to the car by royal protection officers, and Kate with a group of friends fifteen minutes later.

Later that day, Wills admitted to Kate that he felt their ongoing charade was "ridiculous." Within hours, they boarded a plane for yet another holiday together. This time, he promised her, things would be different.

One year after they were first photographed sharing an intimate moment on a ski lift, the couple returned to Klosters with a new, decidedly more open attitude about their romance. Now they held hands, whispered in each other's ears, and playfully jostled each other in full view of the other skiers. During lunch at a village café, Kate unself-consciously plopped herself in Wills's lap and wrapped her arms around his neck.

Since this March 2005 ski trip was ostensibly billed as a "stag week" for the altarbound Prince of Wales, Kate's mere presence

among the thirty-odd guests was significant. All the more revealing was the ease with which she interacted with the male members of the Royal Family, especially Charles and Harry.

In the absence of his girlfriend Chelsy Davy, who had not been
invited, the Spare needed some cheering up. At Klosters' Casa
Antica, once a favorite hangout of Diana's, Harry drowned his
sorrows in Red Bull mixed with vodka. Chelsy's absence notwithstanding, the soused prince insisted on telling every girl in
the room that he did not wear underwear—an admission that
prompted their friend Guy Pelly to strip down to his black silk
boxers and take to the dance floor.

Oblivious, William and Kate drank wine, snuggled in a corner, and, when the mood struck them, clung to each other on the
dance floor. The mood was so mellow that, when a reporter for
the *Sun* asked if he and Kate would also be thinking of marriage,
he didn't hesitate to answer. "Look, I'm only twenty-two, for God's
sake," he blurted. "I'm too young to marry at my age. I don't want
to get married until I'm at least twenty-eight or maybe thirty."

The offhand comment would prove to be prophetic. Right
now, all eyes were on someone else's wedding—one that had been
delayed for thirty-five years. The wedding of Charles and Camilla
had been problematic from the beginning.

With polls showing that fully 93 percent of the British people
did not want Camilla to be their queen, Charles pledged that
when he became king, she would become the country's first "princess consort." (It would turn out to be an empty promise, since he
has no choice in the matter, according to English law, Camilla
automatically becomes queen when Charles becomes king.)

Charles had made another promise not only to his future subjects, but to his sons. Out of respect for the memory of Diana, not
to mention the public's enduring resentment toward Camilla for

her role in destroying Diana's marriage, Charles's new wife would not be known as Princess of Wales. Instead, she would settle for a lesser title that Diana had also held: Duchess of Cornwall.

Then there was the matter of the ceremony itself, which had to be shifted from Windsor to city hall—Windsor Guildhall—because the castle itself could not legally be used for a wedding. In what could only be described as an obvious snub, the Queen refused to attend the civil ceremony; Her Majesty would agree only to showing up for the postceremony blessing and reception at Windsor Castle.

By way of calming the waters, Clarence House arranged for a feel-good press conference and photo op midway through Charles's stag week. Father and sons posed gamely for photographers atop a stone wall, William and Harry looking every bit as euphoric as their father was sullen. Even though microphones were everywhere, a fidgeting Charles griped about the reporters who were just yards away. "I can't bear that man," Charles said of respected BBC royal correspondent Nicholas Witchell as Witchell stood directly in front of him. "He's so awful. He really is. . . . Bloody people. I *hate* doing this."

Far more media-savvy than his father—a talent that Wills picked up watching his mother charm reporters—William tried to get the press conference back on track. "Keep smiling," he murmured to Papa under his breath, "keep smiling."

If it was all an act, William seemed terribly convincing. Asked what he thought of the upcoming wedding, he enthusiastically replied, "Very happy, very pleased. It will be a good day." He even joked about his responsibilities as a witness at the civil ceremony. "As long as I don't lose the rings," he cracked, "I'm all right!"

To the surprise of royals watchers, Kate's name was missing from the guest list for both the wedding and the reception.

William explained to her that it was simply a matter of protocol, but both admitted to friends they were "relieved." They knew the press would be clamoring for photos of Kate if she showed up, and Wills did not want to worry about her safety. Nor did he want anything to distract from the Couple of the Hour.

What neither Wills nor his girlfriend knew was that Camilla had insisted that several high-profile women be excluded—Kate chief among them. "After all those years hiding in the shadows and being excluded herself," a longtime friend said, "she wasn't going to share that moment in the sun with any woman if she didn't have to. The Queen was another matter, of course."

Kate took it all in stride, promptly returning to the sanctuary of the farmhouse in St. Andrews. Once there, she alternated between studying for her final exams and watching live coverage of the royal wedding on television.

William handed out the rings at the brief civil ceremony, then tried to ignore people waving banners that read ILLEGAL, IMMORAL, SHAMEFUL as he stood outside waiting for the newlyweds to emerge from Windsor Guildhall. "Well, I'm happy with that," he said to Camilla's son, Tom. "Yup, me, too," Wills's new stepbrother answered with a nod.

The archbishop of Canterbury apparently wasn't. Rowan Williams had agreed to perform the blessing at Windsor Castle only if the couple agreed to apologize publicly and effusively for their adulterous behavior. So Wills, Harry, Granny, and the rest of the Royal Family looked on as Charles and Camilla knelt in the transept of St. George's Chapel at Windsor and acknowledged their "manifold sins and wickedness."

Watching it all on their flat-screen TV in Bucklebury, Kate's Middleton relatives agreed that contrition of some sort was in order. They, like nine-tenths of their countrymen, had never understood how Charles could choose someone like the painfully plain and famously unkempt Camilla over Diana. "Why would you swap?" Carole's brother, Gary Goldsmith, asked, echoing the Middleton clan's sentiments. "*What* were you thinking?" Nor did the Middletons find it easy to condone the adulterous affair that destroyed the marriage of the Princess and Prince of Wales and drove Diana to bulimia and suicidal depression.

Of course, now that Camilla might someday be queen of England *and* Kate's mother-in-law, a noticeable shift took place in the family's attitude toward her. "For years all you heard was 'Poor Diana' and 'That horrid Camilla,' " a longtime friend of the family recalled. "That's all anyone was saying, really. Now she's just *wonderful* as far as they're concerned. Can't blame them now, really, can you?"

The Queen could scarcely conceal her displeasure as she remained stone-faced the entire wedding day, occasionally casting a withering glance at her son's aging bride. Her Majesty did, however, finally agree to pose for the first time with Camilla and Charles and gave her permission for William and Harry to do the same.

The Heir and the Spare were, despite all the pain Camilla had caused their mother, genuinely fond of her. Although Charles never actually kissed his bride during the ceremony and the reception, his sons kissed her warmly as they departed. They also got into the spirit of things by tying Mylar balloons on the newlyweds' Bentley, scribbling PRINCE + DUCHESS across the windshield, then pelting them with confetti as they left the castle for their honeymoon at Balmoral.

William was not far behind, heading for Scotland and St. Andrews the next day. He may not have been "the studious type," as his friend Jules Knight pointed out, but Wills needed to hit the books if he had any chance of passing his exams in late May.

For someone trying to study, the distractions were formidable. That spring Operation Paget—Scotland Yard's lumbering official investigation into Diana's death—yielded one jaw-dropping disclosure after another. Perhaps topping the list was the existence of a letter, signed, sealed, and handed to Paul Burrell for safekeeping just ten months before her death, in which Diana predicted her own death at Charles's hands ("My husband is planning an accident in my car, brake failure and serious head injury in order to make the path clear for Charles to marry.") Diana also told her lawyer, Lord Mishcon, that she believed Charles was plotting to murder her.

New evidence suggested that French officials may accidentally have switched the body of Dodi Fayed with that of the driver, and that the blood sample proving Henri Paul was drunk may have come from another corpse altogether. With the toxicology tests done on Diana's body in Paris now called into question, royal coroner Michael Burgess now stated that he could not rule out exhuming Diana's body.

Not surprisingly, the ghoulish prospect of seeing his mother's body dug up was "deeply upsetting" to William. Moreover, it made concentrating on studying for his all-important finals that much more difficult. According to Boyd, Knight, and other classmates, Kate stepped in to keep Wills focused. "If it wasn't for Kate," said one, "Will would have crumbled with all that was going on. She quizzed him, went over notes with him, just did whatever it took to keep his mind on what was important."

Even as more details of Operation Paget surfaced ("They, the machinery, are going to blow me up," she had told her friend Roberto Devorik), Wills and Kate both aced their exams. On May 25, 2005—the last day of finals—the couple joined Fergus Boyd for a stroll on Castle Sands, the tiny beach directly below six-hundred-year-old St. Andrews Castle where students took their annual (and brisk) May Day Dip. The three had been fast friends for four years—three of those spent living under the same roof. Now, Kate said wistfully, "Things will never be the same."

It would be another month before graduation day, but Will and Kate had already begun thinking in earnest about their future as a couple. During their three years living together at St. Andrews under the guise of simply being roommates, they were essentially left alone to go about their business as any married couple would.

Now that they were leaving college to begin their lives in the real world, the press was no longer obligated to leave them alone. Their every move would be scrutinized, analyzed, and chronicled for public consumption by the ravenous tabloid press. Outside the cloistered confines of St. Andrews—and living apart for the first time since they'd met—how could their love survive?

William hoped that a new deal could be brokered: he would be following his brother to Sandhurst the following January, and he believed he should still be entitled to the privacy afforded by a hands-off approach. Since Wills would be living in a barracks anyway, he and Kate would have to be more inventive in finding ways to get together. "They know things are changing and they're both a little scared," Carole told a neighbor, "but they're both up for it."

Meanwhile, Wills was intent on proving to Kate and to the world that as a couple they were far from over. Seven months after Edward van Cutsem's wedding, when Kate stayed home and her rival Jecca Craig showed up instead, the prince and his girlfriend attended the wedding of Edward's younger brother Hugh to Rose Astor.

The ceremony, held in the picturesque Cotswolds hamlet of Burford, was a milestone of sorts—the first time, incredibly, that Wills and Kate had ever attended a public event as a couple. So stringently controlled was the social calendar of the future king that, before asking Kate along as his date, Wills first had to secure the approval of the powers that be at Clarence House.

Although they were supposedly there together, Kate, clad in a floral-print skirt, white wool jacket, and black hat, arrived at the church alone. She then had to content herself with perusing the program while her date, in his role as usher, escorted guests to their pews. All eyes were on Kate when Wills guided a beaming Jecca Craig to her seat. Wearing her trademark poncho and rakish cowboy hat, Jecca whispered into the Heir's ear and then, said a guest, "tossed back her head and laughed. You had to wonder what Kate was thinking."

Jecca's appearance at yet another wedding attended by William did not seem to bother Kate in the least. Immediately after the ceremony, the two dashed off in his black VW Golf—shadowed by his bodyguards, of course—to spend the night together at the sixteenth-century King's Head Inn. Over breakfast at the inn the next morning, they shook their heads at a photo of Kate that ran in one of the London papers. It captured the moment when a gust of wind blew Kate's floral print up à la Marilyn Monroe's famous subway-grate scene in *The Seven Year Itch*.

Two weeks later, they made a cozy pair at the Beaufort Polo Club, where Australia played England for the coveted Argentine Club Cup. Sitting in the stands, eyes concealed behind sunglasses, they unself-consciously held hands throughout the match. At one point, they locked eyes as she stroked his leg, clearly blasé about what might be captured on film and peddled to the media. During this dreamy encounter Kate screwed up her courage enough to tell William why she liked watching polo from a distance: she was allergic to horses.

William and Kate would be the undisputed stars of the next event they attended: their graduation from St. Andrews on June 23, 2005. Still suffering the effects of a bout with the flu, the Queen nonetheless showed up with her husband; it was the first time that Prince Philip had ever attended a family graduation. They had, as one might imagine, the best seats in Younger Hall—front row center of the mezzanine—and were flanked by Harry, Charles, and Camilla.

Wearing a black miniskirt beneath her academic robes, Kate sat downstairs with the rest of the St. Andrews graduates. Five rows behind her sat William, nervously chewing on his lower lip. Once she had her art history degree safely in hand, she flashed a smile in William's direction and he grinned back. Her Majesty, dressed in canary yellow, watched it all from her catbird seat in the mezzanine. "Nice girl," she said to Prince Philip, who nodded in agreement.

Before Dean of Arts Christopher Smith had even finished saying "William Wales," the hall erupted in cheers. In the blinding glare of a thousand camera flashes, William walked briskly to the stage and knelt before university chancellor Sir Kenneth Dover. Pausing for just a moment, Sir Kenneth tapped Wills lightly on the head with a scarlet cap that reputedly contained a scrap of cloth from the trousers of Protestant reform leader John Knox. Beadle James Douglas then attached Will's academic hood to the collar of his robe, and, at long last, Wills was given his master of arts degree in geography.

Vice-Chancellor Brian Lang seemed to have William and Kate

in mind when he rose to give his commencement address. "I say this every year to all new graduates: you may have met your husband or wife." Lang paused for the expected laugh, then continued, "Our title as 'Top Matchmaking University in Britain' signifies so much that is good about St. Andrews, so we can rely on you to go forth and multiply."

Kate and William rolled their eyes in mock disgust, Harry shook his head, Camilla laughed, and the Queen managed a faint chuckle.

Following the ceremony, everyone filed outside to mingle with the other graduates and their families. Wills bent down to kiss both Prince Charles and his grandmother, then dashed off in search of Kate, his gown billowing in the wind.

Still wary of appearing too forward in the presence of the monarch, Kate hung back with her parents on the far side of the courtyard. Once he found her, Wills impetuously took Kate's hand and told her he wanted to introduce her and her parents to Prince Charles and the Queen.

Kate, ever mindful of appearing to overstep her bounds, was reluctant to foist her sometimes overeffusive mum on an unsuspecting monarch. "Are you sure, William?" she asked. After careful consideration, he decided that the fateful meeting might best take place at another time.

After witnessing the disastrous marriages of Charles, Andrew, and her daughter Princess Anne, the Queen concluded that their courtships had been too short. Her Majesty now firmly insisted that members of the Royal Family should date someone for a full five years before settling on a mate. "After all," she told Prince Philip, "look at Charles and Camilla."

Having dated William steadily since their first year in college, Kate was nearly four-fifths of the way home. She had not only coped with the vagaries of royal life—the stringent security measures, the constant scrutiny—but she had done so with grace and charm.

Just as important to the Queen, Kate had shown a degree of loyalty and discretion that was markedly absent in her daughters-in-law Diana and Fergie. Kate had always gone out of her way to make William's life easier—even when it meant staying in the shadows while other young women, including ex-girlfriends, grabbed the limelight. In short, Kate was giving the Queen every reason to believe she truly loved him.

The Queen and Charles both credited Kate with rescuing William from the deep hole of depression he had fallen into during his first semester at St. Andrews. "She is good for him, I think," the Queen told Charles within earshot of a St. Andrews faculty member on graduation day. Charles nodded in agreement. "But," the Queen added rhetorically, "where do we go from here?"

It was still unclear if Kate, a college graduate who might wish to pursue a career of her own, would be happy to give up her own identity for a life of groundbreakings, tree plantings, wreath layings, ribbon cuttings, and endless walkabouts. William was certainly not looking forward to this part of the job. He made it clear that, unlike his father, he would not take on a full schedule of ceremonial duties immediately upon graduation. "It's not that I never want to," he explained. "It's just that I'm reluctant at such a young age to throw myself into the deep end."

Another, more onerous issue was being talked about behind palace doors. Several of the Men in Gray suggested that Kate should be disqualified as a potential royal bride because of her middle-class background. Kate's parents had earned millions from their party-supply business, but they had never moved in aristocratic circles. "We just don't know what skeletons might be rattling in their family closet," a courtier said. "We know an awful lot about the other girls Prince William has dated, but really almost nothing about the Middletons."

It boded well for Kate that she seemed as grounded as Diana was high-strung, but the Palace worried that a relative might do something embarrassing. "The Queen was sick of all the scandal and the drama," Brooks-Baker had said. "She wanted a nice, obedient girl from a lovely, hopefully rather boring, family."

For the time being, Big Willy and Babykins were determined to enjoy themselves. They held each other close on the dance floor at the St. Andrews Graduation Ball and two days later partied at the members-only club Boujis in South Kensington. Club regulars William and Harry, said Boujis manager Jake Parkinson-Smith, "are very ordinary, nice guys. They feel very safe because their pals come. . . . It's the English aristo set. They all know each other, they all went to Eton together and all play polo together, so it's all very comfortable and happy."

A little too happy, perhaps. Inside the club's private Brown Room, Wills and his friends knocked back several crack babies, a lethal combination of Chambord, vodka, champagne, and passion fruit juice served in a test tube. Kate, whose favorite drink those days was Jack Daniel's and Coke, took the high road and nursed a single glass of champagne throughout the evening.

After dancing until 1:00 a.m. on the postage-stamp-size dance floor, they once again took care to throw off the paparazzi by departing separately. First out the door was Kate, who smiled for the cameras as she climbed into her waiting BMW sedan. Unlike William, Harry, and nearly all their friends, who routinely stumbled out of clubs looking disheveled and bleary-eyed, Kate resolved never to be photographed looking wasted. In addition to never overimbibing, she always made a last-minute trip to the ladies' room to check out her hair and makeup before being confronted by the photographers who lurked outside. "They'd love it if I walked outside looking wrecked," she said to a bartender at Purple. "I'm not going to make it easy for them."

The morning after downing a half dozen crack babies, Wills nursed a hangover as he boarded a royal jet bound for New Zealand. In addition to spending time with the touring British and Irish Lions rugby team, the prince performed his first solo engagements as the Queen's official representative at ceremonies in Wellington and Auckland commemorating the sixtieth anniversary of the end of the Second World War.

William was between wreath-layings when terrorist bombs exploded in the heart of London, killing fifty-two commuters. No political figures or royals had been targeted, but Wills was understandably concerned that Kate was especially vulnerable. Although she warranted no formal protection when Wills wasn't around, he asked that, as a personal favor, someone from his detail check in on her.

Kate and William had been apart less than three weeks, but already rumors were afoot that their graduation from St. Andrews signaled an end to their romance. William put that notion to rest on July 17, when he whisked Kate—along with a dozen friends—off to what he considered "the most magical place on earth": Africa.

It was the third time William visited his old friend Jecca Craig at Lewa Conservancy, her family's eighty-six-square-mile wildlife preserve nestled in the foothills of snowcapped Mount Kenya. As before, he would spend a month at Lewa checking fences, digging trenches, and tracking endangered species such as the Grevy's zebra and the black rhino.

This was Kate's first trip to Africa, however, and she instantly fell under the continent's spell. The prince's party spent the first day hiking up to the Il Ngwesi, an exclusive lodge perched at fifty-six hundred feet on the edge of the Ngare Ndare River. The lodge was made up of six thatch-roofed cottages called *bandas*, and Will and Kate had one with a fireplace, a net-covered king-size (what else?) bed, and a veranda with a heart-stopping view of Mount Kenya all to themselves.

Inevitably, the tabloid press back in London suggested that Kate had gone to Africa to keep tabs on her man, with friction between the two over his friendship with Jecca. Kate apparently needn't have been concerned. Jecca had fallen in love with British financier Hugh Crossley after Crossley was injured climbing Mount Kenya and wound up recuperating at the Craig estate. The four quickly became fast friends, and, as if to prove it, Kate proudly wore the same broad-brimmed rancher's hat that had become Jecca's trademark.

Laboring under the hot equatorial sun paled in comparison to what Wills faced when he returned to the UK in August. Before he could enter Sandhurst in January 2006, he had to take the academy's grueling entrance exams to prove that he was mentally and physically up to the task. The Regular Commissions Board test consisted of problem-solving tasks, written exams, interviews, and an assault course. He passed easily—just as Harry had the year before—and now fretted about having to salute his little brother. "I'm sure he can't wait," William said. "How humiliating!"

To celebrate that he was now officially Sandhurst-bound—a result that was never much in doubt—William took Kate to the Collection, a former warehouse and Porsche garage that had been transformed into one of the hottest restaurants in Chelsea. From there, it was back to the VIP room at Purple for sambucas and dancing. The prince strolled over to the DJ with some special requests that he wanted to dedicate to the woman he now openly referred to as "my girlfriend." They danced to "Fall to the Floor" by Starsailor, and the BodyRockers' "I Like the Way (You Move)" before exiting the club at 1:30 a.m. This time, tellingly, they made no attempt to conceal that they had been there together.

Before long, duty called. On September 3, William sat in the royal box alongside the Queen and Prince Philip at Scotland's Highland Games while his girlfriend shopped alone on Kensington High Street in west London. "She went through the racks and never made eye contact," said a clerk at Topshop, one of the boutiques where Kate shopped that day. "She seemed preoccupied."

A few weeks later, Kate was noticeably absent when William sounded an airhorn at Falmouth Harbor to welcome their friend Oliver Hicks home after the bearded adventurer had rowed solo from North America to the Isles of Scilly. The record-shattering feat took Hicks, who had known both Wills and Kate for years, more than four months.

When Hicks rowed in, several dozen people rushed toward the edge of the dock to greet him. Billionaire Richard Branson, one of Hicks's sponsors, shook Hicks's hand and then sprayed him with champagne. Then, Hicks recalled, "Willy came along and pulled my hat down over my eyes and then they carried me off to the pub."

Once again, the press seized on Kate's being a no-show to suggest the couple had broken up. In truth, she had been there all along, but stayed away from the crowds so that she wouldn't further distract from Hicks's moment of triumph. According to Hicks, the couple had actually spent the weekend with him. "They are together," their adventurous friend protested. "The reason they never confirm their relationship is because they don't want to make it open season for people to ask questions."

The next evening, they both attended the Institute for Cancer Research charity gala at Whitehall. Much was made of their being seated at separate tables, and that William was obviously ignoring her. He seemed to have reverted to old habits, dancing with Kate only once and shamelessly flirting with several giggly young women. While William danced with one particularly attractive blonde, Kate sulked in a corner.

Kate knew what was making her prince behave this way, but she also understood she could do little about it. William was yet again being forced to relive the details of his mother's death, this time for Operation Paget investigators. Lord Stevens had long dreaded the prospect of having to interview members of the Royal Family—particularly Charles, William, and Harry—as part of his interminable official investigation.

First up was William, who was grilled for more than two hours by Lord Stevens and two Scotland Yard detectives. Most significantly, the prince stated that he did not believe his mother had any intention of marrying Dodi Fayed, a claim repeatedly made by Mohamed Al Fayed as the basis of his theory that Diana had been assassinated to prevent her from marrying a Muslim.

The strain of having to answer investigators' questions took its toll on Wills's most important relationship. "Whenever all the madness about his mother got to be overwhelming," one of his oldest Eton chums said, "Will went a little wild. More drinking, more girls. It was his way of saying, 'Oh, fuck you all.' "

The Palace gave him little time to wallow. In an attempt to give the prince a sampling of various employment experiences, William was put to work at three jobs in rapid succession before his Sandhurst term began.

First, Wills donned an apron and straw boater to work behind the counter at the Chatsworth Farm store, part of the thirty-five-thousand-acre Chatsworth Estate in Derbyshire. One of England's most impressive stately homes, Chatsworth was owned by the Duke and Duchess of Devonshire. Like many stately homes, Chatsworth could only survive by opening its doors to paying guests.

In addition to working at the farm store, Wills also cut meat in the Chatsworth butcher shop, tilled the soil, picked apples, and worked in the bakery. Unlike other workers however, he stayed for free in a sixteenth-century stone hunting tower on an escarpment overlooking Chatsworth House that normally rented to guests for $1,600 per week. Climbing the narrow, winding staircase each night to his room at the top of the tower, the prince was afforded a sweeping view of the estate's manicured grounds four hundred feet below.

Before he left for his next job, the future king scrawled in the guest book, "A wonderful place to stay but don't try to tackle the stairs once you have a drink!" With a nod to his regarding Highgrove as his own gentleman farmer's scaled-down version of Chatsworth, the prince signed the guest book simply, "Will, Gloucestershire."

Next up was a job working for HSBC Investments, an asset-management firm. Wills was "particularly keen" to work with HSBC's Charities Investment Services team so that he could learn how to raise more money for his various causes—particularly the homeless. Wills's brief exposure to the financial sector also included visits to such venerable institutions as the London Stock Exchange, Lloyd's of London, and the Bank of England.

Wills's final task would take place later in the year, when he joined an RAF Mountain Rescue Team in North Wales. Unlike his other on-the-job-training assignments, this one called for William to show off his newly acquired skills to the press—including the mock rescue of an injured climber.

With cameras clicking, Wills rappelled down the face of a two-hundred-foot cliff while attempting to steady a stretcher filled with ballast to simulate a human body. Handling reporters with his customary easy charm, Wills looked down at them from the cliff top before beginning the simulated rescue. "You're just waiting for me to fall over," he joked, "aren't you?"

William embraced these carefully planned work experiences with characteristic gusto. But he chafed at the growing realization that his life was not his own; it would all be mapped out for him in excruciatingly precise detail by the omniscient Men in Gray.

Kate faced the opposite problem. Now that she and Will were no longer cohabitating, she was left to her own devices. The royal bodyguards who had shielded both Kate and William from the press were gone. Unless Kate was in the company of the prince, she was not legally entitled to any VIP treatment or any special protection from law enforcement.

Kate also faced some tough decisions about what, precisely, she was supposed to do with her life. William complained to her incessantly about being overscheduled, of having little say in day-to-day matters. But Kate, with no official role and no readily apparent employment prospects, was floundering.

Encouraged by the success of Party Pieces, Kate decided to launch her own company designing and selling children's clothes online. She failed to take into account, however, that her parents had already built a thriving mail-order business before they took their company online. The Middletons had also managed to get Party Pieces in on the ground floor of Internet sales. Thirteen years later, the odds were stacked ten-to-one against any Internet start-up succeeding—odds that got even stiffer when it came to marketing children's clothing online.

With no backup plan, Kate divided her time between shopping and working out. By Christmas of 2005 she had shed ten pounds and, with the help of image consultant Katherine Hooker, worked on adding more sophisticated outfits to her limited wardrobe of jeans, boots, white shirts, and plaid skirts.

Gradually, almost imperceptibly, Kate evolved from a fresh-scrubbed English coed to a polished, sophisticated, self-assured beauty. That made her even more desirable to the paparazzi. "She is young and gorgeous and really has the makings of a fashion icon," said one. "Kate has everything Diana had, including her own sort of mystique. Whether she will be able to use it all the way Diana did is another matter entirely."

Since her Chelsea flat was located directly across from a bus stop, Kate made an easy target. Just as they had with Diana, photographers jumped out from between parked cars and bushes, then chased her as she tried to make her getaway on foot. On one occasion, she jumped on a No. 19 bus to elude them—only to be trapped on board.

None of this made it easy for the prince and his girl to have their customary trysts at her place in Chelsea. That fall, the German magazine *Das Neue* ran photos of Wills leaving Kate's flat after spending the night. For anyone reading the magazine, it would be easy to pinpoint the exact location of the apartment where the future king and his lover were spending their nights. A large red arrow pointed to the flat, along with a caption that called it "The Love Nest."

Kate had been rather philosophical about the press. She had gamely smiled when asked to turn her face toward the camera and had never scowled, made a rude gesture, or struck a photographer—things the paparazzi had come to expect, even from certain members of the Royal Family.

William genuinely feared for her safety. He demanded that Clarence House do something to protect Kate. The Queen's law firm, Harbottle & Lewis, swung into action, sending a letter to newspaper editors admonishing them to leave Prince William's girlfriend alone. The royal barristers also accused several photographers of pestering Kate in violation of rules established by the Press Complaints Commission.

Ever mindful of the fate that had befallen his mother, William wanted to go a step further. Pressing for even tougher legal action, he cited the case of Princess Caroline of Monaco. Grace Kelly's daughter had succeeded in getting a court order prohibiting the German press from publishing photos of Caroline or her children. If photographers continued in their relentless pursuit of his girlfriend, William wanted his grandmother's lawyers to argue Kate's case before the European Court of Human Rights.

Clarence House was more than happy to oblige, flooding editors' offices with dire-sounding threats and admonitions. Going on the offensive quickly backfired. Rather than blame William, who had enjoyed a cordial relationship with Fleet Street, journalists fingered Kate as the real control freak. "Kate Middleton wants the privacy of a nun, yet she chooses to go out with Prince William," wrote the *Sun*'s deputy editor Fergus Shanahan. "She can't have it both ways."

Kate took the criticism that should have been aimed at William without complaint. She also said nothing when, along with Harry's girlfriend, Chelsy Davy, she was pointedly excluded from the Royal Family's Christmas celebration at Sandringham.

Diana would have empathized. After her divorce from Charles, she was barred from Sandringham and forced to spend the holidays apart from her beloved sons. Until this Christmas of 2005, when as Charles's legal wife she became the second-highest-ranking woman in the kingdom, Camilla had also been prohibited from sharing in the Windsors' holiday festivities.

It remained to be seen when—or indeed if—Kate would ever be deemed worthy of the prized invitation. For now, she celebrated Christmas as she always had, with her family in Bucklebury.

Kate didn't have to wait long to meet up with her handsome prince. The main house at Sandringham was still off-limits to nonfamily on New Year's Eve, but the "cottages"—actually sizable guesthouses—that dotted the estate were another matter. The couple rang in the New Year at one of these, then departed the next day for Switzerland. Wills had only one week of freedom before entering Sandhurst, and he wanted to make the most of it.

Toward that end, Clarence House led Fleet Street to believe that the royal lovers were headed for Verbier. Instead, they sneaked off to Klosters, some two hundred miles to the northeast. It would be two full days before the press caught up with them—enough time to ski undisturbed during the daylight hours before retreating to their romantic chalet at night.

Savoring these few moments of freedom, the two accomplished skiers went off-trail to ski down Casanna Alp, then stopped for a moment to catch their breath and drink in the magnificent view. Wills drew Kate to him and for a few breathless moments kissed her.

Much to the couple's chagrin, the paparazzi had finally landed in Klosters and were lurking a few hundred feet away, telephoto lenses at the ready.

It was the first time anyone had captured Kate and Wills kissing on film, and Fleet Street made the most of it. Not surprisingly, several newspapers employed the same corny but irresistible headline to accompany their front-page photos of the prince and his girl in the clutch: KISS ME KATE.

Kate had a surprise of her own up her sleeve. The next day, on the eve of his arrival at Sandhurst, Wills and Kate headed to her Chelsea flat for what he once described as "the usual"—a shower, some takeout, and a DVD. Wills's royal protection officers were in on the secret, but when she pushed open the front door and thirty of their friends shouted, "Surprise!" the man of the hour flinched. Wills turned around to see his bodyguards standing behind him. "Well?" the prince cracked. "Aren't you going to shoot them?"

Before everyone moved on to a French restaurant in the heart of Mayfair, the somewhat questionably named Kilo Kitchen & Bar, Kate led the others in a champagne toast to Wills's success as a cadet. The ultimate outcome was, of course, preordained. As king, William would automatically become the commander in chief of Britain's armed forces, Sandhurst or no.

The surprise party was more than just a send-off for William. It was also a de facto birthday celebration for Kate, who was turning twenty-four in two days. Unfortunately, Will wouldn't be there on Kate's actual birthday to watch her blow out the candles on her cake. Once he was enrolled at Sandhurst, he would be banned from leaving the academy grounds for five weeks while he and the 268 other cadets underwent basic training.

Arriving with his father at Sandhurst in a driving rain, William was greeted by the academy's commandant, Major General Andrew Ritchie. Appearances notwithstanding, Ritchie and the other officers wanted to make it clear that William would be treated like any other cadet. "Background goes right out the window once training begins," Lieutenant Colonel Roy Parkinson said. "If someone steps out of line, they're stamped on, whether they're a prince or not."

From Harry, William had learned what to expect. The first phase at Sandhurst consisted of brutal physical training, drills, and never-ending spit-and-polish inspections. As they had with the Spare, some of the more grizzled instructors seemed to take an almost perverse pleasure in putting the screws to a member of the Royal Family. William and Harry bonded over having had drill sergeants scream, "You 'orrible little prince!" at them as they scrambled under barbed wire and marched until their feet bled.

William survived the "hell on earth" portion of his academy training, and Kate rushed to spend a romantic weekend with him at Highgrove—just one week before Valentine's Day. By this time, Charles had become so fond of his son's girlfriend that he gave his explicit permission for Kate and William to stay in the same room whenever she visited.

Their reunion was interrupted by yet another embarrassing scandal, one that called into question William's judgment when it came to picking his friends. This time, William and Kate had joined his chum Guy Pelly and his cousins Peter and Zara Phillips—Princess Anne's children—for a drink at the Tunnel House Inn, one of their favorite hangouts in the neighboring Cotswolds village of Coates.

During the evening, Pelly, who had already been blamed for introducing Prince Harry to marijuana, openly smoked a joint—a lapse that was captured on video and broadcast the next day. Pelly complained that he had been framed—that a "pretty girl" had handed him something he thought was a cigarette. No one suggested that any of the royals present were doing drugs, but once again it appeared that Wills was running with a wild crowd.

As nettlesome as the latest drug-related incident was, it paled in comparison to what Carole Middleton believed was the couple's biggest problem. With Prince William locked away at Sandhurst for forty-four weeks, Kate no longer had a royal role to play—unless steps were taken to give her one. The longer Kate was home twiddling her thumbs, the deeper the public perception would be that she had fallen out of favor. "And before long," well-known British publicist Max Clifford said, "perception becomes reality."

Before he returned to Sandhurst the next day, Wills promised Kate that she would have a more public role in his absence. But when a month passed with no royal invitations, Kate took matters into her own hands.

On March 17, 2006, she and a girlfriend decided to go by themselves to the prestigious Cheltenham Gold Cup, one of the highlights of the Thoroughbred racing season. Determined not to go unnoticed, she wore a long beige coat, black gloves, and a tall, Cossack-style mink hat. Her outfit had the desired effect. As she checked out the horses in the paddock and mingled with friends in the crowd, photographers dogged her every move.

Although she had not formally been invited, Kate was now approached by an aide to Prince Charles, who had been disturbed to hear that she was being hassled by the press and asked her to join both him and Camilla in the royal box. Even without her Willy around, Kate exuded confidence and ease in the presence of his father and stepmother that startled many onlookers. Charles and Camilla were clearly as comfortable in Kate's company as she was in theirs, treating her as they would any member of the family, with a daughterly familiarity that did not go unnoticed by reporters.

Kate had won Charles over long ago, but until this point Camilla had been a challenge. For all her earthiness—Camilla still loved to "muck around" the gardens at Highgrove in her mud-caked Wellingtons—the Duchess of Cornwall had proven herself a skilled courtesan who, for obvious reasons, viewed other women warily. She was the woman who dismissively called Diana "Barbie" and whose nickname for the princes' attractive nanny, Tiggy Legge-Bourke—perceived by both Diana and Camilla as a rival for Prince Charles's affections—was even more unkind. Camilla routinely referred to Tiggy as "Big Ass."

Now it appeared that Camilla was at last in Kate's corner, in large part because William's girlfriend seemed nothing at all like the other woman who loomed as large in death as she had in life. When Tom Parker Bowles suggested that the stylish, beautiful Kate reminded him in some ways of the young Diana, Camilla snapped, "Kate and Diana? Are you mad? No, no, no. Kate and Diana are absolutely nothing alike. Not at all!"

The shift in Camilla's attitude—the duchess now joined her mother-in-law the Queen in boosting William's longtime love as a potential princess—was evident to Kate. "Camilla is very sweet to me," she said at the time. "She is very warm and very funny, and she doesn't take herself too seriously." Yet, Kate went on, Camilla was "nervous" about fulfilling her royal duties. "I don't blame her. It's all a little scary."

Kate's appearance at Cheltenham—the first time she was seen at a public function with members of the Royal Family sans William—was a masterstroke. Her standing was bolstered even more the following day when Wills was given leave to return to Eton to play the Field Game—a cross between soccer and rugby—as part of an "old boys" alumni team.

At last intent on letting the world know how much they cared for each other, they hugged and kissed without hesitation, in full view of hundreds of spectators. Cadet Wales threw back his head and laughed when Kate reached up to check out his new military buzz cut—a style that, unfortunately, exposed the bald spot he had been concealing for more than two years with an artful comb-over.

Now that they were being more public about their feelings for each other, Wills worried that the paparazzi would become even more aggressive in pursuit of his girlfriend. Months earlier, Kate had met with officials at Clarence House and the Scotland Yard detectives who oversaw Wills's security detail. They could only advise her on what measures she might take to protect herself, including hiring her own private security.

Kate, however, was not about to ask her parents to pay for a bodyguard. Aside from the obvious expense, she also worried such a move would invite a drubbing from the press. "She's right, of course," Charles replied when Wills laid out the case for providing Kate with a royal protection officer. "I suppose they'd just say, 'Who in blazes does she think she is?' if she went out and did it herself." As March 2006 drew to a close, Prince Charles paid out of his own pocket for a bodyguard to watch over Kate now that she was apart from his son, by her own account, "ninety percent" of the time.

As William and Harry proved time and again, armed bodyguards could protect their clients from everyone but themselves. On April 12, William, Charles and Camilla, Prince Philip, and the Queen—who had not visited the military academy in fifteen years—all showed up for Harry's graduation from Sandhurst. Chelsy Davy had flown all the way from Cape Town, and Kate, intent on not overshadowing Harry's girlfriend, graciously chose to stay home.

The ceremony itself went off without a hitch. The Queen, reviewing the new officers as they stood stone-faced with their swords raised, paused for a moment before her red-faced, beaming grandson. After all the medal-bedecked Windsor men had an opportunity to salute each other, Harry was off to put on his dress uniform for the extravagant ball held on the grounds of the military academy.

Now that he was Second Lieutenant Wales, Harry was on his best behavior. William was another matter. Without Kate there to rein him in, Wills was soused by midnight. Fortunately, he wasn't a mean drunk—Wills was known for breaking up fights when his friends under the influence turned belligerent—but he was a loud one.

Wills roared at a fellow cadet's dirty jokes, then repeated them at the top of his lungs. Later, he reeled around the dance floor, plowing into other dancers and accidentally tipping over a table. Perhaps his biggest mistake was laughing too loud when cadets did a scathing impersonation of a general and then offering his own, even more insulting version. One of a number of senior officers who were shocked by Wills's behavior took the prince aside. He ordered Wills to return to his barracks.

Commandant Ritchie, enraged at the reports he received concerning the Heir's behavior, phoned Clarence House early the next morning. He told Prince Charles that such "crass and ungentlemanly" behavior was "unacceptable" in an officer—and grounds for summary expulsion if it ever happened again.

For someone who had always lived in fear of disappointing his family, William scarcely seemed chastened. The very next night, the celebration continued at Boujis, where the princes downed crack babies and crack daddies (a crack baby, only double) until dawn. This could not go unnoticed by the powers-that-be at Sandhurst; the next morning tabloids had a field day running pictures of the smashed princes and their equally bombed girlfriends stumbling out of the club. Equally disturbing was their bar tab for the evening—$4,200.

William's grandmother was not amused. "When my sister and I were young," the Queen said, "our friends would arrange parties in their homes and we had quite a lot of fun. We did not go to West End nightclubs."

William's defiant streak was not entirely new; partying too hard in public was one of the ways he could flout authority when he felt he was losing control of his life. He was feeling the public pressure to marry Kate, surely. But that, he assured everyone, was something only the two of them could decide.

Whether he would be allowed to fight alongside his fellow soldiers in Iraq or Afghanistan was also becoming a major issue— and a source of frustration for William. Like Harry, William had continued to demand that, following graduation, he be assigned to combat duty. Granny was grateful that the decision was not hers to make. The government and the military would have to determine whether the risk—of, say, being kidnapped and beheaded on videotape—could be tolerated.

Harry would be given his chance to fight alongside his comrades when the time was right. But this was not an option for William. Regardless of how strongly he felt about it, the military was not putting the heir to the throne directly in harm's way.

Understandably, Kate was relieved that the man she loved was not likely to be dodging bullets in a war zone. But she also worried that his mounting frustrations over not being allowed to serve were fueling another need of his: a need for speed.

Even behind the wheel of his sedate VW Golf, William was at times an aggressive, even reckless, driver. Five years earlier, he had even tried to drive Lord Bathurst, a seventy-six-year-old Highgrove neighbor, off the road. Lord Bathurst offered a heart-pounding version of the encounter: "He went on the grass to overtake me. . . . I thought he'd stop. . . . I didn't know who it was!"

Motorcycles, however, were Wills's true love. Behind his helmet he could be anonymous and free, and he now owned two new superbikes capable of reaching speeds in excess of 160 miles per hour—a Honda CBR 1100XX Blackbird and a Yamaha RI.

At first Kate was characteristically hesitant to tell William what to do. She was aware, however, that on three separate occasions he had rocketed so fast and so far ahead of his bodyguards that they lost him. Now Kate was telling Wills that she didn't want him taking any chances and pleaded with him to slow down.

William shouldered a lorryload of frustrations that caused him to party too hard and drive too fast. But this side of his personality members of the Royal Family only read about in the papers. Just one week after his wild and widely reported night at Boujis, William was the cynosure of decorum as he sat next to the Queen at her eightieth-birthday dinner in the white-paneled dining room of the newly refurbished Kew Palace. On the other side of Granny sat Charles, who chatted amiably with the Queen before rising at the end of the dinner to toast her.

William's assigned place at the table next to Her Majesty was not merely symbolic. Not only was he second in line to the throne, but William continued to be the people's overwhelming favorite to become the next monarch. But Charles, who would wait longer than any other heir apparent to inherit the crown, was not about to step aside. "I'm," he said when Diana famously declared him unfit to be king, "not going anywhere."

Nevertheless, given that Charles's time on the throne would almost certainly be short—he would be well into his sixties or perhaps even his seventies before finally becoming king—William stood to reign for a long time. In light of this—and the Queen's wish to extend the reach of the monarchy well into the twenty-first century and beyond—she was now inviting her grandson to sit in on secret meetings to plot the future of the monarchy.

Founded in 1992 with the Queen as its chairperson, The Way Ahead Group was made up of the highest-ranking members of the Royal Family and a half dozen anonymous senior advisers. To free the monarchy from political influence, no member of government—including the prime minister—was privy to what went on during the group's closed-door sessions.

Many of the decisions made by The Way Ahead Group had already had a major impact—from the sovereign's agreeing to pay income taxes to finally taking steps toward ending primogeniture, the centuries-old rule that places male children ahead of female children in the line of succession.

Admission into this sanctum sanctorum of royal decision-making—MI5 swept the conference room inside Buckingham Palace for bugging devices before each of the twice-yearly meetings—was a distinct honor. But it also meant Wills was being expected to assume more royal responsibilities even as he trained to be a soldier. "It's all getting to be," he told Guy Pelly, "too much."

At the end of April 2006, William took advantage of a break from training at Sandhurst to sweep Kate off on yet another adventure—this time to the exclusive island enclave of Mustique in the Grenadines. Mustique (a variation on the French word for mosquito) had royal connections stretching back to the late 1950s, when British real estate tycoon Colin Tennant—now Lord Glenconner—bought the fourteen-hundred-acre island and gave a little piece of it to the Queen's rebellious sister, Princess Margaret.

Although nothing on Mustique outshone Tennant's own Ali

Baba–style, domed estate, the princess's Les Jolies Eaux ("The Beautiful Waters") came close. When building her lavish villa, Margaret fell in love with the garden designer Roddy Llewellyn. He was seventeen years her junior. Their scandalous affair led to Margaret's sensational divorce from Lord Snowdon and put Mustique on the map as a hideout for the notoriously rich and famous.

Mick Jagger bought a home on Mustique in 1971, and soon he, David Bowie, and the rest of Mustique's seventy residents were busy dreaming up ways to keep their private paradise private.

They would, of course, make an exception for William and Kate. In exchange for making a donation to a hospital on nearby St. Vincent, Jigsaw fashion moguls John and Belle Robinson waved the usual $14,000 weekly rental fee and lent the couple Villa Hibiscus, their stone-walled hilltop estate overlooking Macaroni Beach.

Blissfully free from the prying eyes of the press, Kate and William spent the next week frolicking in the crystal blue surf, challenging billionaire Richard Branson, a longtime island resident, to a tennis match, playing beach volleyball with locals, and sipping margaritas and mai tais at the only two watering holes on the island, Firefly and Basil's Bar. After a languid afternoon spent swimming off Branson's yacht, they headed for an evening of off-key karaoke at Basil's Bar. While Kate doubled over with laughter at their table, Wills performed cringe-inducing renditions of Frank Sinatra's "My Way" and Elvis's "Suspicious Minds," the latter accompanied by the appropriately inappropriate pelvic swivels and thrusts.

No sooner had they arrived back in England than newspapers carried photographs of the couple in their bathing suits, hosing themselves off on the deck of the yacht. Mustique, it turned out, was not as paparazzi-proof as everyone had been led to believe.

William seethed yet again—not over the invasion of his privacy, but the loss of hers. "She shouldn't," Wills told his handlers at Clarence House, "have to give up her privacy just because of me."

While the Crown's solicitors worked on a solution to the vexing problem of protecting Kate, the couple made another high-profile appearance—this time at the wedding of Will's stepsister, Laura Parker Bowles, to Harry Lopes, grandson of the late Lord Astor of Hever and a onetime Calvin Klein underwear model.

Wills and Kate had technically attended a society wedding together, but the Lopes–Parker Bowles nuptials marked her first invitation to a Royal Family wedding. Wearing an embroidered, cream-colored coat that showed off her deep Caribbean tan—not to mention a striking ostrich-plumed hat—Kate provided an undeniable touch of class to the proceedings. When she and an equally sun-burnished William walked into St. Cyriac's Church in the rural Wiltshire town of Lacock, the result was predictable. "There was," the church's Reverend Sally Wheeler recalled, "a terrific buzz."

Kate kept the buzz going after William returned to Sandhurst, staying on the party circuit and looking as if she had no intention whatsoever of seeking gainful employment. After attending the fashionista-studded launch of a new boutique, she made another splash a few nights later—this time cheering on Wills's old pal Hugh van Cutsem during the amateur boxing match that was the centerpiece of the Boodles Boxing Ball. Judging by the stories that ran the next day, fewer journalists were interested in who won the match than what Kate was wearing—a cornflower blue gown by the U.S. designer BCBG Max Azria.

At a party to celebrate Wimbledon thrown by the ubiquitous Sir Richard Branson, Kate once again showed up without her prince. Substituting for Wills on the dance floor was resident court jester Guy Pelly. Despite his headline-grabbing antics, Pelly, strangely enough, was one of the few people Wills trusted to escort Kate around town.

Amidst the swirl of wedding receptions and parties that summer, there were also moments of sadness. In early July, William and Harry were among the mourners at the funeral of Camilla's father, Major Bruce Shand. The quintessential English gentleman, Major Shand had moved into Clarence House with his daughter and was a grandfatherly presence in the lives of the young princes.

At the same time, both of Kate's grandmothers were fighting for their lives. Carole's chain-smoking mother Dorothy, the driven matriarch who had passed her own social ambitions on to her children, battled lung cancer for four months before succumbing to the disease on July 21, 2006. She was seventy-one. "Dorothy came from nothing, but she always behaved like a queen," said a Goldsmith cousin. "She was completely thrilled that her own granddaughter might really become one." As for Dorothy's role in the family's ascent: "Dorothy pushed Carole, and Carole, well, *encouraged* Kate. None of it would have been possible if it weren't for Dorothy. None of it."

By cell phone from Sandhurst, William did his best to console Kate. Since they would go weeks at a time without seeing each other, the phone was their lifeline; they spoke to each other two or three times a day and texted each other constantly.

When she heard that William had pulled a tendon in his knee, Kate left a sympathetic message on his cell phone. When he checked his messages, however, it looked as if the one from Kate—which he had yet to read—had already been sent to his mailbox as if it had already been listened to and saved.

Top aides to both William and Harry were experiencing the same thing with their cell phones, but at first they simply ignored the phenomenon as some sort of technical glitch. However, when details of William's knee injury—which had been known to only three or four people—surfaced in the *News of the World*, William became convinced his conversations were being bugged.

His suspicions were confirmed when Harry's escapades in a strip club resulted in the *Sun* headline HARRY BURIED FACE IN MARGO'S MEGA-BOOBS. STRIPPER JIGGLED, PRINCE GIGGLED. Chelsy blasted her boyfriend for his behavior, but it was William's cell phone message teasing Harry about the incident that ended up in the *News of the World*. Under the headline CHELSY TEARS A PIECE OFF HARRY, the story quoted Wills's message verbatim.

In mid-August, three men were charged with obtaining PIN codes and hacking into the phones of William, Harry, and their aides. One of them was *News of the World* royals editor Clive Goodman, who eventually pleaded guilty to charges of eavesdropping.

Under normal circumstances, it would have been a perfect time for William to gloat. He had always suspected that the press would stop at nothing to invade his privacy, and here was the proof.

Unfortunately, on August 16, 2006, the *Sun* ran frontpage photos showing Harry grasping sportscaster Natalie Pinkham's breast while a blotto William looked on. The accompanying headlines DIRTY HARRY and THE BOOZE BROTHERS—not to mention additional shots of them whooping it up with several scantily clad young women—embarrassed the princes and enraged the Palace.

Before their military superiors could reprimand them, however, it was pointed out that the offending photos had been taken at Pinkham's birthday party three years earlier. Chelsy Davy had little to complain about; the pictures were taken well before she and Harry began their affair. William was another matter. The *Sun* photos were taken well into his relationship with Kate.

The Heir seized the chance to make it up to her when they flew on a private jet to the Mediterranean island of Ibiza, the fabled playground for the rich and famous off the coast of Spain. With their four-man security contingent and a dozen pals in tow, they chartered a yacht for nearby Espalmador. There they visited the uninhabited island's famous mud baths, where William gamely slathered his body in black goo and then stood with his friends knee-deep in the surf. Kate declined, choosing instead to remain on the yacht and sunbathe.

For the entire week on Ibiza, the couple stayed with Carole Middleton's younger brother, Gary Goldsmith, at his pink, tile-roofed $8 million villa high in the hills overlooking the island's trendy Cala Jondal beach. Goldsmith's place was easy enough to find: the owner's logo—the initials GG—were spray-painted in gold on an outside wall. (The initials were also tattooed on his right shoulder.) Another white stucco wall was emblazoned with the owner's credo: IT'S GARY'S WORLD—YOU JUST LIVE IN IT.

A founder of Computer Futures, a firm that recruited staff for the computer industry, Gary Goldsmith reportedly reaped a $60 million windfall when the company was sold in November of 2005 for more than $400 million. At forty-one, Uncle Gary now owned a variety of properties, including a $2 million London town house. In the wake of two failed marriages, however, he now spent most of his time here, in the pleasure palace he somewhat indelicately christened La Maison de Bang Bang.

The minute the royal party walked up the steps that led to the villa's front door, Kate saw that staying with her bald, portly uncle might prove problematic. With the prince's royal protection officers walking a few yards ahead of them, William and two of his chums burst out in adolescent laughter as they walked past the elegantly lettered LA MAISON DE BANG BANG sign.

With only the housekeeper there to greet them, they surveyed the kitschy decor that featured a white grand piano, several pinball machines and video games, a 1950s jukebox, a mosaic-tile *Mona Lisa*, and, propped against a wall in the living room, a pink Raleigh motorcycle circa 1980 emblazoned with the requisite initials GG in gold.

William's bodyguards were more concerned about the obvious lack of security. The house had no alarm systems, no guard dogs, walls, or fences, and no surveillance cameras. As it turned out, this may have been the least of their problems.

As they waited for their host to show up, William and Guy Pelly tossed around a ball in the living room, inadvertently striking a cabinet that contained Gary's collection of glass pyramids. Several crashed to the floor, shattering. When Goldsmith arrived, he surveyed the damage and then walked up to Prince William.

"Hey, you fucker!" Goldsmith bellowed—the first words, he later boasted, that he ever said to the prince. "Did you break my glass pyramids?"

With Kate looking on in shock, William apologized, and Goldsmith quickly changed the subject. "So what do you think of the place?" he asked his guests.

" 'La Maison de Bang Bang,' " Wills replied. "Catchy name. Your idea?"

"Well, I preferred 'Can Aveline.' Pronounced 'Can I have a line.' " Goldsmith said, making a not so subtle allusion to cocaine use. "Either that or 'Cumalot.' "

Goldsmith's reputation for throwing some of Ibiza's wildest parties was well earned. Appropriately enough, the owner of La

Maison de Bang Bang was not only a connoisseur of pornography who frequented the island's raunchiest live sex shows, but he also boasted of paying as much as $1,000 a night for the services of local prostitutes. "Mention you know Gary from Cala Jondal," he said as he handed a new friend the name and phone number of his favorite pimp. "There's loads of Brazilian girls here."

Of more concern was Uncle Gary's cavalier attitude toward drugs. From an ornately carved wooden box on his coffee table, Goldsmith blithely doled out marijuana, cocaine (which he snorted using a rolled-up hundred-euro note), and ecstasy ("Two pills," he would instruct a guest as he pressed them into his palm. "Do half at a time, every hour").

Kate's uncle was something of an expert when it came to the consumption of recreational drugs. To anyone who would listen, he offered tips on how to stretch one's cocaine supply ("If you put it on a warm stone, it will blow up to three times the size") and how to consume the drug ecstasy ("You never snort that. It's the pure stuff. . . . You take one tab at a time").

Although he apparently did not deal himself, he did not hesitate to offer putting others in touch with his suppliers—both in London and on Ibiza. "You need me as a friend," he told a visitor from London whom he had just met. "I have a company that delivers to your door. . . . I can get cocaine to your door here, too."

"He was amazing fun and really caring," a friend told writer Rebecca English. "But like a lot of people who are the life and soul of the party, he had a very dark side."

As he had with so many of his substance-abusing friends, William simply preferred to look the other way. His bodyguards felt differently. "We knew this guy was a ticking time bomb," one recalled. "You can't have all these drugs and prostitutes around and no security to speak of. It was crazy that Prince William was staying there—but he didn't want to offend his girlfriend."

If nothing else, William and Kate seemed to be enjoying themselves at La Maison de Bang Bang, especially when several of Gary's island friends stopped by to show Wills how to mix tracks on Goldsmith's DJ decks. "Yeah, it was brilliant," Gary later recalled. "And they told him he needs a shout: 'The King's in da house!' "

Loud partying aside, Kate did not want to give the press more ammunition than it already had. When Wills and Pelly began tearing up and down the street in mopeds, she came out of the house and began scolding them. "Anyone could be watching," she said. "Go out the back and stop behaving like this."

Having shown his niece and her beau a good time on Ibiza, Gary soon found himself welcomed into their tight-knit circle of friends. Occasionally he would lunch with the couple in London or join them for dinner at the Middleton family manse in Bucklebury.

William's presence at the Middleton family table had become commonplace since he began his army training. Those weekends that he didn't spend with Kate at the Middletons' flat in Chelsea, he drove the thirty-three miles from Sandhurst to Oak Acre in Bucklebury.

Since William had only known the turmoil of his own parents' bitter marriage, the Middletons' ostensibly happy family life was a revelation. He enjoyed being in their company, and they, in turn, treated him like one of their own. The Heir and his girlfriend's parents had grown so close that William began calling Michael "Dad."

The level of familiarity was, one houseguest pointed out, "easy, breezy, and at times naughty." Even the less-than-genteel Gary was surprised when, over dessert, Kate's breasts suddenly became the topic of conversation. "They were talking about boobs at the time," Goldsmith recalled, "around the table at my sister's house." When Kate complained about the size of her own, her prince would have none of it. According to Gary, William proclaimed that "more than a handful is a waste."

Gary jokingly chastised the prince not only for using such language in front of Carole, but for using it to describe her own daughter. "Now you must put on the hankie of shame," Gary intoned to William, who promptly draped a napkin over his head and bowed in mock contrition.

For all intents and purposes, Kate and Wills seemed to be weathering their new situation well that September 2006. Before returning to Sandhurst after their Ibiza idyll, they made a last stop at Boujis. This time, when they left the club at 3:30 a.m., they made no attempt to avoid the paparazzi. Instead, they laughed and tussled playfully with each other for the benefit of photographers in the backseat of their black Range Rover.

Five days later, the real world intruded once more when Kate's paternal grandmother, Valerie Middleton, died of lymphoma at age eighty-two. William's own grandmother, meanwhile, was taking steps to move his relationship with Kate along.

The Queen had always wanted both William and Harry to make full use of her beloved Balmoral, but the house they were sharing was obviously too cramped for two princes *and* their girlfriends. She decided that Harry should have the existing house all to himself, and that she would give William a newly renovated, 120-year-old gamekeeper's cottage in a part of Balmoral known as Brochdhu. Behind the striking, sky blue front door of the gray stone cottage were four fireplaces and three upstairs bedrooms with bay windows. The romantic hideaway was intended as a sanctuary for the couple—and, as far as the Queen was concerned, an ideal honeymoon spot.

The Queen had done more than just set the couple up with new digs at Balmoral. Since new titles are traditionally bestowed on newly married royals, she had thought long and hard about what to call William and his bride. She had her staff research the available titles, then picked two that she thought were particularly appropriate for a future king and queen. According to senior palace officials, William and Kate would probably become the Duke and Duchess of Cambridge. Two lesser possibilities were his being named Duke of Clarence (the title was tarnished by scandals linked to its last holder, Edward VII's son Prince Albert Victor) or Duke of Sussex, a title more likely to be bestowed on Harry when he married.

For William, even the most routine walkabout or ribbon-cutting seemed fraught with meaning. When he reopened the Winnicott Baby Unit of St. Mary's Hospital in London—the very maternity ward where he was born—nurses thrust a newborn in his arms. Wills rolled his eyes when he read what was written on her T-shirt: LITTLE PRINCESS. Asked if being surrounded by burbling babies made him feel "broody," Wills winced. "I don't know about that," he replied. "Not yet."

Talk of parenthood was the last thing Kate wanted to hear. She had more immediate problems. If Kate was expected to sit on the sidelines and wait, then she wanted to earn a paycheck while she did it. Over the months since Kate and William had stayed at Belle and John Robinson's villa in Mustique, Kate had gone out of her way to attend promotional events for the Robinson's Jigsaw chain of stores. Now, she approached Belle directly and asked for her help.

"She genuinely wanted a job," Belle Robinson said, "but she needed an element of flexibility to continue the relationship with a very high-profile man and a life that she can't dictate." Kate signed on with Jigsaw in late November, working four days a week as an assistant buyer for the company's junior accessories line.

Joining the workforce made Kate no less appealing to the paparazzi. At the end of each workday, photographers stationed themselves at the end of the drive leading up to Jigsaw's front door waiting for the world's most envied part-time assistant buyer. "Listen, do you want to go out the back way?" Belle Robinson asked Kate on that first workday.

"To be honest," Kate replied with a sigh, "they're going to hound us until they've got the picture. So why don't I just go, get the picture done, and then they'll leave us alone."

Robinson was impressed. "I thought she was very mature for someone her age," she said, "and I think she's been quite good at neither courting the press nor sticking her finger in the air at them."

Kate had shown much more savvy than either William, Harry, or Prince Charles when it came to massaging the press. When William invited her to join the royal shooting party at Sandringham in early December, she made the calculated decision to be photographed traipsing behind her rifle-toting prince carrying a brace of pheasant he had just shot.

Predictably, the images of a smiling Kate holding a half dozen dead game birds infuriated the same animal-rights groups that routinely denounced the royals for their love of hunting. "It turns your stomach," said Andrew Tyler, director of a group called Animal Aid. "I would have hoped that she might have talked some sense into William . . . but sadly, she is offering her support to his brutal habit and seems happy to join the latest generation of blood sport enthusiasts."

Yet the photos also proved to the public at large—not to mention the Queen—that Kate and the Royal Family were a perfect fit. "I think she knows," Robinson said, "*exactly* what she's doing."

Charles was now ready to act on his long-held conviction that Kate should be his daughter-in-law. With the Queen's blessing, he also did his part to insure the couple's smooth transition to married life. Plans went ahead for an eighty-five-hundred-square-foot, neoclassical stone "starter palace" on the Duchy of Cornwall's nine-hundred-acre Harewood Park Estate, located some fifty miles from Highgrove in the Wye Valley of Herefordshire. Once owned by the Knights Templar during the Middle Ages, Harewood Park was confiscated by Henry VIII and over the centuries became the site of a succession of stately homes. By the mid-twentieth century, Harewood Park had fallen into such disrepair that it was used for bombing practice by the SAS (Special Air Service), Britain's most elite special services unit.

Prince Charles purchased the property in 2000 with idea of turning the property into a model English village—until Kate Middleton came along. Built around a courtyard from recycled bricks, timber, and slate, the new Harewood Park would boast six ground-floor reception rooms, six bedroom suites, fourteen bathrooms, a library, a swimming pool, tennis courts, formal gardens, stables, an orangery, and a chapel. Most important to the ecologically correct Prince of Wales, Harewood Park would be the first truly "green" palace in the kingdom.

For the time being, Cadet Wales and his girlfriend made do with stolen weekends at her flat and the occasional night out to hip spots such as London's Archipelago (he had crocodile, she had wild boar), Pangea, and of course Purple and Boujis. With Will's full consent, she also hit clubs during the week or on those weekends when he was required to remain at Sandhurst.

For all of these excursions without her Big Willy, Kate was escorted by the wacky but nonthreatening Guy Pelly. There was not much Pelly, or for that matter, anyone else, could do to stop the paparazzi from harassing her. When news photos showed Kate wading to her car through a sea of photographers and jostling reporters, William turned to the law firm favored by the royals, Harbottle & Lewis. The firm's first step was to have private investigators covertly videotape the paparazzi as they harassed her. The newspapers were then presented with a choice: either leave Miss Middleton alone or risk having the tapes shown in court.

As so often happened, the press backed off when faced with the threat of legal action, only to return to business as usual within one or two weeks. Soon photos surfaced of Kate outside her flat, arguing with a parking warden who had just given her a ticket. Later, when she somehow locked herself out of her own apartment, she stood on the steps while photographers snapped away and she phoned the first person she could think of—William.

Interest in all things royal would be triggered on December 14, 2006, by the release of Operation Paget's *Inquiry Report into the Allegation of Conspiracy to Murder*. The massive dossier (832 pages) agreed with the conclusion reached by French authorities in 1999: Diana was the victim of a drunk-driving accident.

The report's conclusions did not come as a surprise to either Wills or to Kate; Lord Stevens had met with both of Diana's sons at Sandhurst the night before the report was released. As soon as he left, William called Kate to tell her that he didn't buy the theory that Diana was the victim of a drunk chauffeur behind the wheel.

"They killed her, pure and simple," Wills told Kate, repeating his long-held and publicly expressed belief that the press chased Diana to her death. "If the paparazzi hadn't been chasing after her like they always did, they wouldn't have been speeding."

What William didn't tell Kate was that, at his urging, Clarence House was scrambling to find new ways to keep the press at bay. Nor did he mention his nightmare visions of Kate's violent death in a crash caused by the press—an accident that took place not in Paris this time, but in the heart of London.

Kate is a lovely girl . . . who happens to be going out with a boy called William who happens to be a prince. That's all.
—*Middleton family friend Gemma Billington*

He's lucky to be going out with *me*.
—*Kate, to yet another friend who said she was lucky to be dating William*

You can't string her along forever.
—*Prince Philip, to his grandson William*

6

December 15, 2006

Sandhurst

"I love the uniform," Kate whispered to her mother as William marched by with an SA80 rifle on his shoulder and the distinctive scarlet sash of the sovereign's banner holder slung across his chest. "It's so, so sexy."

The Sovereign's Parade marked Cadet Wales's graduation from Sandhurst, and since this time Kate was not invited to sit with the Royal Family, she wanted to make certain William could spot her with her parents in the general stand. Enveloped in a crimson wool coat, wide-brimmed black hat, high black leather boots, and elaborately stitched black leather gloves, Kate was such a standout even in this crowd that at one point Prince Charles could be seen pointing her out to the Queen from across the field.

Palace officials took pains to explain that only members of the Royal Family could sit in the royal enclosure. Kate could scarcely complain about being snubbed. She and her parents sat in the front row of the general stand, next to two of William's godfathers—Norton Knatchbull (Baron Brabourne) and King Constantine of Greece.

Harry had found it impossible not to break up when his grandmother reviewed the troops as they stood stern-faced and ramrod straight, and Wills was no different. The Queen, braced against the December chill in a red wool coat of her own, paused in front of the Heir just long enough to break him up and then moved on.

"For those who are to be commissioned today," the Queen told the 233 graduating cadets, "a great deal will be expected of you . . . and you must be all these things in some of the most challenging environments around the world."

Like Harry, William was set to join the Windsor-based Household Cavalry's Blues and Royals. (They would not be the only royals to serve in the regiment; their aunt, Princess Anne, was an accomplished equestrienne who already held the rank of colonel in the Blues and Royals.)

In view of the conflicts in Iraq and Afghanistan, both princes were also due to undergo extensive training in desert warfare. From there, their military career paths would sharply diverge. To familiarize himself with all branches of the service, the future commander in chief would serve in both the Royal Navy and the Royal Air Force as well as in the army.

Ironically, precisely that future role as head of Britain's fighting forces would in all probability preclude him from seeing action. Although it was ultimately up to the prime minister, one veteran diplomat observed, "There is simply no way they are going to put him at risk." The reason: "William is the last best hope for the monarchy." Harry was an entirely different matter: "Prince Andrew was allowed to fight in the Falklands. If Harry wants it, and he does, he'll get to fight in Iraq or Afghanistan. But William? No, I don't see it."

All of which was fine with Kate. While she was immensely proud of William for wanting to fight for his country, she did not want him in harm's way. "He thinks he's invincible," she told one of their pals from St. Andrews, "but he's not. There would be a price on his head. I just hope they tell him he can't go."

Kate herself was catching plenty of flak at home. The same reporters who declared that Kate's presence at Sandhurst signaled an imminent engagement announcement sniped at her mother for furiously chewing gum throughout the entire ceremony. "Unfortunately," wrote Julia May in the *Age*, "dozens of photographers caught every unladylike chomp." For Carole, May continued, "opening the papers the next day was a rude initiation into the media-driven world that her daughter has graced without putting a foot wrong in five years."

The explanation was simple enough: Carole was struggling to overcome a thirty-year smoking habit, and she was chewing nicotine gum. Ironically, because Carole was a smoker, the Middleton home was one of the few places where William felt free to light up.

Carole's nonstop gum-chewing in the presence of the Windsors wasn't the only thing that ruffled the feathers of royals watchers. Spectators at Sandhurst claimed they heard Carole ask where she might find the "toilet," as opposed to the more acceptable *lavatory*. Such faux pas were held up as evidence that the former flight attendant with working-class roots that stretched back to the coal mines of County Durham was too "common" to become mother-in-law to a future king.

Since invitations to spend Christmas at Sandringham were

still reserved for family members and fiancées, Kate and William once again spent the Christmas holidays apart. This time the Middletons, undaunted by the unflattering newspaper stories about Carole, decided to spend $8,000 to rent a baronial thirty-room Georgian mansion in Scotland for Christmas week. They invited William to join them there for New Year's Eve, but he didn't show. For the first time since 2003, William and Kate did not ring in the New Year with a kiss.

For the next week, Kate bided her time in silence. Although she was about to celebrate her twenty-fifth birthday, William was understandably distracted; that same day he was due to report for duty with the Blues and Royals. The farewell party at Highgrove, thrown by Prince Charles the night before Wills was to move into Combermere Barracks in Windsor, was the kind of genial Royal Family get-together Kate had become accustomed to over the past two years. Charles and Camilla both greeted her with kisses on both cheeks, and everyone wished her a happy birthday, but Kate was under no illusions about the purpose of tonight's celebration—to toast the launching of the future monarch's military career.

The morning of January 9, 2007, marked the beginning of a new and treacherous phase in the relationship. It was, Kate noted wistfully to a former roommate, the first birthday she had spent apart from her Big Willy in five years.

To the public at large, their romance could not have seemed more solid. "She is perfect princess material," gushed *Tatler*'s Geordie Greig. "She is the epitome of an effortlessly stylish English rose. She has qualities you can't create or manufacture. Her unaffectedness makes her particularly attractive. In many ways that makes her a Diana II." Concurred Deirdre Fernand in the *Sunday Times*, "Her elegance, dignity, and beauty certainly make her the People's Choice. Kate is what we need. . . . In her case beautiful does not mean bonkers. She is unlikely to throw herself downstairs, tell all to a tabloid reporter, become a phone pest or watch her lover perform heart surgery. The time is ripe for the announcement of an engagement," Fernand continued, echoing the sentiments of millions. "What better start to the new year than the prospect of a royal romance, officially sanctioned?"

So convinced were Woolworth executives in England that by January 2007 the chain had already begun selling a line of souvenirs "commemorating" the couple's nuptials. In stores across the UK, their smiling faces appeared on plates, cups, dish towels, cell phone covers, even mouse pads.

Emerging from the front door of her town-house flat in Chelsea, Kate was instantly blinded by a score of flashing cameras. A small army of photographers had camped outside her door, dispatched by tabloid editors who sensed that an engagement announcement was in the air.

"Bloody hell!" Wills shouted after a Clarence House staffer showed him the photos of a grim-faced Kate rushing past photographers on her way to work. "I do not want the same thing happening to Kate that happened to my mother. We must do *something.*"

The Crown could do little to protect Kate physically. Prince Charles had only provided her a privately paid-for bodyguard for a short time before being advised that it was not appropriate; until she became engaged to William, Kate would not be legally entitled to her own officers from SO14, Royalty Protection branch.

Scotland Yard, meanwhile, did what little it could. For a few weeks in early 2007 when the hysteria over a possible royal engagement reached a fever pitch, guards were stationed outside her flat and assigned to escort Kate to work.

The lawyers at Harbottle & Lewis also swung into action. On Kate's behalf, they lodged an official harassment complaint with the Press Complaints Commission, specifically citing a *Daily Mirror* photographer who chased her down the street as she walked to work. Clarence House issued a statement describing William as "very unhappy at the paparazzi harassment of his girlfriend. He wants more than anything for it to stop. Miss Middleton should, like any other private individual, be able to go about her everyday business without this kind of intrusion. The situation," the statement concluded ominously, "is proving unbearable for all those concerned."

Wills did what he could to keep Kate from cracking under the strain. For the next few weeks, he partied with Kate in London at clubs such as Mayfair's Polynesian-themed Mahiki (Guy Pelly was now marketing director there) and Boujis, where he gave her a diamond-encrusted, green enamel Van Cleef & Arpel's compact for Valentine's Day. The compact, which was decorated with the image of a polo player about to hit a pearl, was eighty years old and set the prince back $17,000.

Kate was crestfallen. She had expected a ring. "She thought he was finally going to propose to her on Valentine's Day," said a friend from St. Andrews. "When it didn't happen, Kate was crushed."

It scarcely helped matters when he returned to Boujis with his hell-raising pals Arthur Langdon, Will van Straubenzee, Jack Mann, and Hugh van Cutsem for a boys' night out. Hitting the dance floor, he grabbed twenty-four-year-old public relations executive Tess Shepherd and, as she later recalled, "started twirling me around." At one point, Wills pulled Shepherd toward him for a warm embrace and, according to some witnesses, a torrid kiss.

The pretty blonde denied that their brief encounter was anything approaching erotic. "It's not true that I snogged him," Shepherd insisted. "It was an embrace but not a French kiss." As for the impact all this would have on the royal romance: "No," Shepherd admitted, "I don't think I'll be very popular with Kate."

That would be a masterpiece of understatement. Shepherd's denials only fueled speculation that trouble was brewing for William and the young woman now being routinely derided in the press as Waity Katie. "Will was letting off steam and Kate understood that," said a member of their pub-crawling posse. "But it was still hurtful and embarrassing."

Trying to repair the damage, Wills took Kate to the chic Swiss resort town of Zermatt on March 4 for a weeklong holiday on the slopes. As usual, the prince insisted on bringing his entourage—the always amusing Pelly, of course, and four other well-connected buddies. The couple confined themselves to their romantic chalet while the others made the rounds of Zermatt's après-ski clubs, leading everyone—their friends included—to conclude that all was well.

It wasn't. William and Kate managed to get away to attend the National Hunt Festival west of London in Cheltenham—another premier horse-racing event—but the tension between them was palpable.

To be fair, William had plenty on his mind. His brother had been told in late February that he had gotten his wish to fight. Despite heightened concerns that he would be targeted by terrorists, Harry received his orders to ship out for Iraq with the rest of the Household Cavalry Regiment's A Squadron in May.

Frustrated in the knowledge that his combat training was probably just a futile exercise, William nonetheless arrived in

Dorset on March 16 to begin a ten-week course in tank warfare. Kate, waging a public relations war of her own, plowed ahead on her own.

Just one year earlier at the Cheltenham Gold Cup, Kate was asked at the last minute by Prince Charles and Camilla to join them in the royal box—a huge step toward establishing her as a probable royal bride. Rather than just show up and hope to be invited, this year Kate wrangled a formal invitation. Once she arrived wearing a jaunty beret and an eye-catching periwinkle blue jacket, Kate was escorted by royal protection officers directly to the box.

The next day's papers were filled with photos of Kate cheering for the horses she bet on to win, and jumping up and waving her arms when they did. However convincing her performance, Kate realized she and Wills—now immersed in the world of hotheaded young officers training for battle—were growing further and further apart.

Just how far started to become apparent on March 22—Second Lieutenant Wales's first night on the town with the rest of the hard-drinking men known throughout the British army as the "Booze and Royals." At Elements, a nightclub in the nearby town of Bournemouth, William knocked back pints of Stella Artois with sambuca chasers while dozens of women in skimpy outfits took pictures of the prince with their cell phones.

"Word went round that William was there playing cheesy eighties music, so we went to take a look," recalled eighteen-year-old Ana Ferreira, a stunning brunette international-relations student from Brazil. "He was dancing, looking a bit wooden—I don't think he would be any good at the samba! But there were lots of girls hanging around him."

Soon, he had Ferreira on one side and her friend Cecilia on

the other, posing for pictures. With his right hand, a grinning Wills reached down and grasped Ferreira's breast—an image that ultimately made its way into the papers. "I was a little bit drunk myself," she remembered, "but I felt something brush my breast. I thought it couldn't be the future king, but now that I've seen the picture, it's no wonder he's got a smile on his face! He has big, manly hands and certainly knows what to do with them." (Later, Ferreira e-mailed the photo of William and his wandering hand to her family in Brazil. "My mother thought it was very funny," Ferreira said. "She is pleased I met Prince William even though he was a little naughty.")

Later that same evening, Wills was "a little naughty" yet again—this time with a six-foot-tall, blond, nineteen-year-old performing arts student named Lisa Agar. "Come on," he said, grabbing Agar's arm and leading her to the dance floor. "Show us how it's done. You're too good for this place."

"He was being very flirty and I was quite taken aback but just went for it," said Agar, who chalked up his behavior to too many pints followed by too many shots of sambuca. "I call that stuff rocket fuel," she said. "It does give you a huge hit very quickly and gets you rolling drunk."

As the evening progressed, the rocket fuel had its desired effect. "He was very touchy-feely and quite pissed," Agar said. "He was not a shy boy and didn't talk about Kate."

Around 3:30 a.m., Wills invited Agar back to the barracks for a nightcap. When she balked, the prince pressed her. "Are you coming back?" he asked. "It'll be a laugh. Come on. We need to go."

Agar and a friend followed the soldiers back to the base and were led into the barracks lounge. They spent the next twenty minutes "lying about on a leather chair and sofas," Agar recalled.

In the end, she wondered if the prince was depressed over problems in his relationship with Kate. At 4:15 a.m. the prince announced that he would have to get some sleep, and Agar left. "Strangely, I felt sorry for William," she said, "and I thought maybe he was cheering himself up."

When Wills and Kate dined on March 31 at the aptly named King's Head Inn in the Cotswolds with their old friends Hugh and Rose van Cutsem, much of the conversation centered on their wedding less than two years earlier. But the van Cutsems' talk of marital bliss did little to mask what one of their party called the "strange fog of disillusion" that had settled over Wills and Kate.

Kate told her mother and her sister that William had "changed"—the result, she believed, of the physical distance between them and the enormous strain that distance was putting on their relationship. "I think it's really tough on her," said artist and longtime family friend Gemma Billington, "but she handles it well. . . . It's funny how you think people are different, but we are all just muddling our way through life. Whoever you happen to be going out with, you have to take the rough with the smooth."

Things were, in fact, far more serious than Kate imagined. Now that he was embarking on a military career, William complained that his relationship with Kate felt "confining" and "claustrophobic." More important, the recurring nightmare he was having about her being chased to her death by the paparazzi was making him ever more anxious.

William went to his father for guidance. Ironically, Prince Charles's affection for Kate was precisely what led him to recommend dumping her. He did not bother asking if Wills and Kate were in love; when asked that question after proposing to Diana,

Sporting a new beard after weeks at sea, William joined the rest of the Royal Family for Christmas at Sandringham in 2008—without Kate.

As a guest at Sandringham on other occasions, Kate was taught to shoot by Prince Philip. Here, she joins William on a grouse hunt in Scotland in 2009.

44

Lying low for months, Kate and William finally surfaced together in May 2009 at a polo match in Ascot. A photographer caught them stealing a kiss in the parking lot after dinner at the Potting Shed Pub in not-so-romantic-sounding Crudwell.

45

47

motorcycle fanatic who owns two
perbikes, capable of reaching speeds in
cess of l60 miles per hour, William (shown
ere racing in Africa) also relishes the fact
at he can go unrecognized beneath the
elmet. With the Queen's blessing, Kate has
eaded with William to slow down.

46

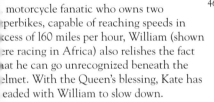

48

"Who? Me?" At the wedding of their pal
Nicholas van Cutsem in August 2009,
the groom told Wills, "You'll be next."
According to a fellow search-and-rescue
pilot, at the RAF advanced helicopter
graduation ceremonies in January 2010,
"You couldn't have pried them away from
each other." The same was obviously true
three months later when they took off
on a snowmobile in Courchevel, France.

51

52

April 29, 2011. The groom and his best man Prince Harry were the first to arrive at Westminster Abbey. Wearing an ivory silk and lace wedding gown by Alexander McQueen designer Sarah Burton and a diamond tiara loaned by the Queen, Kate strode confidently into the abbey on the arm of her proud father Michael Middleton. Kate's maid of honor, sister Pippa, carried the nine-foot train.

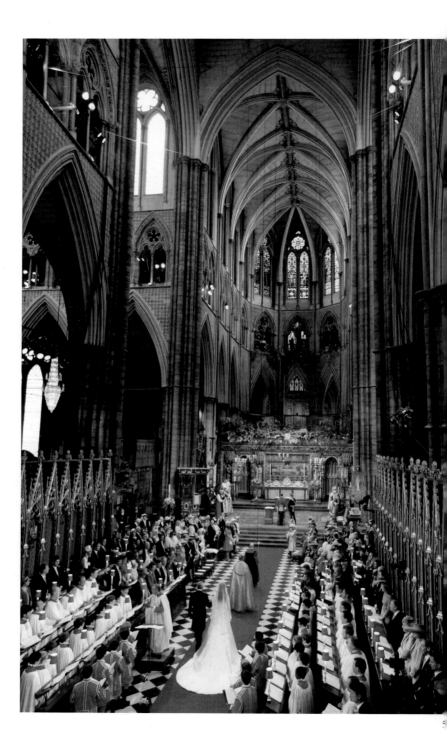

Westminster Abbey has been the site of every coronation since 1066, as well as the site of fifteen previous royal weddings—yet perhaps none more important than this one, witnessed by two billion people worldwide. "I thought," William whispered to Kate and his future father-in-law, "this was going to be a small family affair."

55

56

William and Kate exchanged vows before Archbishop of Canterbury Rowan Williams. Following Diana's lead, Kate omitted the word *obey* from her wedding vows. William slipped the wedding ring on Kate's finger. Later, she transferred her famous engagement ring to her left hand.

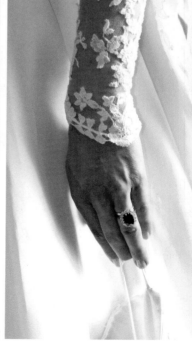

57

William and Kate walked back up the aisle—finally man and wife after nine years—and emerged to cheers from the crowd. Outside, Carole Middleton, the Queen, and Camilla breathed a collective sigh of relief. Riding in the same horse-drawn carriage used by Charles and Diana at their wedding in 1981, Kate and William waved to the more than one million people who lined the procession route to Buckingham Palace.

At Buckingham Palace, Kate's train hit a snag as she emerged from the carriage, then she made her way inside with her bridesmaids and pages in hot pursuit.

On the balcony moments later, what everyone has been waiting for—not one but two balcony kisses.

64

The official family photo. From left (not counting bridesmaids and page boys): Camilla; Philip; Charles; the Queen; Harry; William and Kate; Michael, Carole, James, and Philippa (Pippa) Middleton.

After the wedding breakfast hosted by the Queen, the newlyweds surprised the crowd by driving out the front gates of Buckingham Palace in an Aston Martin convertible for a victory lap before heading to nearby Clarence House. Later, Kate and Camilla left Clarence House for a party in the newlyweds' honor thrown by Charles at Buckingham Palace. The next morning, the Duke and Duchess of Cambridge strolled the palace grounds.

66

67

Charles famously answered, "Whatever love means." But he did ask his son if he planned to marry "in the end."

Pointing out that he was just shy of his twenty-fifth birthday, William told his father he was not ready to promise marriage to anyone. Then end it now, Charles urged his son. By stringing her along, Papa said, William was being "completely unfair to Kate." Equally important, Charles, who had been pressured by his own father to marry Diana, was not about to make the same mistake with his own son.

Charles knew from experience that William was likely to be seen as a cad for callously breaking up with the loyal Miss Middleton for no apparent reason. Before handing his poor grandmother yet another public relations grenade, it was best to give her fair warning. Rather than approach the Queen directly, William asked his grandfather, Prince Philip, to convey the news to her.

"The Queen was disappointed, of course," a former Palace equerry said. "Prince William and Miss Middleton had been together such a long time. But it was not the Queen's decision to make. She did not wish to interfere one way or the other. She did not want him rushing into a commitment if he wasn't absolutely certain this was the one."

Eager to escape from the London scene, Kate joined her mother in Dublin for Gemma Billington's art exhibition at the city's Urban Retreat Gallery, followed by a quick visit to the National Gallery of Ireland. It was a very different scene back in Dorset, where Wills and his fellow Booze and Royals officers were causing a commotion at a bar called Bliss. An audience of several hundred had paid to hear acoustic guitarist Dan Baker. "This gig," Baker later said, "was the pinnacle of my career. I've practiced for years in the hope of a chance to perform like this."

Baker was in the middle of a song when one of Wills's group climbed onto the stage, grabbed the microphone, and yelled, "Please stop playing these crap songs. The prince wants dance music!" After a few minutes of awkward silence, the prince and his raucous army buddies departed. Baker understandably claimed to be "staggered" by the incident. "It was," he said, "the rudest thing I've ever experienced."

Nursing a hangover the following morning, William was unprepared for the news that Second Lieutenant Joanna Dyer, one of his closest friends at Sandhurst, had been killed along with three other British soldiers by a roadside bomb in Iraq. William was already in the midst of a total reassessment of his priorities. Now the shocking death of a comrade-in-arms convinced him that some major changes were in order.

Since 2003, William had spent at least part of the Easter holiday in the warm embrace of the Middleton clan. This year, however, he declined their invitation without explanation—another ominous sign. Instead, Wills agreed to meet Kate that weekend at her London flat.

Kate had always been careful not to overplay her hand. She never complained about his nightclub antics and for six years had remained mum on the subject of marriage. But now that she was forced to deal with the paparazzi on her own while Wills was serving in the military, Kate needed a commitment—and the promise of royal protection that came with being a royal fiancée. "It wasn't just 'I want to be a princess,' " noted a former member of Wills's royal protection squad. "There were some genuinely scary moments when the crowds and the press were chasing her. She was, to some extent, afraid."

Alas, William was—for the time being, at least—unwilling

to make a commitment. Nor was he willing to maintain the status quo. Since Kate was still not entitled to royal protection, the threat to her safety was simply too great. "The press will make your life unbearable as long as we're together," he reportedly told her. "I don't want you suffering the way my mother did."

Kate was not willing to give up quite so easily. She asked him to consider all that they had been to each other, what he really wanted out of life—and how they could make their relationship work. "She told him," a friend from Bucklebury said, "that he made her happy and that she believed she made him happy, and that was all that mattered in the end. But he just shook his head and said that for someone like him, it wasn't that simple."

The next day—April 11, 2007—William called Kate at Jigsaw on his cell phone. She excused herself, went to a back conference room out of earshot of the other buyers, shut the door, and for the next hour heard Wills sputter the reasons he was breaking up with her. "I can't . . ." he stuttered. "It just isn't going to work. It isn't fair to you."

This time, Kate could not face the paparazzi who were camped in front of her office. She left at 3:00 p.m., slipping out a side door and driving directly to Bucklebury. Once home, she was not the only one crying on Mum's shoulder. Facing the same commitment issues, sister Pippa had just ended her two-year-long relationship with Hong Kong banking scion J. J. Jardine Patterson.

After breaking up with his girlfriend on his cell phone, William placed another call—to Windsor Castle. The Queen was preparing to leave for a two-day visit with the Earl of Carnarvon at Highclere Castle, where, among other things, the orgy scene in Stanley Kubrick's *Eyes Wide Shut* was filmed. According to a senior courtier, the Queen "had to sit down to hear the news.

She was very disappointed, of course, because of all the hurt that would be caused." Rather than prolong the agony, the Queen agreed that Clarence House should leak the news that afternoon.

Bracing for the inevitable headlines, a devastated Kate holed up in Bucklebury with her family. Wills, on the other hand, made the calculated decision to reclaim his title as the world's most eligible bachelor. Shortly before midnight on Friday the thirteenth, the prince and his band of bar-hopping buddies showed up at Mahiki, where they knocked back mai tais, piña coladas, and zombies as well as several $700 bottles of vintage Dom Pérignon—all at a total cost to the prince of over $17,000.

As the Rolling Stones classic "You Can't Always Get What You Want" blasted over the sound system, Wills waved his arms in the air and shouted, "I'm *freeeee*." Then he launched into an exaggerated soccer-goal victory dance. "I'm really happy," he insisted to his friends within earshot of other patrons. "Everything is fine. Let's drink the menu."

More than three hours later, a melancholy and bleary-eyed Wills, looking physically and emotionally drained, straggled out a back door and into a waiting limousine. It had been a tough day, but it was going to be even tougher tomorrow.

WILLS AND KATE SPLIT screamed the front-page headline in the next morning's *Sun*. IT'S OVER! chimed in the *Daily Mail*. "The future king and his long-term girlfriend Kate Middleton," the *Times* solemnly intoned, "have parted."

The matter was of such national significance that the prime minister felt compelled to make a statement. "They are a young couple," Tony Blair said. "We've had the announcement. Fine. They should be left alone."

Taken by surprise, Fleet Street scrambled to find plausible reasons for the breakup. The most popular theory: the Middletons were too common and too crass ever to be accepted by the royals. There was, after all, Carole's nasty gum-chewing habit—not to mention her use of the word *toilet* and a predilection for saying "Pardon?" when she didn't hear someone, as opposed to the royal practice of simply saying "What?"

The Queen's real opinion remained behind palace walls. Over the years since Diana's death, the monarch had learned the hard way that she could not survive without the love and affection of her middle-class subjects. She could not, under any circumstances, appear arrogant or elitist. At Her Majesty's urging, the Palace vehemently denied ever saying anything remotely critical of the Middletons.

It was not enough—at least as far as William was concerned. Just four days after telling Kate they were finished as a couple, Wills called to assure her that none of the nasty stories about her family were coming from his camp. "Don't worry," she replied. "Of course I know that."

Kate also knew that she could not afford to look as pathetic as she felt. Her hair pulled back and her tears concealed behind her trademark oversize sunglasses, the prince's former girlfriend slipped into a pair of low-rise jeans and a gray striped T-shirt before heading out the door. With her brother, James, serving as her chauffeur and her only protection against a paparazzi onslaught, Kate first dropped by her apartment to fetch her tennis racket. "A very confident move and a very shrewd one, too," said publicist Max Clifford, who suggested that Kate could now write a kiss-and-tell memoir for $8 million. "The message that sends is 'I'm still in the game.' "

Then Kate popped into her Jigsaw office to retrieve a cardboard box full of files to work on at home. "She was determined not be thrown off the rails by this," a coworker said. "Now that she was by herself out in the big world, she wanted to focus on herself for a change."

Nevertheless, the wound was still fresh when she returned to work a week a later. According to Jigsaw staffer Philip Higgs, Kate was clearly "very emotional and on edge" during this period. At one point, after being asked for the umpteenth time if she was all right, Kate snapped. "It's because of his daddy!" she blurted out, taking her coworkers by surprise.

"Everyone raised their eyebrows," Higgs said of Kate's uncharacteristically candid comment. "In the heat of the moment she'd given us a glimpse of what she really thought, what was really going on behind the scenes. Normally, Kate is very quiet. She'd been trying to keep it together and hide her real feelings, but she got a bit angry about it and momentarily lost her cool. That happens sometimes when people are being nice to you and you're upset."

Once again, Carole Middleton stepped up. She would play a key role in mapping out Kate's strategy to win back her prince. "He'll change his mind," she reassured her daughter. "For now, just let him know you have a life. He'll realize soon enough it was a mistake to let you go."

What better place to make a splash than Mahiki, site of Wills's own "freedom" party the week before. Wearing a 1970s minidress and knee-high boots, she danced and flirted for hours with several men, including architect Alex Shirley-Smith. "She was dancing in the middle of a group of about five guys, who all seemed a lot more drunk than her," he said. "Was she having a good time? Let's just say she was certainly *trying* to have a good time." When the DJ put on James Brown's "Sex Machine," Kate, according to Shirley-Smith, "flicked her hair and looked over her shoulder at me. The next thing I knew she had twirled backwards towards me so her back was up against me. She started doing some very sexy moves and she was absolutely gorgeous."

Guy Pelly snatched Kate away, but she turned and winked at Shirley-Smith. Later they reconnected on the dance floor. "You've got some moves," he told her as they danced to EMF's "Unbelievable."

"So have you," Kate replied.

With that, Kate was pulled away by another man—a six-foot-two-inch-tall friend of the family Oli Packer. They, too, Shirley-Smith recalled, "were doing some pretty steamy dancing."

The scene was repeated just a few days later. After dinner with friends at Mango Tree, a Thai restaurant in Chelsea that she had frequented with William, Kate was off to another of their favorite hangouts—the VIP Brown Room at Boujis. Short of actually running into William at one of their old haunts, Kate seemed to be doing everything possible to make him jealous. At Boujis, she hit the dance floor again, winking and flirting and grinding up against a succession of men.

Kate also intended to lose a dress size, get toned, and thumb her nose at convention—all by joining the Sisterhood, an all-women rowing crew that vowed to beat the all-male Brotherhood in a twenty-one-mile race across the English Channel. The group's leader, Emma Sayle, modestly described the fourteen-member Sisterhood as "an elite group of female athletes talented in many ways, toned to perfection, with killer looks and on a mission to keep boldly going where no girl has gone before."

The group Sayle had assembled was colorful, to put it charitably, and no member of the Sisterhood was more colorful than Sayle. The daughter of a high-ranking English diplomat, Sayle had attended Downe House, the posh boarding school Kate had briefly attended. Vowing to "either be a millionaire or in jail by the age of thirty," she launched Club Fever, a sex club for "liberated couples and single women." From there, she headed up French Letter Day, a service that promised to fulfill its clients' sexual fantasies, from orgies to bondage and anything in between. After French Letter Day, Sayle founded Cake, a women-only club where members pole-danced and dessert came in the shape of a penis.

More recently, Sayle had become infamous as the proprietor of Killing Kittens, an upscale swingers club that catered to wealthy couples and single women—what Sayle called "the world's sexual elite." Members and their guests wore masks (though often little else), and among the services offered was a $5,000 "Dungeon Break," in which a member could spend an entire weekend manacled in the dank dungeon of a West Yorkshire castle. Killing Kittens also offered a chilling, twelve-hour "Kidnap Experience," a ticket to the "Mile High Club" (sex aboard a private jet), and a $6,000 transgender makeover.

Sayle was not the only member of the Sisterhood with questionable credentials. Her best friend at Downe House, Amanda Cherry, was just nineteen when she embarked on a scandalous affair with her forty-one-year-old married social studies teacher, Ian Goodridge. He left his wife and two children to marry her.

Another member of Kate's Sisterhood was self-described "reportage artist" Anna-Louise Felstead. Called A-L by her friends, Felstead made the rounds of strip clubs and fetish parties in search of material. Rounding out Kate's motley crew were a part-time masseuse, a champion female bodybuilder, a supermodel, a full-contact kickboxer, a stuntwoman, and a sex-toy marketer.

"Helming is a key role," Sayle said, "and Kate will be responsible for yelling orders, keeping rhythm, and also keeping morale high. . . . It's a tricky job, like standing on a wobble board in the gym. But Kate's very gifted and capable. She's not on the team as a token celebrity."

To make the point that she was now steering her own course in life, Kate was photographed standing at the stern of the Sisterhood's dragon boat, manning the helm. "God," William said wistfully when he was shown the photos. "Isn't she beautiful? Takes your breath away."

Kate's regimen—into the boat at 7:00 a.m. for an hour-long row up the Thames three times a week—was having the desired effect. Down to a size four, she no longer had to dress the part of a princess-in-waiting. Out went the more tailored jackets in favor of micro-miniskirts, formfitting wrap dresses with plunging necklines, and shimmering black sequined outfits worn with tall boots, large hoop earrings, and bangle bracelets.

While Kate showed off her new look in London's most high-profile nightspots, Wills did his best to appear uninterested. He was anything but. "Seeing her out dancing and having a good time," Harry told Chelsy Davy, "it's just driving him absolutely crazy."

The Heir had other pressing issues on his mind—not the least of which was the upcoming tenth anniversary of his mother's death. He and Harry had already planned a church service for August 31, 2007—an event that would reunite both sides of their fractured family. For the People's Princess, however, her boys wanted to do something, well, for the people. Only a pop concert would do—"a *big* concert," Wills insisted. The net proceeds—which would amount to some $2.5 million—were earmarked for Diana's favorite charities.

Scheduled for July 1, which would have been her forty-sixth birthday, the star-packed Concert for Diana at London's new sixty-three-thousand-seat Wembley Stadium was already shaping up to be the pop event of the decade. The lineup would be headed by Diana's old friend Sir Elton John, whose moving "Candle in the Wind 1997 (Goodbye, England's Rose)" tribute was the biggest-selling single of all time, and include Rod Stewart, Duran Duran, Kanye West, Tom Jones, Nelly Furtado, Fergie (of the Black Eyed Peas), Joss Stone, comedy by Ricky Gervais, and special music written for the occasion by Andrew Lloyd Webber. Since Diana had been its patron, there would also be a performance by the English National Ballet.

The first twenty-two thousand tickets put on sale sold out in four minutes. Amidst all the hype, William wanted to make sure that "first and foremost, the evening is for her—it's all about remembering our mother. It's got to be the best birthday present she ever had."

As usual, William had taken on the lion's share of responsibility for putting on the Concert for Diana. That, coupled with the stress over the breakup, had plunged the Heir into another of his dark moods.

This time, as he prepared to ship off to Iraq, it was the Spare's turn to worry about his brother's precarious state of mind. When officers from the Household Cavalry threw a farewell party at Mahiki for Harry's Iraqi-bound squadron on April 27, he was careful not to do anything remotely inappropriate. He and Chelsy arrived at eight thirty, had one drink, and left. "Harry," said a fellow officer, "was on his very best behavior." William, on the other hand, "was clearly on a mission to get as drunk as possible."

Arriving with Guy Pelly through a back door at 11:00 p.m., William rang up another $8,000 bar tab splurging on Dom Pérignon, tequila shots, and Coconut Grenades, a frozen blend of passion fruit, coconut, and rum. Soon he was on the dance floor with Sir Richard Branson's daughter, Holly, dirty-dancing to the Kinks classic "You Really Got Me."

(Sir Richard was not exactly thrilled at the prospect of his daughter becoming seriously involved with the Heir. "Nothing against William," he said, "but the life the royals lead, and the responsibilities that go with it, are very difficult.")

Before having to be helped out of the club at three thirty the next morning, William spent an hour talking to another attractive blonde. At one point, he leaned over and—in full view of dozens of club patrons—kissed her.

In mid-May, Kate called for reinforcements. Now that Pippa had graduated from Edinburgh and was free of her filthy-rich boyfriend, the Middleton girls decided to hit the party scene together. Their first stop was a high-profile book party held at Asprey jewelers in Mayfair and attended by a slew of royal friends. One of them was former cocaine addict and Windsor chum Tara Palmer-Tomkinson, who used to greet the adolescent Will by thrusting her hand down the front of his pants. "Keep your chin up," Palmer-Tomkinson told Kate. "Don't let them get you down. You'll be fine."

Fine, indeed. "In the weeks since her apparent heartbreak," Laura Collins and Louise Hannah wrote in the *Daily Mail*, "she has never looked better . . . or happier. Far from appearing shattered, Kate sans William is cutting a frankly far sexier figure."

Although four inches shorter than her five-foot-nine-inch-tall sister, Pippa was nevertheless regarded as the more flamboyant of the two. She was also the most overtly ambitious. Pippa "makes no secret at all of it," said a fellow student at Edinburgh. "She wants power and money. . . . She was very charming about it, but quite ruthless in cultivating the 'right' friends."

Cultivate them she did. Before she began dating the wealthy J. J. Jardine Patterson, she cozied up to the Duke of Northumberland's son George Percy and to the son of the Duke of Roxburghe, Ted Innes-Ker.

Photographed hand in hand and smiling broadly as they arrived at club after club, Kate and Pippa were soon dubbed the Wisteria Sisters because, as one wag put it, they were "decorative, terribly fragrant, and have a ferocious ability to climb."

As helpful as Pippa's presence was in raising Kate's already sky-high profile, other men remained the key to making the Heir jealous. Finally, on May 26, 2007—exactly six weeks after their breakup—Wills invited Kate to Clarence House for a drink. By all accounts, they took the first tentative steps to mending their relationship. "It was like old times," Kate told her sister. "He sounds like he wants to get back together, but isn't sure. We'll see . . ."

Kate's strategy: apply more pressure. In one evening alone, she was photographed at Mahiki uncomfortably close to real estate investor Charles Morshead, eyeglass magnate Jamie Murray Wells, and—the pièce de résistance—Jecca Craig's old movie-star-handsome, shipping-heir flame Henry Ropner. When she and Ropner weren't singing along to "I Walk the Line" and "Ring of Fire" (it was the club's Johnny Cash Night), they were knocking back Fog Cutters—a lethal combination of cognac, gin, dark rum, and fruit juices.

The next day, she was summoned back to Clarence House for another secret tête-à-tête with Wills. Apparently, this time things turned amorous. By the time she accepted his invitation to attend the Household Cavalry's salacious "Freakin' Naughty" extravaganza—a Moulin Rouge–themed barracks party marking the end of troop leader training—Kate had clearly won back her prince's heart. Mingling with other guests dressed in "saucy" attire, William and Kate—who wore a starched white nurse's uniform with lots of décolletage—never left each other's side. "He was following her around," said one senior officer, "like a lost puppy." Shortly after midnight, they kissed. Moments later, he took her hand and led her back to his quarters. Kate did not leave until the following morning.

For the time being, Fleet Street was completely in the dark about the couple's reconciliation. Before that bombshell was dropped, Kate—with Wills's blessing—jetted off to Ibiza for a four-day vacation with friends. Once again, Kate managed to fly beneath the radar, spending entire days lazing on Cala Jondal beach and nights at Uncle Gary's La Maison de Bang Bang. Three weeks earlier, Carole's brother had married for the third time in a brief civil ceremony, and now Kate and William were both invited to return for a $400,000 church blessing. Unfortunately, the new Mrs. Goldsmith, growing increasingly distraught over Gary's heavy drug use, would leave him just days before the blessing. Kate's mother pleaded with her to reconsider ("He needs a good woman to pull him through. Please come back"), but to no avail.

Kate was well on her way to getting her own love life back on track. Tanned and rested after her holiday on Ibiza, she returned in time to pay another secret visit to Wills, and to wish him a happy birthday. There would be even more cause for celebration than usual. Now that he was turning twenty-five, Wills could begin collecting at least $600,000 in annual earnings on the $10 million he had inherited from his mother. This was on top of his own allowance and expenses already fully covered by his father and the Queen.

Still intent on being seen alone at as many high-profile venues as possible, Kate showed up in the stands at Wimbledon before pulling off another cloak-and-dagger operation. It was June 30—the eve of the Concert for Diana—and while Kate was watching Maria Sharapova clobber her opponent in straight sets, William and Harry were at rain-soaked Wembley Stadium checking out rehearsals.

Beneath umbrellas and with a giggly Joss Stone standing between them, the princes took a handful of questions from reporters. It had already been announced that Kate Middleton had been invited to sit in the VIP section, so the question was on everyone's lips. "How," asked one intrepid reporter, "are things going with Kate?"

"I've got lots of friends coming, so everyone's going to be there tonight," William replied sheepishly while his brother looked bemused.

"Very well avoided, William," Harry said.

"Yes," William added without missing a beat. "Very diplomatic."

What neither prince knew at the time was that on that day—Saturday, June 30—history came perilously close to repeating itself. As Kate maneuvered her black Audi through the slick, rain-swept streets of central London, she looked in her rearview mirror and saw a car following dangerously close to her rear bumper. Suddenly, she swerved to avoid a second car that was trying to come between them. When Kate realized she was actually being chased by four cars full of paparazzi, she pulled over, got out of her car, and confronted them. Standing in the driving rain, she pleaded with the photographers to stop tailgating her. "It is so dangerous," she told them. "There is going to be an accident. Someone is going to get killed." The photographers refused.

That night around nine, Kate parked her Audi at the Ritz

Hotel in Mayfair. Then, her face partially concealed beneath her umbrella, she walked the five blocks in the rain to Clarence House. Once inside with William, she handed her car keys to a footman, who later retrieved her car from the hotel parking lot and stealthily slipped it into Clarence House at 1:45 a.m.

Conspicuous in knee-high black boots and a clinging white minidress, Kate took her place the next day in the royal box—two rows behind William, Harry, Chelsy Davy, Diana's brother and sisters, and ubiquitous royals hangers-on Thomas van Straubenzee and Guy Pelly.

After Elton John opened the concert with "Your Song," he introduced "the two people who have made this all possible." Kate seemed to be fighting back tears as sixty-three thousand concertgoers—many cheering, some weeping—rose to give William and Harry a standing ovation as they stepped up to the microphone to address a television audience of nearly 1 billion people in 120 countries. Wearing open-necked shirts and chinos, they seemed overwhelmed at first, but quickly pulled it together. "This event is about all that our mother loved in life—her music, her dancing, her charities, and her family and friends," Wills said. "We just want you to have an awesome time."

For the next six hours, William and Kate never made eye contact as they clapped and danced and in some cases sang along to the music. When the group Take That sang their hit "Want You Back for Good," all eyes were on Kate and William as they swayed—separately.

The brothers returned with Elton John to close the show, and this time William became emotional as he thanked everyone for making the concert a success. "This is how," he said, "our mother will always be remembered."

The $500,000 afterparty, held in a club specially constructed backstage at Wembley just for the night, was a bacchanalian eyeful that featured acrobats swinging overhead and nearly naked dancers gyrating in cages. Hundreds of brightly colored tropical fish swam in a tank beneath the Plexiglas dance floor.

At first, William and Kate stayed in their separate corners. When he seemed to be spending too much time talking to Joss Stone, Kate said to Pippa in mock indignation, "Hmmm . . . Willy's ignoring me." As the DJ, Erick Morillo, pumped up the volume, Kate took to the dance floor. A male admirer began pawing Kate and was promptly dragged away by a burly bouncer.

Yet when the DJ began playing "I Like the Way (You Move)"—the BodyRockers hit Kate and Wills had always called "our song"—a sweat-drenched Wills jumped onto the dance floor, grabbed Kate, and kissed her passionately. Since they hadn't had a chance to speak all evening, she pulled him close to tell him how wonderful the concert had been. "Well done, darling," she said.

Clearly they had both decided to let the world know that they were indeed a couple again. During a particular steamy session on the dance floor, Wills moved up behind Kate and cupped her breasts ("More than a handful is a waste") in his hands. "It was," said a waiter who watched the whole thing, "pretty X-rated stuff. I think he realized after a bit that they were becoming the show." Retreating to a quiet, candlelit corner, they sat holding hands on a white leather sofa, drinking mojitos, occasionally kissing, and quietly making plans for their future together.

That future did not include immediate marriage plans, and that was fine with Kate. They were, after all, only twenty-five. But Wills also made it clear that he loved her, and that he could not see himself marrying anyone else. For now, they agreed to share their lives as they had since 2001.

"Is it true, William?" the Queen asked, somewhat breathlessly. She had ostensibly summoned her grandson to Windsor Castle to congratulate him on the Concert for Diana. But she really wanted to hear about Kate. "Are you seeing each other again?"

William and Harry had always both felt a deep affection for their grandmother, but that didn't mean that even as children they would ever wrap their arms around her or jump in her lap. She was the Queen—head of state and virtual embodiment of the entire nation—so even those closest to her treated Granny diffidently. In this case, however, Will reacted to her question with a toothsome Windsor grin.

"Yes, Granny," he said. "Kate and I are back together, indeed. We're very happy."

Her Majesty paused for a moment, then clasped her hands in front of her. Her purse dangled from her right forearm. "Well, yes, then," she said, nodding approvingly. "I'm glad to hear it. She's a nice girl."

I was young. I'd had a few drinks. What can I say? I wish I'd kept my big mouth shut!

—*William, on his remark that he would marry at "twenty-eight or even thirty"*

7

The cars and motorcycles—twelve vehicles in all—swarmed around Kate's Audi as she drove through Knightsbridge on her way to work. They swerved from lane to lane, ran lights and stop signs, pulled close—too close—so they could snap a shot of her behind the wheel or, better yet, elicit a rude reaction. They clung to her rear bumper no matter what the speed, pushing her to go even faster to avoid a rear-end collision. For Kate, even the most mundane trip became a death-defying car chase. Once again, she pulled over and begged them to stop. Once again, they said no. "It's our job," one of them told her. "If you don't wish to be followed, Miss Middleton, I suggest you stop dating a prince."

Only three days earlier, William and Kate had been intimate in front of hundreds of people at the Concert for Diana afterparty—their declaration to the world that they were back together. To the press, however, this was an invitation to ramp up their coverage of Kate. "Nobody knows how terrifying it can be until you're chased by these people," she told a coworker at Jigsaw. "They have no regard for their own lives, much less anyone else's. They'll do anything to get a photo. Anything."

Coincidentally, the very day Kate was being pursued by a

dozen vehicles, Gerrard Tyrrell of the royal law firm of Harbottle & Lewis was pleading her case before the Press Complaints Commission. Pointing to the June 30 chase involving only four cars, Tyrrell told commissioners Kate was left feeling "scared" and "harassed." Since the Press Complaints seemed powerless to do anything to protect his client, Tyrrell made it clear that Kate intended to take legal action of her own.

Scotland Yard had, meantime, finally decided to heed William's pleas. They agreed to provide Kate some level of official protection despite her commoner status. A steel-lined, bulletproof front door was installed at her Chelsea flat, along with motion detectors, exterior surveillance cameras, a secure line patched directly to William's security minders at Scotland Yard, and several panic buttons, with discreet police patrols of the street and even a small, impregnable panic room modeled on the rooms at the royal palaces.

"It's the standard kit," one former member of the royal protection service said of the new measures, "that we would fit at the home of any middle-ranking diplomat." Cost to the taxpayer: an estimated $60,000, not counting the cost of police patrols, and the man-hours to monitor and maintain the surveillance devices. A drop in the bucket, of course, compared to the Royal Family's total annual security bill of more than $200 million.

Such pressing public interest was a problem that Charles and Camilla might have devoutly prayed for. "They are old and boring as far as the public is concerned," one veteran royals correspondent confided. "All anyone cares about are William and Harry—and the women they will eventually marry."

Still, Camilla was now the second-highest-ranking woman in the realm, after the Queen. Camilla would remain so even if Kate married William; despite Charles's earlier assurances to the contrary, nothing would prevent Camilla from becoming queen once her husband ascended to the throne.

All of which made an invitation to Camilla's sixtieth birthday celebration at Highgrove on July 22, 2007, one of the most coveted of the season. Now that Big Willy and his Babykins were back together, a last-minute invitation was hastily dispatched to Kate at her flat in Chelsea.

Coming so close to the tenth anniversary of Diana's death, the black-tie gala at Highgrove struck several of the princess's pals as, in the words of one, "extremely tacky." The Queen, still sensitive to such criticism, chose not to attend.

Behind the event were Charles's former valet Michael Fawcett and Camilla's younger sister, Annabel Elliot. Diana had confronted Camilla about her affair with Charles at Annabel's fortieth birthday party. As for Fawcett, who had left the Prince of Wales's employ to become a high-end party planner, Diana claimed the two men were "too close. What can one do," she asked, "when your husband is in an unhealthy relationship with a servant?"

William, who had fully embraced Camilla as his stepmother in the interest of making Papa happy, had learned to push such unpleasant thoughts out of his mind. Kate, who had never met Diana and had nothing at all to do with William's Spencer relatives, found it easy to do the same.

Once again, Kate dazzled in white, mingling easily with aristocrats and such celebrity guests as Joan Rivers, Stephen Fry, Edward Fox, and Dame Judi Dench. Taking to the dance floor, William mouthed the words to "It Had to Be You" to Kate as they held each other close.

"Well," Joan Rivers said, "I guess it's back on."

So much so that Clarence House now asked Kate to bow out

of her boat race across the English Channel. Her presence might turn the event into a media circus, and a flotilla of boats carrying photographers might swamp Kate and her crew. "The wash," Sayle conceded, "might capsize us."

Also wary of being capsized was the Queen, who was shocked by the racy résumés of some Sisterhood crew members. "When the Queen read about sex clubs, S and M, and the rest of it," said a junior staff member at Buckingham Palace, "she wasn't eager to have the Royal Family dragged into it." Her Majesty, a devourer of tabloids and racing sheets, was especially taken aback by the name of Sayle's club for swingers. " 'Killing Kittens'? My word," she asked, nonplussed. "What on earth . . . ?"

"What I don't want," Sayle said in her defense, "is for people to say, 'Look who Kate's got involved with—a big sex-party orgy organizer.' She's not stupid, she's aware of it. It's all very aboveboard, and I've never denied it."

Whatever the real reason, Kate pulled out of the Sisterhood in early August—but not before she was asked by her fellow crew members to pose covered only in paint for a promotional calendar. "She is strongly considering it," Sayle said. "We are leaning on her a bit." Not surprisingly, Kate declined.

It was eighteen months since Wills and Kate had been away together—most of that time taken up with Wills's training at Sandhurst. Now they were eager to make up for it. On August 16, 2007, Wills and Kate arrived by seaplane on the tiny Seychelles island of Desroches in the Indian Ocean. Traveling without an entourage for only the second time in their six years together, they checked into their suite overlooking a lagoon under the aliases Martin and Rosemary. Over the next week, they swam, snorkeled, and scuba dived in the turquoise surf or simply stretched out on the white sand beach. Denied access to the island, newspapers were left to their own devices. The *Sun* was particularly inventive, pasting the couple's faces on a still of Burt Lancaster and Deborah Kerr kissing passionately on the beach in *From Here to Eternity*.

Back in London after their romantic interlude in paradise, Kate was given her first security pass to Clarence House—in effect, a key that allowed her to enter and leave at will, without having to have her name placed on a list at the gate. Although it was a far cry from false reports that Kate had actually moved into Clarence House, being given full access was another clear sign that, wrote columnist Rebecca English, the relationship was going "from strength to strength."

One of Kate's greatest strengths was being able to keep up with the royals as they went around, as Diana used to say, "killing things." At Balmoral, Kate once again donned camouflage gear (and a pair of dangling pearl earrings), picked up a rifle, and joined William and the others as they hunted stag.

The next morning's papers carried photographs of Kate lying prone in the mud and carefully taking aim. The reaction was immediate, and expected. "It is very sad that Kate has been sucked into such activities by William," said Barry Hugill of the League Against Cruel Sports. "We hope this is not Kate's way of trying to endear herself to our royals." Another animal-rights activist took square aim at Kate. "How sad," Brigitte Bardot said. "She was trying to win him [William] and his family. But this is not the way to get a man. And I do know one or two things about it, you know."

More often than not, William and Kate were the ones being hunted. After a night of intense drinking at Boujis—their first public outing as a couple since they got back together—the two left the club at 2:00 a.m., smiled while photographers snapped away, and climbed into the back of Wills's waiting Range Rover. As the car pulled from the curb with a royal protection officer behind the wheel, a mob of photographers took off after them in cars, on motorcycles, even on foot.

The Range Rover sped down a main road, then zigzagged down narrow side streets, but was still unable to lose the paparazzi. At Hyde Park Corner, the car carrying William and Kate rocketed through two red lights before their pursuers called it quits. "If someone had been killed," the photographer said, "it wouldn't have been our fault. They were the reckless ones, not us."

Clarence House disagreed. "Prince William was concerned by the threatening behavior of the paparazzi in London," said William's official spokesman, Paddy Harverson. "The aggressive pursuit was potentially dangerous and worrying for them." Then, citing the tenth anniversary of Diana's death and the ongoing inquest into the crash, he pointed out that it seemed "incomprehensible, particularly at this time, that this behavior is still going on."

It did, however, give Kate an idea of what to do next. She informed her bosses at Jigsaw that she was quitting—to become a photographer. "Still lifes and portraits," she told her colleagues over a farewell lunch in the corporate dining room. "I'm thinking of curating the work of other photographers, or maybe even opening my own gallery. The possibilities are endless."

That evening, she was clearly in the mood to celebrate. While William spent the closing days of his army service at the Windsor barracks with his Blues and Royals comrades, Kate and Pippa joined Guy Pelly and Holly Branson at Mahiki's annual Halloween bash. Kate arrived in a demure cocktail dress but changed inside into a sexy witch's outfit.

The Wisteria Sisters danced with each other for more than

an hour before returning to their table and downing "blood"—actually a red-colored rum concoction—from realistic-looking hospital IV bags. "They smeared the fake blood all over their faces," said a club patron who was sitting at a nearby table, "and Kate got a pair of vampire fangs and started joking around. They were in hysterics."

Kate wasted no time getting her new career off the ground. In late November, she organized a King's Road exhibition of celebrity snapshots taken by noted British portrait photographer Alistair Morrison. Taken in a photo booth set up in London's swank Dorchester hotel, the snapshots of Tom Cruise, Catherine Zeta-Jones, Sting, Kate Winslet, and other stars were sold at the show with half the proceeds going to UNICEF.

At the exhibition, Kate stressed the difference between a celebrity photographer such as Morrison and the paparazzi who chased her through the streets of the city. "No one," she said with a smile, "was harmed in the taking of these photographs."

As for Kate's own talent as a photographer, Morrison had nothing but praise. "She is very, very good, and it shows," he said. "She takes very beautiful, detailed photographs. She has a huge talent and a great eye. I'm sure she will go far."

Morrison was not the only big-name photographer whose advice Kate sought. She had also made an undercover trip to New York to pick up some tips from Mario Testino, whose portraits of Diana had graced the covers of *Vanity Fair* and *Vogue*.

Coming just months after the Queen's own dyspeptic encounter with celebrity photographer Annie Leibovitz, Kate's foray into photography struck the monarch as "an odd choice. Unless," she told her private secretary, "she sticks to bowls of fruit, or perhaps horses."

At the moment, the Queen was more concerned about what

looked like the unraveling of Harry's career. In a complete about-face, the army brass decided that it was simply too dangerous to send Cornet Wales to Iraq. Publicly, Harry claimed to understand. "I would never," he said, "want to put someone else's life in danger when they have to sit next to the bullet magnet." Privately, he told his family that he was ready to quit.

In late November, the Queen summoned Harry to Buckingham Palace and told him he was going to Afghanistan instead. "I felt a bit of excitement," he later said, "a bit of 'Phew, finally get the chance to actually do the soldiering I wanted to do from ever since I joined.' "

Harry was to serve on the front lines for four months, in the dangerous southern province of Helmand. His job: to guide fighter jets toward suspected Taliban targets. In the interest of making Harry less of a "bullet magnet" in the field, his departure was to be kept top secret. With the exception of the prime minister, the defense minister, and two or three generals, even the top brass were kept in the dark.

Wills and Kate knew, as well as Chelsy Davy. Incredibly, Harry's otherwise undisciplined band of club-hopping, binge-drinking buddies also knew and kept the secret to themselves. It would be ten weeks before the Drudge Report broke the story, forcing Harry's hasty departure from the war zone.

Once again, Kate and Wills spent Christmas apart—Kate joining her family in Barbados and Wills, as always, with the rest of the Royal Family at Sandringham. The Queen still insisted that only royals and their spouses could join in Christmas at Sandringham, which, among other things, included the opening of gag gifts on Christmas Eve. It was difficult to top Prince Charles's favorite Christmas gift: a white leather toilet seat.

Although Kate was not there, a poll by Britain's Discovery Channel, released on December 26, 2007, indicated that perhaps she should be. More than 80 percent of those surveyed said Kate would be a "good addition" to the Royal Family. Moreover, most Britons wanted William and Kate—not Charles and Camilla—to be the next king and queen.

As they had since college days, Kate and Wills rang in the New Year together. But, as had been the case ever since he enrolled at Sandhurst, Wills could not be there when she celebrated her birthday on January 9, 2008. This time, her prince was being called away by another branch of the service—the Royal Air Force.

William's great-grandfather George VI joined the RAF at its inception in 1918. Prince Philip was an RAF pilot, and so was Prince Charles. Forty years after earning his wings, the Prince of Wales now held the vaunted title of air chief marshal.

Eager to become the fourth generation of Windsors to take to the skies, William reported to RAF Cranwell's Central Flying School the first week in January. Kate appreciated what the RAF meant to Wills. Her own grandfather Peter Middleton saw action with the Royal Canadian Air Force in World War II.

It did not take long for Wills to get his wish. After just eight days, he became the first in his class to solo in a light propeller-driven aircraft. Within a month, he had graduated to the faster, more maneuverable Tucano T1.

Kate quickly discovered that her life as an air force officer's girlfriend was very much like her life as an army officer's girlfriend. She turned heads, as she always did, during yet another solo visit to Cheltenham. Escorted by the ever-reliable Thomas van Straubenzee, she landed back in the royal box, chatting away with Princess Anne and William's cousin Zara Phillips. Kate and

Zara had plenty to talk about; they were both wearing trench coats and identical Dick Tracy–style fedoras.

She did not have to bide her time for long. On March 16, 2008, Kate returned with Prince Charles to Klosters, where this time photographers caught Babykins playfully poking Big Willy in the back with a ski pole. "They were openly affectionate on the slopes," another skier pointed out. "They were nuzzling each other, at one point he gently stroked the back of her neck, they kissed. It was pretty obvious they were in love."

As soon as they returned to England, "Flying Officer Wales" was transferred to RAF Shawbury, a base 170 miles northwest of London. There, he fulfilled a dream he had nursed since child-hood, taking the controls of a helicopter for the first time. Perhaps not altogether surprisingly, his instructors were quick to praise their future commander in chief for his flying ability. "I'm very impressed," Commander Andy Lovell said, with Prince William's "natural handling ability."

From Shawbury, Flying Officer Wales continued his helicop-ter flight training at RAF Odiham in Hampshire, a more com-fortable thirty-three miles outside London. It would not be long before William, like other novice pilots before him, decided to buzz the homes of friends and relatives. Trouble was, the aircraft he was flying wasn't a single-engine prop plane, but a $17 million twin-rotor Chinook troop carrier.

For his first training exercise, the prince (code name Golden Kestrel) decided to circle Highgrove. On April 2, 2008, Wills, ac-companied by an instructor and a crew of three, made the hundred-mile round-trip from RAF Odiham to Highgrove. The next day, he decided to impress his girlfriend by flying to Bucklebury, buzz-ing Oak Acre, then practicing landings and takeoffs in a field next to the house. The Middletons were asked to remain inside, where

Kate waved and blew kisses to her aviator prince. The cost for the trips to Highgrove and Bucklebury: more than $41,000.

Wills was only getting started. For the third time in as many days, he flew the Chinook, this time to Northumberland, where he was dropped off so he could meet Kate and drive on to Scotland for the wedding of their St. Andrews pal Lady Iona Douglas-Home to banker Thomas Hewitt. (Lady Iona was the granddaughter of the late British prime minister Sir Alec Douglas-Home.) This trip cost over $36,000.

Amazingly, Wills was still deficient when it came to low-level flying experience. Next, he flew the 128 miles to Sandringham to buzz his grandmother. She was, perhaps fortunately for both of them, at Windsor at the time. The cost for that jaunt was nearly $9,000.

More accustomed to chasing William from nightclub to nightclub, the British press remained unaware for weeks of these taxpayer-funded joyrides. Meanwhile, just twenty-four hours after William buzzed the Queen's house, the Heir joined Charles and Camilla at the Royal Air Force College Cranwell for a gala dinner marking the RAF's ninetieth birthday. While William was praised in the press for "cutting a dash" in his cutaway dress uniform, Camilla's elaborately embroidered evening coat was compared to the rumpled wizard's robe worn by Dumbledore in the Harry Potter films.

The next morning, Kate looked on proudly as Charles, bedecked in gold braid and medals in his role as air chief marshal, presented William with his provisional wings. "He looks gorgeous," she said of Wills's blue dress uniform as they headed off to lunch. It was, significantly, the first time William and Kate had ever been photographed together at an official function.

Even though he had already fulfilled all his training requirements, Wills took off on another exercise the following day—this time primarily to perfect his skills at flying over water. What he failed to tell senior officers was that he was really using the Chinook to pick up Harry at his barracks in Southeast London, then fly on to the Isle of Wight. Once there, they joined twenty-two of their pals at the stag party of their cousin Peter Phillips, who was set to wed Canadian commoner Autumn Kelly. This time, the estimated cost ran to a little over $17,000.

"Sheer stupidity!" shouted Air Chief Marshal Sir Glenn Torpy when he learned of Prince William's five joyrides. Not only had the total tab run to well in excess of $103,000, but Wills's misuse of a Chinook for personal reasons at a time when British troops were fighting in Afghanistan seemed "feckless, at best."

Air Chief Marshal Torpy ordered an investigation into the flights that, not surprisingly, absolved everyone involved. All of the flights were deemed "legitimate exercises."

"All flights undertaken with Flying Officer Wales were planned, briefed, authorized and flown by him, under appropriate supervision, in accordance with extant regulations," read the official report. Blaming "the public and the media" for their "misperceptions," the report conceded, "In retrospect, there was a degree of naivete in the planning of these sorties."

Not so fast. "The average Joe is going to view it as an expensive taxi," one RAF pilot said. "The RAF hierarchy looked bloody stupid for attempting to explain it as anything other than that." RAF-trained pilot and aviation expert Jon Lake described the flights as "ridiculous and inappropriate." He also claimed that by putting a novice such as William at the controls of such a sophisticated aircraft, his life and the lives of others had been put in grave danger.

Sir Glenn worried that perhaps Lake was right. "He is

deeply concerned," said defense analyst Paul Beaver, because "he is ultimately responsible to the Queen for the safety of her grandson."

Wills was resigned to accepting at least some of the blame. "It was a collective error of judgment," a Clarence House spokesman said, "and Prince William is holding his hands up for it as much as the RAF."

For the most part, however, the RAF's most famous helicopter pilot seemed unfazed by all the commotion. The day that a member of Parliament stood in the House of Commons to protest the joyrides, Wills was taken up for spin in a $50 million Tornado fighter jet. "That was the most awesome, most amazing experience of my life," he said after a mock six-hundred-mile-per-hour dogfight with a Harrier jump jet. "It will take weeks for my legs to stop shaking."

Wills's thrill ride aboard the Tornado was not entirely for effect. "Prince William," said an RAF spokesman, "experienced firsthand the combat teeth of the RAF, which you just cannot get from a book."

Of course, the only way to get real firsthand combat experience was to be assigned to a combat zone. Now that William's joyrides had besmirched the royals' otherwise sterling reputation in a time of war, both his father and grandmother agreed that damage control was in order.

With the Queen's explicit approval, Wills was to fly a C-17 Globemaster troop transport to the front lines in Afghanistan and bring home the body of a fallen British soldier. One of the Queen's Royal Lancers, twenty-two-year-old Robert Pearson, had been killed in Helmand Province when his armored vehicle struck a land mine.

The entire trip was to take thirty hours and, following Harry's example in Afghanistan, was to remain top secret. "The Taliban or Al Qaeda would have stopped at nothing to shoot down a plane carrying the future king," said a cabinet member who had been informed of the mission. "We could not take any chances, however much Prince William wanted to see action."

Landing in Kandahar, William put his star power to good use, boosting morale by shaking hands with servicemen and asking them about their families back home. Several inquired about Kate, although none broached the question of marriage. All in all, he told a fellow officer, it was "the most important walkabout I've ever done."

After his return on April 28, he met Trooper Pearson's family at the RAF Lyneham air base and thanked them for their sacrifice on behalf of the Queen. He told them that he was "honored" to make the special trip. A year later, Paul Pearson was at Buckingham Palace to accept the Elizabeth Cross from the Queen on his son's behalf. "Although it was obviously a hard time for us when he died," Pearson said, "we do smile when we think of Robert up there telling people how Prince William flew him home."

For Wills, the thirty-hour mission to Afghanistan was important for other reasons, as well. "He just wanted to know a little bit about what it's like," a Ministry of Defense official said. "He wants to be able to look other military men and women in the eye." Less than a week later, he left the RAF for his next assignment—as a lieutenant in the Royal Navy.

Kate, meanwhile, had received orders of her own. On May 17, she stood in for William at the royal wedding of his cousin Peter Phillips and Autumn Kelly, both thirty. These nuptials, held in St. George's Chapel at Windsor Castle—spiritual home of the Order of the Garter and burial place of ten kings, including Henry VIII—were of special significance. Peter, the only son of Princess Anne and Mark Phillips, was the first of the Queen's eight grandchildren to walk down the aisle.

Her Majesty, Prince Philip, Charles and Camilla, Princes Andrew, Edward, and Harry, and of course the mother of the groom, Princess Anne, were all accounted for. Every senior royal was present with one glaring exception: William.

Strangely, he had chosen to honor a previous engagement. Had the Heir been called away on another image-boosting military exercise, Wills's absence might easily have been excused. Instead, he was off attending another wedding. While the rest of the royals gathered at Windsor, Wills joined his old flame Jecca Craig in Kenya at the traditional Masai wedding of her thirty-two-year-old brother, Batian.

In contrast to the Church of England ceremony back home— Autumn had converted from Catholicism so Peter wouldn't have to give up being eleventh in line for the throne—Wills watched as the newlyweds were given a cow for slaughter. Then he and the other guests (including Masai chief Kip and members of the Samburu tribe) poured milk over the bride and groom—a Masai tradition intended to symbolize good fortune and fertility.

The Queen and Prince Charles were not amused, but they did not attempt to dissuade William from going to Africa. Neither did Kate, who no longer felt threatened by Jecca and had come to accept that the Craig family—and Africa—held a strange power over her prince. "I didn't really understand any of it," Kate told South African Chelsy Davy, "until he took me there."

The distinct upside to William's decision not to be at his cousin's wedding was Kate's presence. This was clear evidence of his faith in her, and, equally important, proof that the royals accepted Kate as a suitable stand-in. To drive home the point, William's grandmother—who for over a year had been telling

William she was eager to meet Kate—seized the opportunity to be introduced to the young woman who stood a good chance of some day becoming queen. "It was in amongst a lot of other guests," Kate later recalled of her first brief conversation with the monarch, and the Queen was "very friendly and welcoming."

It was a banner day for Chelsy, as well. After the Queen met Kate, Harry took the bold step of introducing his girlfriend to the Queen for the first time. Although not as close as Diana and Fergie had been, the two girlfriends spent an inordinate amount of time giggling and whispering on occasions like this. Later, at a lavish reception for three hundred at Frogmore House in Windsor Great Park—a spectacular seventeenth-century royal residence that is also the burial place of Queen Victoria and Prince Albert—Kate and Chelsy cut loose with Harry on the dance floor.

William's conspicuous absence would have gotten more notice had it not been for the next issue of the UK's hugely successful *HELLO!* magazine, which filled fifty-nine pages with candid snapshots from the wedding and the rather rowdy reception that followed. Unbeknownst to the Queen—who was shown mingling with guests in a dozen separate photos—Peter and Autumn had signed a $1 million deal with *HELLO!* giving the magazine total access to the festivities. It was enough that, for the first time in history, rights to a royal wedding were sold to the highest bidder. But when Granny found out that the newlyweds had personally approved each image that ran in the magazine, she was, said a Palace spokesman, "displeased."

William and Harry were more than merely displeased when they realized that their girlfriends appeared in the *HELLO!* piece dozens of times. "The princes are deeply unhappy," a Clarence House spokesman said, "that Miss Middleton and Miss Davy had their privacy invaded in this way." William was more upset at the notion of selling out to the press. "They must," he told Harry, "need the money very badly."

HELLO! had yet to hit the stands when, just a few days after the wedding of Peter Phillips and Autumn Kelly, Kate joined William at a secluded cliff-top villa overlooking Mustique's Macaroni Beach. Amidst the frenzy of speculation over when they would finally tie the knot, Babykins and her Big Willy enjoyed their final week together before he joined the navy.

———

Of all branches of the military, the Royal Family was most closely identified with the navy. Not only had his great-great-grandfather George V, his great-grandfather George VI, and his grandfather Prince Philip attended the Britannia Royal Naval College in Dartmouth, but Prince Charles and Prince Andrew had also gone there. William respected his father for having commanded a minesweeper in peacetime. But it was Andrew, a navy helicopter pilot in the Falklands War, whose military career William most sought to emulate.

One thing about Andrew that William did not wish to mimic was his marriage. Both Andrew and Fergie acknowledged that his long tours of duty at sea had doomed their relationship. William had made that mistake when he chose drinking with his army buddies over seeing Kate. Now he was determined to see her at every opportunity, even if it meant traveling more than 160 miles from Dartmouth to London just for the weekend.

His first weekend off, Wills joined Kate, Harry, Chelsy, and the rest of the usual suspects at the annual Boodles Boxing Ball for charity. This time, Jecca Craig was on hand to cheer on her current boyfriend, Hugh "the Hitman" Crossley, who battled Bear "the Pain" Maclean (and lost). To the astonishment of onlookers, Kate and Jecca laughed and joked as if, a spectator said, "they were best pals. You wouldn't have thought they were rivals at all."

For the most part, Kate grimaced or covered her eyes every time someone landed a punch. Even Wills, who had been yelling words of encouragement at the amateur boxers, blanched now and then when a fist found its mark.

William and Harry had an important reason for being there. The black-tie event raised $250,000 for the Starlight Foundation, a charity begun by former *Dynasty* star Emma Samms to grant the wishes of seriously ill children. The wish of nineteen-year-old singer Bianca Nicholas, who suffered from cystic fibrosis, was to sing at the ball and—most important—to meet Diana's sons.

The Heir and the Spare notwithstanding, Nicholas—and everyone else at the event—appeared equally taken by Kate. The next day's front pages were dominated not by the princes, but by the image of Kate in a coral pink, floor-length gown by the Brazilian designer Daniella Issa Helayel. Issa had become Kate's designer of choice, the woman behind countless glamorous outfits that landed Kate in fashion spreads and on several best-dressed lists. It helped that Issa gowns were supplied gratis to the princess-in-waiting.

A week later, Kate and William were together again, this time at Windsor Castle to witness his investiture into the Order of the Garter. It was the most solemn and historically significant royal ceremony she had attended to date, yet another sign that she had been fully embraced not only by William's family but also by the string-pulling Men in Gray.

Kate, dressed in a dark suit with tiny white polka dots and a black-and-white "fascinator" (British fashion lingo for a headpiece), walked with a formally attired Prince Harry to the Galilee Porch of the church. There they waited with Camilla and Prince Edward's wife, the Countess of Wessex, for William to make his entrance with his father.

When William finally appeared in his knight's getup—a blue velvet cloak, a garter (what else?) buckled just below his left knee, and an elaborate, floppy hat festooned with ostrich and heron feathers—Kate gasped, "Oh my God!" before she and Harry dissolved in giggles.

For all the hilarity—William struggled to maintain his composure when he saw Kate's and Harry's reaction—this was the highest honor the monarch could bestow. Created by Edward III in 1348, the world's oldest order of chivalry was based on Arthurian legend and was in essence the king's own Round Table. It's motto: "Evil to him who thinks evil." Since Knights of the Garter were personally chosen by the Queen, they included her husband, children, and several high-ranking cousins as well as former prime ministers, a few captains of industry, as well as the kings of Sweden, Norway, and Spain and the queens of Denmark and the Netherlands. William became the one-thousandth knight inducted into the order in its 660-year history.

"They will probably have to give it to Prince Harry, too," commented the *Times*' Alan Hamilton. "He will have to behave himself, as knights deemed to have 'degraded' the order can be thrown out." Although Japan's Emperor Akihito is a Knight of the Garter, his father, Emperor Hirohito, was stripped of his garter—as was Kaiser Wilhelm before him. "Mere high jinks in nightclubs," Hamilton allowed, "would probably be forgiven."

Without doubt, Kate appeared to have charmed her way into the hearts of all the people in William's life who counted. She was so comfortable in the company of the Queen, and under the stuffiest of circumstances, that she felt free to be herself—even if it meant giggling at centuries-old tradition.

Kate also knew it was important not to overplay her hand—or overstay her welcome. She did not, for example, accept every royal invitation sent her way—not even when it came personally from the woman Diana had called Top Lady.

Since neither William or Harry would be able to attend Ascot that year, the Queen had invited Kate to host a table for ten at the royal enclosure. Wary of appearing too eager, Kate politely declined. "She's been advised," one of the Middletons' friends told the *Daily Mail*, "to take a backseat, publicity-wise. So she'll only really step out in any sort of royal capacity she absolutely has to and when she's with William."

The day after Ascot—Saturday, June 21—was quite another matter. To celebrate Wills's twenty-sixth birthday, the couple joined Harry and Chelsy at Highgrove. After watching England wallop New Zealand in the Williams de Broe international match at the nearby Beaufort Polo Club, William and Kate partied with two hundred others under a tent set up on the grounds. Fueled by copious quantities of champagne, Wills did what was fast becoming his signature dance, waving his arms wildly and looking, as observer Sarah Jellema put it, like "a helicopter attempting to land in an unusually fierce tailwind." They both, said another guest, "seemed really happy, just larking around and letting off steam."

The need to let off steam was understandable. No one at the party but Kate knew that Wills had just spent twenty-four hours submerged aboard the nuclear submarine HMS *Talent* off the coast near Plymouth, taking part in a clandestine exercise that simulated tracking down and attacking an enemy sub. Once his time on the *Talent* was up, the sub surfaced and he was plucked from the deck by a Sea King helicopter.

Now, Sublieutenant Wales shipped off aboard HMS *Iron Duke*, a forty-nine-hundred-ton frigate bound for the Caribbean. Working alongside officers from the U.S. Drug Enforcement Administration, Prince William and his 184 shipmates spent the next five weeks crisscrossing the waters off South America and Central America in search of cocaine smugglers.

The prince had been at sea just four days when, while scouring the horizon as part of a six-man crew aboard a Lynx helicopter, he spotted a suspicious-looking fifty-foot speedboat northeast of Barbados. The Lynx chased the boat, then hovered above the craft until it was boarded by armed U.S. coast guard officers. Before the boat sank, they seized forty-five bales of cocaine. Street value: $80 million.

"This was a substantial haul which will significantly disrupt drug supplies that may have been headed for Europe," said a Ministry of Defense spokesman. For his part, William "played an important planning and surveillance role in part of a successful team operation." The *Iron Duke*'s commanding officer, Mark Newland, said William and his crewmates were off to a "fantastic start."

Things got even dicier a few weeks later when the Lynx helicopter William was aboard opened fire on smugglers some 110 miles off the coast of Colombia. Before their boat sank, three crew members jumped to safety; they were later pulled aboard the *Iron Duke* and turned over to Colombian authorities. After the harrowing incident, his superiors explained, "Prince William returned to ship to resume his normal duties as officer of the watch."

Most of Wills's naval training was not nearly so exciting. Back at Dartmouth, he had learned how to drop anchor—but only after losing a crate of beer on a bet that he could do it on the first try (it took two). Now he put that skill to use on the volcanic island of Montserrat, where he led a beach landing as part of a hurricane-disaster exercise.

Once on the island, Wills took his team up a winding forest road and encountered a simulated bus crash. After summoning a medic, he prioritized the "injuries," clambered over a barrier to calm a boy who was convincingly screaming in pain, then led paramedics to the ersatz victims. Declaring the mission a success, Commander Newland noted that William's ability to lead came as "second nature" to him.

Back in London, Kate was on a training mission of her own—called upon yet again to substitute for William at a royal wedding. This time it was the marriage of George Gilman to the Queen's cousin Lady Rose Windsor, youngest daughter of the Duke of Gloucester (her father became duke when his elder brother was killed in a plane crash in 1972) and twenty-fourth in the line of succession. The Duke of Gloucester and his family now lived in the royal residence William once called home, Kensington Palace.

William and Kate had never been apart for so long. When his five-week stint at sea finally came to end, they met up once again on Mustique. Their days, as usual, were filled with water sports, their nights with drinking at Firefly and Basil's Bar.

This time, they had plenty of company. In addition to all of Kate's immediate family, more than one hundred VIPs showed up to celebrate the fortieth anniversary of the Mustique Company, the firm set up by landowners to run the island. At Basil's Bar, island homeowner (and one of Princess Margaret's favorite drinking buddies) Mick Jagger sang "Satisfaction," "Jumpin' Jack Flash," and "Brown Sugar" while Wills and Kate rocked out on the dance floor.

On Mustique Wills also first mentioned the idea of getting a tattoo—something dramatic, like the angel that sprawled across the shoulders and back of soccer star David Beckham. William had discussed the idea with his mates aboard the *Iron Duke*. "He said the only thing stopping him was his girlfriend," one crew member said. "He was worried she would think it was a bit too chavvy [tacky]." He was right.

Although William and Kate seemed to be stumbling over each other as they left the nightclub Raffles in the predawn hours of August 15, the adjective *tacky* was rarely applied to Miss Middleton. The same, sadly, could not be said for the rest of her family. The gum-snapping, supposedly "insufferably middle-class" Carole Middleton was still being lambasted in certain circles. By this time the UK flight-attendant line "Doors to manual"—roughly the British equivalent of "Will flight attendants please secure the cabin doors?"—had been used so often in describing Kate's mother that it had become a running joke throughout Britain.

Fortunately, the world had yet to learn about Uncle Gary Goldsmith and his drug- and hooker-filled La Maison de Bang Bang. Palace officials wanted to keep it that way. In early 2008, royal protection agents worried that Gary's wildly hedonistic ways would embarrass William—and by extension the entire Royal Family—approached Kate's uncle and warned him to "modify" his lifestyle.

"They have been onto me," Gary admitted, "and I've got to keep a low profile and be a good boy. I am going to stop all the drugs and clean up my act." That would turn out to be a tall order. Not long after he was warned, London police were called to the Park Lane Hilton after he was reported running through the lobby and then out into the streets of Mayfair in a "distressed state."

Enter Kate's little brother James, who had dropped out of the University of Edinburgh after one year to start his own business in the fall of 2007. Actually, the Cake Kit Company was more or less James's independent fiefdom within the Party Pieces empire. The basic concept was similar: to simplify home baking by supplying the disposable baking tin, cake mix, icings, decorations, even the candles.

Acknowledging that he didn't "look like your average baker," Kate's wiry, jeans-clad brother nonetheless insisted that baking was in his blood. "I have great childhood memories of my mother baking, and I was always a willing participant," he cracked, "especially if it meant I could revarnish the kitchen floor with treacle."

That wholesome image changed in late August, when photographs surfaced online showing James in a variety of compromising poses. In one, he was shown wearing a polka-dot dress that he borrowed from Kate; in another, a French maid's costume complete with ripped fishnet stockings, a lacy cap, and full makeup. In that last shot, he holds a bottle of beer in one hand, his crotch in the other. Another shot taken at the same party shows James and other men either in French-maid costumes or nude, two of whom are jokingly engaged in simulating an oral sex act.

Another shot showed the then twenty-one-year-old James stretched out naked in front of a fireplace, beer in hand, his genitals deftly concealed behind a row of towels. In other photos, he is seen out with his buddies, getting ready to consume dozens of drinks lined up before them. In one picture, he makes a not-so-regal gesture at the camera using his middle finger.

These would seem tame compared to pictures that appeared a few months later showing James and his pals using a dead squirrel as a prop in a variety of grotesque tableaux. Although much of the public anger this time would come from England's outspoken animal-rights activists—in another shot he is cheerfully holding up a half dozen dead game birds—the new batch of photos posted online also showed the future king's prospective brother-in-law in various stages of undress, and in suggestive poses and situations that seemed ill-advised, to say the least.

When an enterprising reporter brought the photos to the Middleton home in Bucklebury, Carole and Pippa sat on their living room couch and leafed through them. Carole showed no reaction, but when they were asked if the flamboyant gentleman in the photos was James, a seemingly delighted Pippa laughed before answering, "Oh, yes!"

Neither of Kate's siblings had been particularly shy about capitalizing—socially, at least—on their family's connection to the royals. James more than kept up with the "Party Princes," as William and Harry had been dubbed in some quarters. But unlike his sister, James not only appreciated the attention of the paparazzi but courted it. "James used to get miffed if he wasn't recognized by them when he first left university," said one of the young men who often accompanied Kate's brother to the clubs. "It's even worse now if they don't spot him. He can get quite upset."

Carole Middleton understood her son's frustration. "James . . . has business projects which he wants to talk about," she said, "but then it's difficult when everything else is going on around him and people don't just want to know about his projects."

Pippa, whose own social ambitions had been well documented, also took a job for which her social connections made her particularly well suited. She now handled marketing and public relations for Table Talk, an event planner. Kate's sister shared their brother's wild streak. When guests at a particularly rowdy party decided to form a human pyramid, Pippa shed her clothes, wrapped herself in toilet paper, and climbed to the top.

Pippa seemed to welcome the publicity that came her way. But when her digital camera was stolen, she frantically called police to report it missing. Less than an hour after the camera vanished from the seat of Pippa's car, two men contacted the *Sun* offering to sell the images on the camera's flash memory for $90,000. Among the more than forty pictures of William and Kate cavorting on Mustique were shots of Kate doing yoga on the beach in her bikini, and of the couple snuggling poolside or simply together in the water, gazing into each other's eyes. If a shot of William's camping it up in a woman's hat—so reminiscent of the scandalous James Middleton photos—ever made it into the papers, it would have been hard to put out of one's mind.

William and Kate were distraught. They had no compunction about being amorous around Kate's family, clothing on the island was kept to a minimum, and they had no idea just how risqué some of the photos might be. Some of the photos might at the very least show them smoking—a habit that Kate now shared with her boyfriend, but that they both took considerable pains to conceal. (William, who was nearsighted, also went out of his way not to be photographed wearing the glasses now required whenever he was behind the wheel of his car, careening about on one of his souped-up motorcycles, or at the controls of a military aircraft.)

Fortunately, the *Sun* did not pay for the photos. Instead, they took the matter directly to the police. By the end of the day, Scotland Yard detectives, accompanied by royal protection officers, had arrested two men and recovered the flash memory.

It was all resolved by the time Kate and William attended

the wedding in Salzburg, Austria, of Household Cavalry officer Rupert Evetts and Chiara Hunt, the sister of their St. Andrews classmate Olivia Hunt. Although Kate and William each seemed to have achieved the status of professional wedding guest, this was the first time in three years that they had actually attended a wedding together.

Before they walked into the church, he tenderly placed his hand on her shoulder and bent down to whisper in her ear. That simple gesture—along with the fact that Wills had asked that Charles's bodyguard Dominic Ryan be assigned specifically to Kate for the day—sparked a frenzy of speculation that an engagement announcement was in the air.

Such gossip was dismissed out of hand by Clarence House more or less routinely. "We simply do not," the refrain went from William and Harry's private secretary, Jamie Lowther-Pinkerton, "comment on Prince William's private life." Behind the scenes, no issue was more fraught than the increasingly probable marriage of Prince William and Kate Middleton.

"The general feeling was 'What in blazes is he waiting for?'" said a senior staff member at St. James's Palace. "We knew that after all this time, if he dumped her again, he'd look like a terrible cad." And if Kate did the dumping? "If she called it off, everyone would blame him anyway, for keeping her waiting all that time. Not good."

———

At Buckingham Palace, the Queen often asked her private secretary, Christopher Geidt (Geidt replaced Sir Robin Janvrin in 2007), and other senior staff members for updates on the personal lives of family members—Harry and William in particular. Invariably, the Queen asked these questions as she did paperwork in her study, and in an offhand manner that belied the gravity of the matter at hand.

With its soothing teal wallpaper, expansive windows, and overstuffed furniture, the Queen's study at Buckingham Palace was both a working office and an oasis of calm. Framed family photos and knickknacks—items that staff were instructed never to touch—covered the eighteenth-century carved wooden desk, along with the Queen's famous red boxes and blue boxes brimming with matters of ceremony and matters of state.

As her corgis napped on the Aubusson carpet, the Queen would ask how Miss Middleton was faring alone while her prince was hunting down drug smugglers in the Caribbean or—as was now the case—doing his final months of training with Britain's elite special services, focusing on reconnaissance and counter-terrorism techniques.

"The one thing you can't say about her is that she's impatient," the Queen remarked at one point.

"No, ma'am," replied one of the three advisers in the room. "That's a very good quality."

"Yes," the Queen agreed wanly, pausing for a moment as if to imply Kate may have hung around too long. "It usually is . . . admirable."

The Middleton siblings' shenanigans were of little concern to the monarch; she put them in the same category as Harry's periodic and largely harmless hell-raising. As for Kate's parents, the Queen was, if anything, sympathetic. When she read the flurry of stories suggesting that the Royal Family viewed Carole Middleton as an unsuitable mother-in-law for William, the Queen made her displeasure known. "What rubbish," she said. "I have absolutely nothing against gum. *I* chew gum!"

What did trouble the Queen was Kate's apparent lack of any gainful employment since she'd left Jigsaw. Even Diana was working several jobs when she met Charles—three days a week as a kindergarten teacher and one day a week caring for an American family's baby boy. (One of the employment agencies Diana signed up with, Solve Your Problems, also sent her out on the odd housecleaning job.) That Kate seemed to spend all her time at society weddings, polo matches, ski resorts, and nightclubs—or on the beach at some exotic locale—irked Granny.

"The Queen has a job to do, and she does it full stop," said Prince Philip's cousin the Countess Mountbatten. "She expects everyone in the Royal Family to work hard, and they all do." According to another courtier, the head of the Firm wanted to make sure of one thing: "The Queen is just sick to death of dealing with women who wouldn't behave. Diana, Sarah Ferguson, her own sister, Princess Margaret—she feels they all had too much time on their hands."

The issue became even more pressing when William met with the Queen privately at Windsor and dropped a career bombshell of his own. Instead of simply becoming a full-time royal once his smorgasbord of military training was over, Wills wanted to sign up for a minimum of five years with the RAF as a search-and-rescue pilot. "I love flying helicopters," he told her. "It's what I want to do with my life."

The Queen was delighted, even though it meant he would be risking his own life plucking injured climbers from mountaintops and stranded recreational boaters from the sea. It was, William stressed in the wake of his little brother's highly publicized service in Afghanistan, a way to "serve in the forces operationally" without being deployed to a war zone.

Now that William and Kate faced at least five long years of

being separated weeks, even months, at a time, the Queen felt it was more important than ever that Kate get a job. In fairness to Kate, she had been working for Party Pieces full-time, primarily focusing on updating the company's website and preparing its catalogs. She had not publicized this because she feared it would look as if she were using her connection to William to promote her family's business. "You would think," she told her mother in a moment of exasperation, "that this was something they of all people would understand."

Since her daughter's strategy of flying below the radar was clearly not working, Carole took matters into her own hands and posted a glossy photo of Kate on the Party Pieces website. Kate Middleton, the site now made crystal clear, was a full-time member of the Party Pieces staff.

Kate's work record wasn't the only thing that seemed to be bothering the Palace, however. The Men in Gray were also grumbling that, while William focused on raising money for the inner-city homeless and Harry was building an orphanage for African children orphaned by AIDS, Miss Middleton seemed to have no philanthropic interests whatsoever. "Charities," the Queen had said, "are a big part of the job."

"Precisely what job is that?" Kate might have asked. With no formal position in the family—not even as a fiancée cooling her heels in the wings—Wills's girlfriend received none of the royal perks but was being expected to perform the role anyway.

Nonetheless, she got the message. With William busy being briefed on counterinsurgency warfare by Chief of the Defense Staff Sir Jock Stirrup as part of his special forces training, Kate skated onto a roller rink in yellow hot pants, a green sequined top, and pink leg warmers—all in the name of charity.

Joining with Holly Branson and banking heir Sam Waley-

Cohen, grandson of a viscount and an amateur jockey who had competed in the Grand National, Kate organized the Day-Glo Midnight Roller Disco to help raise money for a new surgical ward at Oxford Children's Hospital. The cause was close to the hearts of Kate and the princes. Tom's Ward was named in honor of Sam's brother Tom Waley-Cohen, a classmate of Kate's at Marlborough and a friend of both William's and Harry's. Tom was stricken with bone cancer and died in 2004 at age twenty.

Proving the adage that no good turn goes unpunished, Kate took the inevitable spill and wound up sprawled spread-eagle on the floor. Although she took the awkward moment in stride, laughing as she was helped to her feet by Sam Waley-Cohen, her unfortunate pose on the floor had been caught on film. "The Queen already thinks that Kate is something of a show-off," a courtier told Richard Kay. As for the Men in Gray, they were, said Kay, "appalled at what they saw as a most unladylike display."

Yet, almost entirely because of Kate's profile-raising presence, the Day-Glo Midnight Roller Disco raised more than $200,000 for Tom's Ward. "Kate has been fantastic in using her contacts," Sam Waley-Cohen said. "She threw herself into it—literally!"

At around the same time, Kate approached Emma Samms with an idea to benefit the actress's Starlight Foundation. Kate had been so moved by Bianca Nicholas, the cystic fibrosis sufferer who sang at the Boodles Boxing Ball, that she convinced her parents to donate Party Pieces goodie bags to ten thousand sick children over the holidays. "What a great thing they are doing," Samms said of the Middletons' contribution to the Los Angeles–based charity she started in 1983. "And what a great change it will make for these kids." She was also "thrilled" that Kate had decided to lend her considerable cachet to the foundation.

Kate welcomed the kind words, particularly coming amid criti-

cism from royal quarters that she was an uncharitable, unem-
ployed slacker. No sooner had those misconceptions been put to
rest than she was being accused of being a self-important snob
who had turned her back on her friends.

First came widespread reports that Kate had e-mailed friends
insisting that from now on she be known only as Catherine. It
never happened, but Kate had been known as Catherine well
into her teenage years. Her family still called her Catherine, and
on the rare occasion, Wills did, too.

More surprising was the accusation that she now regarded herself as too good for her old friends. That fall, St. Andrews pal
Jules Knight cornered Kate. "Listen, Kate," he said, "everyone just
wants you to be happy and wants the best for you, but it's a shame
you haven't been in touch."

"Oh, I know," she conceded. "I've been really bad, I should
really contact them, but it's been really difficult because I've been
so busy."

"These are people who care about you a lot," Knight continued, "and I think they are a little bit hurt that you haven't been
in touch. We care about you and hope you're okay."

"Oh, please send my love to them," Kate told Knight. But
weeks later it appeared she had still made no effort to contact
them herself.

Wills and Kate were still close to a number of their college
buddies—Olivia Hunt, Fergus Boyd, and Mili d'Erlanger, for
example—but others in their St. Andrews circle had felt slighted
of late. "There was a very tight group of friends, and now they
are in London and they don't really have any contact with Kate,
some girls in particular," Knight added. "It's not like they want to
be friends with Kate because of her position. . . . I don't want this
to sound like sour grapes." But, he concluded, "Several of Kate's

old friends are upset that she's made a conscious decision not to stay in touch. They feel she's turned her back on them."

In all likelihood, she had. Kate's rarefied world was now filled with princes and dukes, viscounts and ladies—and the occasional shipping heir or billionaire's daughter. Fewer places were left at the table for old chums; William's relatives and friends, for obvious reasons, had to take precedence. "Once you've signed on," Diana had once said of the Royal Family, "you are expected to leave your friends behind. You take on their friends. They have no interest whatsoever in taking on yours."

A month after Kate took her roller-rink tumble, the Heir and the Spare were given leave by their commanding officers to journey to Africa. They were on a special mission to raise money for the Nelson Mandela Children's Fund, UNICEF, and Sentebale, Harry's charity for children orphaned by AIDS in Lesotho. Eager to slake their thirst for adventure, the brothers competed against a hundred others in the Enduro Africa off-road motorcycle rally, tearing across more than a thousand miles of rugged African terrain on their Honda CRF 230 cc bikes.

The princes, who along with other participants paid a $3,000 entrance fee, did not make the trip alone. Throughout the eight-day event, they were accompanied by ten staff members and security officers. Although the rally raised $300,000, it cost British taxpayers more than $80,000 to fund the princes' adventure.

It was not as if Wills were suffering from a lack of excitement in his life. As he wound down his stint with Britain's special services, the prince resumed looking for drug smugglers in the Caribbean—this time with the coast-guard-like Special Boat Service (SBS).

In keeping with seafaring tradition, Wills returned that December 2008 with the beginnings of a beard. "Oh, my God," Kate said when she met him for the first time in weeks. "What in heavens is *that?*" When he rejoined the RAF in a few weeks, the facial hair came off—long before he had the chance to shape it into the full beard for which kings Edward VII and George V (not to mention their cousin Czar Nicholas II) were famous.

For the time being, Babykins appeared to take great pleasure teasing Big Willy about his whiskers. During another shooting party at Sandringham for which they would take the inevitable drubbing from animal-rights activists, Kate on several occasions stroked his beard and then burst out laughing. "Kate loves to tease him," said a pal who has accompanied them to every Sandringham shoot, "and Will loves to laugh at himself. They have more fun together than any two people I've seen."

Perhaps. But this year, like all the others, Kate was banned—along with every other nonroyal—from spending Christmas Eve and Christmas Day at Sandringham. She was allowed to join Wills on December 26, Boxing Day in Britain, as she had been in 2005 and 2006. But even then, she would not be setting foot in the main house; with other friends of the young princes, she would again be staying at Wood Farm, one of several houses on the sprawling estate grounds.

Although it was now a favorite hangout for young royals and their guests, the rooms at Wood Farm had not always been filled with laughter. Sadly, Wills's great-great-uncle Prince John, the youngest son of King George V and Queen Mary, was hidden from public view at Wood Farm because he suffered from epilepsy. He died there in 1919 at the age of thirteen.

Until Boxing Day, Kate whiled away the holidays with her family at the Middletons' new favorite winter playground, Mustique. Sun, sand, and surf aside, the waiting game Kate was being forced to play was taking its toll—especially on Mum. "You see, I feel very vulnerable about everything," Carole said during an unguarded moment. "I'm not a celebrity and don't want to be one. Celebrities have minders and PR people. I don't want a PR person and wouldn't want to have to pay to employ one. I haven't asked for all this."

Carole Middleton did have her own life, her own career. She admitted it hurt that she was still singled out as a crass plebeian who may have foiled her daughter's chances of being queen. Her only real defense mechanism was to bury herself in work. "I'm concerned about my business; that's my focus," she said. "I don't want the attention to detract from that. I'm also worried for my family. I have three children—not just Catherine."

Not that Kate's princess-in-waiting status wasn't good for business. Eighty-four princess-themed items were now sold on the Party Pieces website—five of which were added after Kate's photo appeared on both the website and in the catalog. There were princess dresses, tiaras, dolls, wands, treasure chests, tablecloths, place mats, cups, dishes, sharpeners, and even a Pink Princess trike for around $450.

Carole may have felt "vulnerable," but the demand for children's party favors was anything but. Even in the middle of global economic collapse, Party Pieces posted record earnings as 2008 drew to a close.

Nor did James seem particularly attuned to the sensitivities of the Palace regarding the commercialization of the Royal Family. Asked the following year to bake twenty-one cakes to commemorate the twenty-first birthday of *HELLO!* magazine, James was shown in its pages posing with several cakes decorated with the images of previous cover subjects—including Diana. When his superiors at Buckingham Palace saw the story, said one junior staffer, "They shuddered."

After celebrating New Year's Eve in London—their own long-standing tradition—William and Kate joined Charles and Camilla for a week at Birkhall, the Prince of Wales's private retreat on Granny's Balmoral estate. One evening, Kate was led down a path to a log fishing cabin nestled on the banks of the river Dee. Inside, the table was set for an intimate candlelit supper, with crisp white linen, gleaming Georgian silverware, and vases overflowing with flowers. As temperatures outside hovered around freezing, the lovers dined alone before a crackling fireplace.

That William and Kate had forgone their annual ski holiday in the Alps to spend time at Balmoral seemed to many a sure sign that an engagement was in the offing. Despite its well-established penchant for hyperbole, this time the *Sun* was not far off when it proclaimed MARRIAGE FRENZY AS WILLS TAKES HER TO BALMORAL on its front page.

The Palace denied the rumors, as it always did. But this time, the tabloids got it right. According to a member of the household staff at Balmoral and one of the couple's closest friends, William made good on the "understanding" they had had for years. Having received the enthusiastic blessing of the Queen and Prince Charles, William finally, formally, asked Kate to marry him.

Senior advisers at Buckingham Palace had been working on a timeline for months. William would be getting his wings in January 2010, but his advanced training would extend well into the summer of that year—interfering with plans for a June or July wedding. Since the London Olympics and the Queen's Diamond Jubilee celebrating her sixtieth year on the throne would both take place in 2012, that left the summer of 2011 for a royal wedding. The Queen was delighted with the timing. Coincidentally, Prince Philip would be celebrating his ninetieth birthday on June

10, 2011. "What a lovely birthday present for your grandfather," she told William.

Tentatively, plans were hatched to announce the engagement in early 2011. Until then, it was agreed that their engagement—which would be more than two years old by the time it was announced to the public—must remain a tightly guarded secret.

Nothing was carved in stone. If unforeseen circumstances forced a change in the timing, one backup plan included a wedding to be squeezed into the hectic 2012 schedule, and another a date further in the future—although no one seriously believed Kate would countenance that.

Their romantic getaway in the Scottish Highlands behind them, the couple flew British Airways from Aberdeen to London. Once the plane landed at Heathrow, the crew followed the usual procedure whenever a member of the Royal Family flew commercial. The rest of the passengers were asked to remain seated while William and Kate were escorted off the plane by their four-man security detail. They then rushed to Wills's black Audi S4 4.2-liter, V-8 saloon, which was waiting on the tarmac—alongside two serious-looking black SUVs—with its engine running. As he took their bags, one of Wills's bodyguards remarked that the prince's beard was gone. "Yes," he replied mock-sheepishly, "she made me shave it off."

For Kate's twenty-seventh birthday, William came up with a novel idea for a gift: himself. Although he had spent the night there secretly on previous occasions, this time he made no effort to conceal his overnight stay with Kate and her family in Bucklebury. To insure at least some degree of privacy for the couple, his three-man security detail bunked in a cottage just down the road. William's gift was nothing if not an endorsement for Kate's place in the royal fold: an $800 custom-made Swarovski Optik sniper sight, for shooting stag.

News of Wills's sleepover on the eve of his departure for RAF training was just one more reason for Fleet Street to get itself worked up. Now, it was even being suggested that, in these economically troubled times, the couple owed a wedding to their British people. "Would a royal wedding," the *Evening Gazette* asked its readers, "lift the national mood?" Not surprisingly, most of those who responded believed it would. "It would," agreed Richard Kay, "be a huge boost for the economy."

Two days later, William reported to RAF Shawbury. He was now code-named Golden Osprey, but the taint of his time spent as Golden Kestrel lingered. Neither he nor his superiors at the base's Defense Helicopter Flying School had forgotten about the costly joyrides that had angered taxpayers and left an air marshal scrambling for explanations.

This time, Lieutenant William Wales would not be buzzing the Queen's palace or landing in his girlfriend's backyard. Zipping himself into his regulation green flight suit each morning, he would spend nine hours a day polishing his flying skills on single-engine Squirrels, twin-engine Griffins, and Lynxes before graduating to Sea Kings. On his off-hours, however, he would not exactly be roughing it. Having spent plenty of time in confined spaces in submarines and army barracks, the prince decided to forgo base housing and instead rented a spacious three-bedroom cottage with tennis courts and a swimming pool nearby.

Not to be outdone by his big brother, Harry arrived at RAF Middle Wallop in Hampshire just days after William started his helicopter pilot's training. Still hoping to return to Afghanistan, the Spare signed up for a fourteen-month course learning to fly Apache attack helicopters for the Army Air Corps.

Harry's decision to commit himself to long stretches away from home did not sit well with everyone. In stark contrast to the more stoic Kate, Chelsy Davy threatened to leave her boyfriend rather than wait around for him indefinitely. And she did, adding insult to injury by announcing the breakup on her Facebook page. Their relationship had always been stormy, aggravated by Chelsy's being torn between her comfortable life of wealth and privilege in Cape Town and the life of a royal girlfriend-in-waiting in England.

Always flashier and more earthily seductive than Kate, the blond, bronzed Chelsy would soon be making up with the prince she called Haz. Over the next several years, their sizzling off-again, mostly on-again romance would offer a welcome counterpoint to the steady, predictable hum of the Wills-Kate love match. "She looks sort of like an unmade bed," Diana's friend Richard Kay said of Chelsy. "The passionate attraction between the two of them fizzles and crackles. You can see they just want to rip their clothes off."

Their military careers now firmly under way, William and Harry now took control of their lives as royals. In late January 2009, the princes technically broke away from Charles's household, setting up offices of their own inside St. James's Palace. Headed by Jamie Lowther-Pinkerton, the Household of Their Royal Highnesses Prince William of Wales and Prince Henry of Wales employed Helen Asprey as the princes' private secretary, Miguel Head as assistant press secretary, and former British ambassador to the United States and Israel Sir David Manning as adviser. For the first time, they reported directly to the boys—who now had their own letterhead incorporating their own royal crests—not to their father.

There would still be time for polo; both princes were invariably granted leave when they were needed to compete in an important polo match. Wills would regret letting his guard down during a match at the Beaufort Polo Club near Highgrove, when he decided to relieve himself in a corner of the field. A photographer with a telephoto lens snapped several shots of the royal lapse, and the revealing shots soon appeared in tabloids and on the Internet. WILLS'S CROWN JEWELS EXPOSED! shouted one headline, along with a Palace source quoted as saying this was "not the kind of leak anyone would approve of."

Minor snafus aside, Kate never underestimated how important these matches were to Wills; she took pains never to miss a single one. In January, William and Harry were galloping up and down the field while spectators gathered beneath a marquee, drinking champagne and generally ignoring the game.

At the opposite end of the field, Kate sat alone in a small tent of her own, studying every move of the players. "Why don't you come and join the rest of the party?" asked one of the guests, Kathy Lette.

"I've got to pay attention to every second," Kate replied, never taking her eyes off the action. "I'll be discussing the game in minute detail later on."

"You can't be having fun here," Lette said. "Why don't you play polo yourself?"

"I'm allergic," Kate said without breaking her concentration, "to horses."

The incident offered a revealing glimpse into Kate's determination, even at this late date in the relationship, to keep up with the Waleses—even at the risk of her health. "You certainly get the feeling," said another member of the Beaufort Polo Club, "that she works very hard at making Prince William happy. To the rest of us it might seem a little desperate, but then consider what's at stake."

By this time, weddings were no longer seen as an opportunity to show the royal flag and have some fun. With each came renewed calls for Wills and Kate to finally announce their engagement. "It was like a slap in the face for Kate every time they were invited to another friend's wedding," said a longtime neighbor of the Middletons'. "It was humiliating."

In late March 2009, their St. Andrews pals Emma Barttelot and Freddie Jones announced their engagement. "Prince William's squeeze Kate Middleton," the *Daily Mail*'s Richard Kay observed at the time, "will be biting her tongue again this week." A few weeks later, their friends Annabel Glynne-Percy and Logie Fitzwilliams also announced plans to tie the knot. After initially accepting invitations to both events, Walls and Kate bowed out.

Most surprising of all—particularly for the bride and groom—was their eleventh-hour decision not to show up at the May 23, 2009, nuptials of their old St. Andrews roommate Fergus Boyd to French aristocrat Sandrine Janet. "It cast a damper over the proceedings, inevitably," one of the guests told journalist Tim Walker. "They were hurt when William told them that he and Kate had decided to withdraw. There is no question that Fergus and Sandrine, who also fell in love at the university, have always been fiercely loyal to them."

Clarence House tried to explain away the couple's absence from their close pal's wedding by hinting that certain "Eurotrash" elements would be among the 150 guests. Hardly. The black-tie reception was held at Janet's ancestral home, the fifteenth-century Loire Valley Château de Boumois, and the only unfortunate incident came when the bride's grandmother temporarily lost her wedding ring.

Indeed, the trashiest behavior seemed to be occurring right on the couple's doorstep. A little over an hour into his twenty-second-birthday party at Boujis, a soused James Middleton was photographed being bundled into a cab with a similarly smashed Kate—all while Carole Middleton angrily warned the paparazzi to keep their distance.

Yet nothing would prepare the Royal Family for the bombshell that was dropped on July 19, 2009, when the world finally learned the truth about Kate's bad-boy uncle. In a front-page story titled I CALLED WILLS A F***ER: KATE MIDDLETON UNCLE DRUG & VICE SHOCK, *News of the World* detailed Gary Goldsmith's out-of-control lifestyle on Ibiza.

Tycoon Who Boasts of Hosting Wills's Villa Holiday, read the subhead, *Supplies Cocaine and Fixes Hookers.* To illustrate the point, the tabloid's front page showed a shirtless, tattooed, beer-bellied Goldsmith using a razor to cut lines of cocaine on his kitchen counter.

It was all part of an undercover sting operation in which two *News of the World* reporters posed as hip young Britons visiting Ibiza for the first time. In addition to offering them prostitutes and drugs—he even asked if anyone was interested in "chasing the dragon" (snorting heroin)—Goldsmith openly smoked pot as he bragged about his royal connections.

"We're connected," Uncle Gary replied when asked about his relationship to Prince William through Kate. If they married, Goldsmith said, "I'll be bloodline . . . *bloodline.* Well, after Charles, I'll be the Queen's uncle." Referring to the dreary working-class town that was home to his Goldsmith ancestors, Uncle Gary cracked, "I'll be the Duke of Slough." As for Buckingham Palace, "I'm getting my own room—the Goldsmith Wing."

Kate's uncle also predicted that there would be a royal wedding soon and joked that he would be giving the bride away. "I'm going to be up front," he boasted. "I want a speaking part."

In yet another surreal moment, Uncle Gary turned judgmental when discussing Prince Harry's hell-raiser image. "Wearing swastikas wasn't ideal," he sniped. "Talk about fashion tips, it wasn't the best move he made."

A stunningly naive Goldsmith also told the undercover journalists, "When the press get you, they kill you. They don't know who I am. I'm under the radar." As the reporters left, he pumped his arms in the air. "I'm going to change the royal wave to that," he said, "having it large!"

The revelations concerning Kate's uncle sent shock waves through Buckingham Palace—and the country. As the rest of the Middletons weathered the storm in Bucklebury ("You know we don't ever talk to the press," grumbled Michael Middleton, "and the situation remains the same"), Kate and Wills holed up with Charles and Camilla at Highgrove. Prince Charles, rather surprisingly, was philosophical about the whole thing. According to an official at St. James's Palace, he told Kate to "simply not read any of the papers for a while. This, too, shall pass."

William, on the other hand, would have to take decisive action. Clarence House confirmed that, for the time being at least, he had severed all ties with Kate's uncle and would most certainly not be checking into La Maison de Bang Bang anytime soon. For his part, a remorseful Gary Goldsmith was, according to a friend, "practically suicidal" over humiliating his niece and—more important—jeopardizing the Middletons' chances of being linked to the Royal Family.

Goldsmith had been right about one thing. At Clarence House, said a senior staff member, the wedding of William and Kate "at times seems to be all anybody talks about."

The Queen's reaction, according to senior courtiers, was characteristically muted. Appearances concerned her less than the real security threat posed to her grandson. The Queen even laughed at a cartoon showing her looking out the windows of Buckingham Palace at aliens that have just landed in a flying saucer. "Oh, no," she says to Prince Philip. "Please, God, no! Don't let it be another one of Kate Middleton's relatives."

Just how had the *News of the World* reporters learned about Uncle Gary in the first place? According to a longtime aide to Prince Charles who remained in contact with his former colleagues, security officials who were concerned about William's safety leaked the information—at the behest of certain Men in Gray who opposed the Heir's marrying Kate Middleton on the grounds that her family was "unsuitable. There is still a faction that believes Prince William would be better off marrying someone with a title. Frankly, they believe Kate and her family aren't just commoners, but simply common." This was, the former aide added, "the ammunition they'd been looking for."

At the height of this latest and potentially most embarrassing scandal, William left for the RAF Valley base on remote Anglesey island off the coast of North Wales. There, he learned to pilot a twin-engine Griffin out over the Irish Sea and high into the region's rugged, snowcapped Snowdonia mountains.

Kate could not weather the storm alone. She fled with the rest of her family to paparazzi-proof Mustique, where she could at least work on her tan until the furor died down. Kate was, by all accounts, far less upset than her mother about the damning headlines and, more recently, actual video posted online of Uncle Gary cutting up cocaine in his kitchen.

Ironically, William and Kate would make their first appearance together since Uncle Gary's sex-and-drugs scandal broke at another wedding—one they felt powerless to duck. This time, fellow Household Cavalry Officer Nick van Cutsem, who along with his brothers Edward and Hugh had been the princes' friends their entire lives, was set to wed event planner Alice Hadden-Paton in London.

The ceremony took place near Buckingham Palace at the Guards Chapel of Wellington Barracks—the very place where, just two years earlier, William and Harry held an emotional memorial service marking the tenth anniversary of their mother's death.

On this occasion, William and Harry wore cutaways in their roles as ushers, and Kate made her customary fashion splash, this time in a blue brocade coat over an off-white dress. Despite her tan, she looked, said several other guests, "gaunt."

After van Cutsem and Hadden-Paton had been pronounced man and wife, Wills shook the groom's hand and congratulated him. "You'll be next," Nick said, grinning.

The lighthearted remark hung in the air like a sword of Damocles. Wills and Kate looked at each other, smiled wanly, and made their way to one more wedding reception that wasn't their own.

I am absolutely determined to see William succeed the Queen. I don't think Charles should do it.

—*Diana*

My mother was the People's Princess. I want to be the People's King.

—*William*

8

——

June 2012

Buckingham Palace

She steps out onto the balcony and waves to a sea of more than a million people that fills The Mall from Admiralty Arch to the gates of Buckingham Palace. The roar that rises up from this record-smashing crowd is deafening. Queen Elizabeth II has reigned for sixty years—only three years and seven months shy of the record set by Queen Victoria—and her people are grateful. But the cheers are not simply for a glorious past. They are for the future of the nearly thirteen-hundred-year-old British monarchy—a future that is represented by the family that surrounds her. To the Queen's right stands the next king and queen: the sixty-three-year-old Prince Charles, and his dazed-looking wife, Camilla. But everyone, including Her Majesty, knows that it is the other future king and queen standing here who embody the future of the monarchy: Prince William and Princess Kate. As the beautiful young couple steps up to acknowledge the crowd, the surge in the decibel level startles even the usually unflappable monarch.

If that dream of a thriving monarchy extending its reach into the future is ever to become reality, the Queen has been told, important decisions must be made. Decisions not just concerning William and Kate, but decisions that could determine the fate of the monarchy itself.

Three of the Queen's most trusted advisers—her former private secretaries Baron Fellowes (formerly Sir Robert, Diana's brother-in-law) and Sir Robin Janvrin, as well as her current private secretary, Christopher Geidt—had weighed in on the most pressing problem of all: who should next wear the crown, and when. "It's all," said one of their former aides, "about the numbers. The Queen Mother lived to be one hundred and one, and she was active and alert almost to the very end of her life. Her daughter is eighty-five, and should she live another fifteen years and choose to remain Queen all that time—and I'm not saying she shouldn't—it will have a profound impact."

The Queen was already also Britain's longest-living monarch, surpassing Victoria in 2007. If she stayed on the throne until she was one hundred, Charles would become king at seventy-seven—by far the oldest person ever to inherit the crown. If he reigned for just ten years, William would be fifty-three when he became king. "It isn't," said the adviser, "a very pretty picture."

For the first time, there were serious discussions about when it would be appropriate for the Queen to step aside. Bypassing Charles altogether in favor of William—Diana's devout wish— was out of the question. As Prince of Wales, he was first in line, and no one—not even the Queen—could stop him from asserting his right to the throne.

The solution, **as devised by** several Men in Gray in cooperation with key members of Prince Charles's inner circle, was a compromise worthy of a Metternich. At some point following the Diamond Jubilee in 2012—perhaps upon her own ninetieth birthday in 2016—she would agree to step aside allowing Charles to become king at last at age sixty-seven—still making him the oldest person ever to assume the throne, although at an age when he might still leave his mark on history. (Interestingly, the last William—William IV—holds the distinction of being the oldest new monarch. He was crowned at age sixty-four and, although eight of his ten illegitimate children survived him, died without a legitimate heir seven years later. He was succeeded by his niece, Queen Victoria. Among William IV's direct descendants through his illegitimate children: British prime minister David Cameron, who is the king's great-great-great-great-great-grandson.)

For the Queen to step aside, Charles would, as a quid pro quo, first have to agree to abdicate after some specified time—perhaps at age eighty, after having reigned thirteen years. That would leave a comparatively young and vigorous William and Kate to become king and queen at age forty-seven. "That," the aide said, "would be the point of the whole thing."

"Lots of ideas involving how and when the Queen might step aside have been discussed, of course," said an aide to one of the key strategists in the succession scheme. "But no one really thought there was much of a possibility that she would be willing to. So no one actually talked about it with the Queen until *she* brought it up."

Over the past few years, the Queen had gradually turned over more responsibility to her son. The Prince of Wales was presiding over more investitures and was being given more access to government papers. He was also standing in for the Queen more frequently when ambassadors presented their credentials to the Court of St. James's and even began holding his own regular audiences with the prime minister.

By sharing more of the royal workload, the octogenarian monarch was finally able to take more four-day weekends away from Buckingham Palace and her desk heaped with the dreaded red and blue boxes of state. Yet the Queen never gave any indication that she would consider stepping aside. "She regards the job," said Prince Philip's cousin the Countess Mountbatten, "as a job for life." The Queen's cousin Margaret Rhodes agreed that Her Majesty viewed her duty to the nation as "something so deep and so special" that she would insist on fulfilling it "until the day she dies. I am sure she will never abdicate."

Diana's death, rocking the monarchy to its core, may well have changed all that. "For the first time," said her friend Lady Elsa Bowker, "the Royal Family was truly frightened by how angry they made the people. They almost lost the monarchy. I don't think the Queen could ever forget that." Besides, Elizabeth's own path to the throne was hardly direct. Her painfully shy, stuttering father became George VI only after his brother, Edward VIII, abdicated to marry the American divorcée Wallis Warfield Simpson.

By early 2010, Charles had agreed in principle to the terms of his mother's abdication. However, once he and Camilla were king and queen, there would be nothing to hold him to it. Enforcement, it was determined, would come through making the agreement public. "The people overwhelmingly want William as the next king," said the aide. "If they are told that Charles will make that possible by stepping aside in a few years, and then he reneges, then there will be hell to pay."

In every scenario, one element remained constant: the marriage of William and Kate. While the details of the plan of succession were still being worked out by the Men in Gray, Kate sat by her man on January 15, 2010, and rubbed his shoulders affectionately as he waited to receive his second set of RAF wings—these specifically as a helicopter pilot—from Papa.

Kate stayed home, however, when William left two days later on a whirlwind tour of New Zealand and Australia—his first representing the Queen. The trip was touted as the first in a series of steps to make William a "shadow king," gradually taking on some of the monarch's duties in much the same way his father had done.

William, who was sensitive to his father's having waited to assume the top job for more than sixty years, objected to the term *shadow king* and all that it implied. But the Queen was undoubtedly taking his first trip abroad as her substitute seriously. Included in the prince's entourage was Sir David Manning, Britain's former ambassador, and the Queen's private secretary, Christopher Geidt. Apparently trying to go unnoticed in the crowd, Geidt told reporters that his being in New Zealand was a mere coincidence. "I am on holiday," he tried to explain, "and it was suggested I might like to look in."

Geidt saw a polished young royal who could handle any question with aplomb—including the most frequently asked question of all. At every stop, someone inevitably called out, "When are you and Kate getting married?" Wills, just as inevitably, offered the same three-word reply: "Wait and see."

Back in England, Waity Katie was scoring a public-relations triumph of her own. Claiming that her privacy had been violated when a photographer snapped pictures of her playing tennis, Kate sued and won roughly $7,000 in damages—all of which she then donated to charity.

That March, Wills and Kate sneaked away with her parents on a ski vacation in the picturesque French Alpine town of Courchevel. But even then, paparazzi shots of Kate clinging to her prince aboard a snowmobile and reports that Wills was overheard repeatedly referring to Michael Middleton as "Dad" only sparked more wedding talk.

Within days of their return, speculation reached a fever pitch when the well-connected magazine editor and author Tina Brown declared on her news website the Daily Beast that June 3 and 4 had been "mysteriously blocked out on the palace diaries." Brown predicted that an engagement would probably be announced on one of those dates, with a November 2010 wedding to follow.

The frenzy continued when, on April 17, 2010, the couple attended another wedding—this time of Wills's old flame Mili d'Erlanger to his Eton classmate David Jardine-Paterson. This time, Kate was determined to make a statement, showing up in a flowing scarlet dress with a scarlet hat to match. "How would you like it if someone showed up at your wedding in a bright red dress?" asked one guest. "But I guess she was sort of telling the world to bugger off." Kate was apparently in a different state of mind two weeks later, when she wore an ivory brocade coat and a black pillbox hat to the wedding of yet another pair of St. Andrews pals, Oliver Baker and Melissa Nicholson. "Not many people can say they've had the future king at their big day," a guest said. "But I'm sure that we'd all like to see Wills's *own* big day."

For all intents and purposes, Wills and Kate were already living as man and wife in a three-bedroom stone farmhouse just outside the Welsh town of Blaenau Ffestiniog, not far from RAF Valley air base. Blaenau Ffestiniog, the largest town in the area, was just a few miles from the spot with the longest place-name in Europe: Llanfairpwllgwyngyllgogerychwyrndrobwllllantysiliogogogoch,

Welsh for "St. Mary's Church by the white aspen over the whirl-pool and St. Tysilio's Church by the red cave."

Kate had all but given up her job at Party Pieces so that she could keep William company. But their cozy off-base living arrangement did not come cheap to British taxpayers. Because of their relatively remote location, fifteen extra officers had to be assigned to guard the prince's farmhouse at a cost of more than $2 million. "Prince William is regarded as the highest security risk," a Scotland Yard spokesman stressed. "There is no question that the extra protection is required."

Fortunately, Gary Goldsmith was no longer regarded as an active security risk. William and Kate were simply no longer spending time in the company of Carole Middleton's bad-boy younger brother, either in England or on Ibiza.

Nevertheless, some at the Palace still did not entirely approve of the Middletons. The influence of the naysayers waned as it became increasingly clear that the Queen was genuinely fond of Kate, and that Wills still showed no interest whatsoever in any other woman.

Sniping at the family would continue, however, including reports that Michael Middleton had been inquiring about a coat of arms, and that Party Pieces had been handed a lucrative deal to sell official England World Cup merchandise allegedly because of the family's royal connections.

All this paled in comparison to the year's biggest royal scandal—one that had nothing to do with the Middletons. On May 23, 2010, the *News of the World* released videotape showing Sarah Ferguson, the Duchess of York, soliciting a bribe for access to her ex-husband, Prince Andrew. "Five hundred thousand pounds [$717,000], when you can, to me, open doors," she told an undercover reporter posing as a businessman. Looking nervous, she promised to help secure the stranger a "big deal" using Andrew and his connections. Once she received a wire transfer of nearly three-quarters of a million dollars, Fergie said, "You open up all channels, whatever you need, whatever you want . . . then you meet Andrew." She left the room carrying a computer case crammed with the down payment: $40,000 in cash.

It seemed strange that she did not recognize the modus operandi of notorious *News of the World* undercover journalist Mazher Mahmood. Known as the Fake Sheikh, Mahmood had already exposed dozens of powerful figures and had even nabbed Prince Edward's wife, Sophie, for influence peddling in a similar sting operation.

As soon as the news broke, the duchess issued an abject apology. "I very deeply regret the situation and the embarrassment caused," she said, stressing that her ex-husband, with whom she still lived, knew nothing about it.

Within days, Fergie was on the *Oprah Winfrey Show*, trying to explain that she owed millions of dollars, had been drinking at the time, and simply cracked under the pressure. "I was so out of my mind," she said, "beyond the point of desperation. This had been building up." In telling her story, the duchess made it clear that she was still on the verge of a breakdown. "I can go into hyperventilation and a panic attack right now."

"Right now?" Oprah asked.

"Yes, right now."

"Well, try not to."

Heeding Oprah's advice, Fergie explained that, unlike Diana, she had not pressed for a multi-million-dollar divorce settlement. Although she was given room and board at the Duke of York's official residence, the ninety-acre Royal Lodge estate at Windsor Great Park, Fergie received just $20,000 a year. "I chose friendship," she said, claiming she was attempting to stay in the Queen's good graces, "with the Boss."

The Queen, Philip, and Charles were outraged by Fergie's behavior. That was to be expected. Philip, in particular, had gone on record describing his former daughter-in-law as "vulgar." William's reaction was perhaps more surprising. Although close to his cousins Beatrice and Eugenie, who remained fifth and sixth in line to the throne, he had no sympathy for his former aunt Sarah. "She is a disgrace," he said at a Clarence House staff meeting. "I can't stand these bloody reporters, but there's no excuse for what she did. To think my mother loved her once . . . incredible."

Ironically, Fergie's *Oprah* tell-all would lead to a paying job that helped offset at least a portion of her crushing debt. In early 2011, the disgraced royal is set to chronicle her hoped-for comeback as the star of *Finding Sarah*, her own reality show on OWN, Winfrey's new TV network.

The Fergie scandal had only begun to simmer down when Wills and Kate were broadsided by yet another unsubstantiated rumor. Two years earlier, baseless reports said that the pair had weathered a "pregnancy scare." This time, tabloid reports took the story a step further, claiming that Kate was actually pregnant, and that a "shotgun wedding" was in the offing. Palace spokesmen angrily dismissed the pregnancy reports as "nonsense," but not before checking with William to make certain that indeed they were.

As he embarked on his first rescue mission as an RAF pilot, William was confronted with the sort of life-and-death issue that made all his royal troubles seem inconsequential, if not outright silly. In early June 2010, William was on a training mission aboard a Sea King Mk3 rescue helicopter when news came that a deranged taxidriver named Derrick Bird had gone on a shooting rampage in northwest England's Cumbria County, killing twelve people before turning the gun on himself. When several helicopters were dispatched to the scene of the killings to airlift victims to the hospital, the prince's helicopter was diverted to rescue a young climber who had slipped and tumbled down the side of a mountain in the Snowdonia range.

It was William's first real lifesaving mission, and it would not end well. After following all the procedures he had been honing for more than five months, William and his three crew members retrieved the climber, only to have him die on the way to the hospital. The prince, although disappointed, told Mike France, national fund-raising chairman of a group called Mountain Rescue, that the experience was "amazing—after all the training to see it all work in practice. But it was someone with head injuries. Unfortunately, he didn't survive."

The outcome would be very different a few days later, when William helped guide his chopper to a climber stranded on a ledge atop Mount Snowdon. Suffering from a fractured leg, twenty-one-year-old Ruby Lawrence was treated by medics on the scene and then airlifted to a nearby hospital. Lawrence was unaware at the time that William was at the controls. "It was a shock to find out he was flying the helicopter," she said, "and it's a shame because I wanted to thank him. If I had been up there on my own, I would have died."

As he put his own life on the line to save others, a worshipful public had no concept of Wills's gritty and dangerous new life. With rumors of a royal wedding cresting, the world press ruminated on everything from the venue (it was a toss-up among Windsor Castle, St. Paul's Cathedral, and Westminster Abbey, although the abbey held sad memories of Diana's funeral) and who would design the dress (presumable only British need apply) to who would create the cake (Kate's brother, James?). Diana's famous sapphire engagement ring still had to be coaxed away from Harry, who had chosen it as his principal memento of Mummy, but there was universal agreement that the wedding rings should be simple bands made of gold mined in North Wales—a nod to William's standing as the next Prince of Wales.

Trying to ignore all the wedding chatter, Flight Lieutenant Wales went about his risky business. On September 17, 2010, he officially graduated from the training program and joined 22 Squadron, C Flight, as a search-and-rescue pilot. With a typical tour of duty lasting between thirty and thirty-six months, the Heir could expect to work up to ten twenty-four-hour shifts per month if he had any intention of being promoted to captain. The training and dedication paid off again just two weeks after graduation, when, on his first official shift, William scrambled to rescue a fifty-two-year-old oil worker who had been stricken with a heart attack while working on an oil rig in the Irish Sea. Copiloting "Rescue 122" through a squall, the prince skillfully maneuvered his helicopter so that it could airlift the victim to a hospital. "The prince is proud," Clarence House said in a succinctly worded statement, "to be able to serve."

William was also still hoping to serve his country in other ways: he had not given up his dream of fighting as his brother did on the front lines in Afghanistan. "My heart was in the army and that's why I first joined them," he told a documentary filmmaker, pointing out that many of his fellow officers in the Household Cavalry were still deployed in the war zone. "It's just a pity I didn't get to Afghanistan," Wills went on. "Many people say, 'Well, that's very understandable.' There are some slightly valid arguments as to why not, but many of them are hyped up as to why I couldn't go. I still have hope and faith and a real determination to go out there."

Any attempt to sneak William into Afghanistan for a brief, top-secret tour of duty would, of course, require Kate's full cooperation—and that she would unhesitatingly give. "Kate knows it's what he wants to do," a friend from their days at St. Andrews observed, "and Will has already proven he can handle himself. She has complete faith that he would come back safe and sound."

For the time being, William remained poised to take the controls of his Sea King search-and-rescue helicopter at a moment's notice. There would, of course, be frequent leaves to perform his royal duties and compete in the occasional polo match. He would also find time to party with his friends at the London club of the moment, shoot pheasant at Sandringham and stags at Balmoral, and attend the weddings of friends—all the while with Kate at his side.

For now, home for Wills and Kate was that modest farmhouse in the Welsh countryside near the Isle of Anglesey. With its sandy bays, rocky headlands, dunes, heaths, and broad expanses of green—all silhouetted against the Irish Sea and the blue-white peaks of Snowdonia—Anglesey offered some of the most lushly beautiful scenery to be found anywhere. The last stronghold of the Druids, it was also rich in history and lore, from its moated, thirteenth-century Beaumaris Castle to its Tudor pubs and Georgian mansions.

Sioned Compton was minding the cash register at McColl's minimart in Blaenau Ffestiniog when the young man in the metal-frame glasses reached into his cart and began placing items on the counter: two frozen pepperoni pizzas, a bag of frozen french fries, a bag of salad greens, a head of iceberg lettuce, a bottle of Tropicana orange juice, and two bottles of water.

"That will be twelve pounds [about $19]," Compton said as the frazzled young man searched through his pockets. Then she realized who was standing in front of her. "Oh my God!" she gushed. "You're Prince William, aren't you?"

"No," he said, looking down at his feet. "No, I'm not." By now, Kate was standing next to him, and the clerk could see one of William's bodyguards lurking at the entrance to the store.

Exasperated and embarrassed, Wills turned to Kate. "Can you pay, please? I've not got any cash."

"I don't either," Kate replied before handing over her platinum card to the twenty-two-year-old clerk. Despite Wills's strenuous denials, her name—Catherine Middleton—was printed clearly on the card. Within moments, they loaded up their Audi and sped away.

The entire exchange was captured on the store's security cameras. "I don't know why he didn't just say, 'Yes, I'm William, pleased to meet you,'" Compton said. "It would have made my day. I was disappointed in him, to be honest, but he must have had his reasons."

Notwithstanding the occasional brush with the public, Kate and Wills reveled in their quiet, sequestered life together in this remote corner of the kingdom. One of their favorite spots to relax was Llanddwyn Island, a narrow finger of land that jutted into the sea. Here they strolled along paths that weaved between salt marshes, mudflats, and rolling dunes, pausing to admire the yellow poppies and bluebells that sprouted up around the ruins of Llanddwyn Chapel. William and Kate felt at home here, stretching out on the grass next to a fifteenth-century church built to honor St. Dwynwen. She was, after all, the Welsh patron saint of lovers—Wales's version of St. Valentine—and she gave this speck of land its other name: Lovers Island.

For William, however, the most romantic place in the world

was not to be found in the Northern Hemisphere. In September, he told his father that the time had finally arrived for him to propose to Kate. "Well," Charles replied, nodding in approval, "you've certainly practiced long enough." Charles's blessing was something William desired, but he needed the Queen's permission to wed. During a closed-door meeting at Windsor Castle, William formally asked his grandmother for her blessing. He would later tell one of his cousins that the Queen was "as happy and excited" as he'd ever seen her, with the possible exception of when "one of her horses is racing at Ascot."

William had already approached his brother about Diana's spectacular eighteen-carat-sapphire and diamond engagement ring—the memento Harry had picked out for himself shortly after her funeral—and Harry eagerly obliged. In recent years, they had come to an understanding that the first brother to become engaged would, if he chose, have the option of presenting it to his intended.

In October, William and Kate returned to the one spot he had long regarded as his "second home"—Africa. "When I step off the plane, I'm like, 'Yes, I'm back,' " he told a documentary filmmaker earlier that year. "Africa will hold a special place in my heart for the rest of my life."

During most of their ten-day stay at Lewa Downs, the game preserve owned by the family of his old flame Jecca Craig, William carried the ring—secure in a blue velvet box—in his backpack, worried the entire time that somehow he'd lose it. "I knew if it disappeared," he later confessed, "I would be in a lot of trouble." One morning he borrowed a helicopter and flew Kate to a lake nestled on the slopes of Mount Kenya, some 12,500 feet above sea level. It was the spot, oddly enough, where he staged his mock proposal to Jecca a decade before. This time, with the magnificent Rift Valley spread out before them, William got down on one knee and proposed to Kate. Caught by surprise, Kate did what might have been expected after nearly a decade of waiting for this moment: she burst into tears.

"It was very romantic," she later said of the proposal. Looking at her future husband, she conceded, "there is a true romantic in there." And a true sentimentalist. Giving Kate Diana's ring was, he explained, "my way of making sure my mother didn't miss out on today."

It would be more than month before the world learned the happy news. On the morning of November 16, 2010, Clarence House announced that William and Kate would be wed the following year, in late spring or early summer. When Prime Minister David Cameron, who as a teenager had slept on a London street so he could witness the 1981 wedding of Charles and Diana, announced the news at a cabinet meeting, the ministers responded with cheers and applause. "It's great," Cameron said, "to have a bit of unadulterated good news."

During a reception for leaders of British overseas territories at Windsor Castle, the Queen warmly accepted words of congratulations from her guests. "It is brilliant news," she told one. "It has taken them a very long time." Prince Charles went so far as to say that the long-awaited announcement left him feeling "very old," while William's future father-in-law reacted almost matter-of-factly to the news that their daughter was now on a path to becoming queen. "They make a lovely couple," Michael Middleton told reporters, "they are great fun to be with, and we've had a lot of laughs together."

There were those, however, who took a more jaundiced view. "If she were my sister," said Diana's former private secretary, Patrick Jephson, "I'd tell her to get a good prenup. This is no ordinary marriage, and this last decade has had these terrible divorces." If they did sign a prenuptial agreement—which, despite pressure from several quarters, William was said to be against—it would be a first for the Royal Family.

Appearing for the first time as an engaged couple before a blizzard of flashing press cameras—which offered a startling glimpse of the pressures the young couple faced on a more or less routine basis—they appeared happy, calm, and confident. "We're like little ducks," he later said of their relaxed demeanor, "very calm on the surface, but little feet going like crazy under the water." For one thing in particular, William could be grateful: now that she was officially his fiancee and a future member of the Royal Family, Kate was entitled to her own royal protection officers.

During the couple's first sit-down interview, with England's ITV network, it dawned on the British public that until now they had never actually heard Kate speak. Sounding not unlike Diana, Kate appeared poised and natural. She described William as a "loving boyfriend" who "supported me through good times and also through the bad times." He joked that Kate had "many habits that make me laugh and that I tease her about."

The couple also spoke for the first time about their headline-making split in 2007. "I, at the time, wasn't very happy about it," she admitted, "but actually it made me a stronger person. You find out things about yourself that maybe you hadn't realized." William, who breathed a mock sigh of relief that Kate now seemed to view that difficult period philosophically, agreed that the breakup was "all about finding a bit of space and finding ourselves, about growing up—and it all worked out for the better."

Their relationship now, he said, was "incredibly easy, because we took the time."

Not surprisingly, the memory of Diana was never far away.

"Obviously, I would have loved to have met her," Kate said of her late mother-in-law. "She an inspirational woman to look up to." But William's future wife went on to say that, in the face of the inevitable comparisons to Diana, she intended to "carve my own future." William agreed. "There is no pressure," he said. "No one is trying to fill my mother's shoes. . . . It's about making your own future and your own destiny and Kate will do a very good job of that." Still, she conceded that the prospect of fitting into the Royal Family was "nerve-wracking. I don't know the ropes . . . but I'm willing to learn quickly and work hard. I really hope I can make a difference." Planning for the wedding of the century moved ahead quickly. Within days of their engagement, they announced the time and place on Twitter: April 29, 2011, at Westminster Abbey. Not coincidentally, April 29 is St. Catherine's Day.

The last little girl who pinned a picture of a prince on her bedroom wall and then went on to marry him did not fare well. Even as she walked down the aisle at St. Paul's Cathedral in her gown with the twenty-five-foot train, twenty-year-old Diana knew her marriage was doomed. For the rest of her brief life, the Princess of Wales would struggle with her husband's flagrant and humiliating infidelity, the soul-sapping demands of royal life, fame on an almost unimaginable scale, and her own demons. Until the end, Diana yearned for all she had dreamt of as a young girl—life as a happily married wife and mother. "We would have been the best team in the world," she said wistfully just two months before her death. "But it was not to be."

Without Diana present in their lives, her sons became thoroughly indoctrinated in the ways of the Windsors. They eagerly embraced polo, blood sports, and lives of service in the military. Without their hands-on mother there to steer them clear of trouble, they also meshed with the new generation of club-crawling, hard-drinking, sometimes drug-taking aristocrats. Fortunately, the Party Princes stopped short of squandering the goodwill their mother had bequeathed them.

Most important, the princes bore scant resemblance to Papa's side of the family when it came to the simple business of being human. "They are all so cold," Lady Bowker once said of the senior royals. "They have no heart."

Heart—and an ability to show it by connecting with average people—was something both of Diana's boys seemed to have in abundance. In William, there was something else—a constant visual reminder of Diana, right down to the looking-up-from-a-downward-tilt-of-the-head Shy Di glance. "Do you honestly think people would care half as much about William if he was the image of his father instead of his mother?" a leading member of Britain's Conservative Party once asked. "*Do* you?"

With his own parents' catastrophic marriage as a map for how *not* to proceed in matters of the heart, William charted his own course. Charles had discovered Camilla, the love of his life, when he was only twenty-three. Letting her slip through his fingers, he broke the heart of his first wife and nearly upended the monarchy in his desperate attempt to finally wed the woman who made him truly happy.

William seemed determined not to make the same mistake. Nor did he want to make the blunder his father did when he married Diana—bowing to pressure to take a wife, when in his heart he still harbored doubts.

Throughout their relationship, William's doubts had less to do with Kate than they did with himself. Both he and Harry admired their father, but they also knew that he had spent a lifetime floundering in search of a career beyond that of simply waiting in the wings. William needed a purpose in life, and he found it fly-ing search-and-rescue helicopters for the RAF.

Yet his relationship with Kate would mirror the values of a younger generation. It no longer mattered, as it did when Diana wed Charles, if the heir's bride was a virgin—although, in her zeal to see Kate become queen, a friend went on record insisting that Kate had been a virgin when she began her affair with William. It was also acceptable, as it would never have been a generation earlier, for the couple to openly live together before they married.

There is no doubt that, had she seen them grow to manhood, Diana would have been tremendously proud of both her sons. Given the Spencers' illustrious, centuries-long history of military service—not to mention that she was the patroness of several fighting units—Diana would almost certainly have backed their decisions to embark on military careers. It was Diana, after all, who planted the seed by decorating the princes' Kensington Pal-ace rooms with military paraphernalia, dressing them in fatigues and uniforms, and taking them to bases to ride in armored vehi-cles. "She would have been immensely proud," Richard Kay said, "and sick with worry at the same time."

What would Diana have thought of Kate Middleton? Diana would have been the first to say it scarcely mattered. All that truly mattered, Diana told her sons, was that they find a love and then "hang on to it."

Diana would almost certainly have recognized some of herself in Kate. Both women were beautiful, stylish, athletic, enigmatic, yet at the same time curiously accessible. Each had a mischievous smile, and a wicked sense of humor. Although Diana billed her-self as the People's Princess, Kate was more qualified to claim the title. Unlike the high-born Diana, whose Spencer-family bloodline was even bluer than that of the Teutonic Windsors, Kate was a commoner with working-class roots planted deep in the coal-fields of County Durham. Her creative, hardworking parents had to build a fortune big enough to sustain their children's social ambitions. Diana would have chuckled at the notion that her son and Kate might never have met were it not for the lucrative market in Mylar balloons, paper hats, and noisemakers.

Those who know him best believe the little boy who shoved tissues under his mother's locked bathroom door and brought chocolates to cheer her up is still very much alive in William. After growing up amid the nerve-fraying dysfunction of his parents' calamitous marriage, he cherished most in Kate the qualities his neurotic, self-involved parents ultimately lacked—stability, fidelity, humility, *patience.*

The Queen's mother, Lady Elizabeth Bowes-Lyon, was the last queen not of royal blood; she was also easily the most beloved. She and her husband, King George VI, insisted on staying in London even as bombs rained down on Buckingham Palace during World War II—a singular act of bravery that earned her the undying affection of her people. "Will Kate Middleton," Diana's former private secretary Patrick Jephson asked, "be like Lady Elizabeth Bowes-Lyon?"

During a decade at Prince William's side, dutiful Kate proved that she had the right stuff. She was loyal, discreet, and obeyed every Palace instruction as if she were already a member of the family. Only time will tell if Kate can become the equal in popularity to Diana or the late Queen Mother.

In the meantime, the place of William and Kate in history is already assured. That is his birthright, and now hers as well. One day they will be crowned king and queen of England, the latest in a line of monarchs that stretches back to Egbert of Wessex in the year 829. Their children will be princes and princesses, and one day one of them may well extend the House of Windsor into the twenty-second century. The future of the monarchy, as the Queen and the Men in Gray and the British people know all too well, rests with William and Kate.

Still, there is something here beyond the pomp and the pageantry, the blistering scandals, and the Machiavellian intrigues that define the modern monarchy. Theirs is the story of two young people who found each other in college, came perilously close to losing what they had forever, and pulled back from the brink at the last possible moment. Theirs is the story of private moments stolen for public consumption, of harrowing car chases, of scorching personal dramas played out behind the scenes, of calm heads prevailing in times of panic, and of a singular devotion made stronger by time.

The saga of William and Kate is one thing above all else: a love story.

The affection shown to us by so many people during our engagement has been incredibly moving and has touched us both deeply.

—William and Kate

Be who God meant you to be, and you will set the world on fire!

—The Bishop of London to William and
Kate in his wedding sermon

9

April 29, 2011

Westminster Abbey, London

She stepped out of the classic 1977 Rolls-Royce Phantom VI, and the clouds that had been hanging in the skies over London all morning suddenly parted. A shaft of golden sunlight fell directly on the car, bathing it and its occupants in a kind of eerie incandescence. "It almost looks," said one famously cynical U.S. anchorman who was among the seven thousand journalists covering the event, "as if God is having a hand in this. . . ."

The symbolism was not lost on the young woman who had worked—and loved—for nine years to make this moment happen. There was far more at stake than just her personal happiness, and no one was more keenly aware of this than Kate. Even the car she had arrived in was fraught with meaning. Less than five months earlier, Charles and Camilla had been attacked in the same Rolls-Royce by angry antimonarchist mobs screaming "Off with their heads!" Kate insisted that the same badly damaged car be repaired so that she and her father Michael Middleton could arrive in royal style at the abbey—and at the same time send the unmistakable message that the monarchy was here to stay.

The abbey bells pealed and a collective gasp from the throng, gathered across from Westminster Abbey, turned to cheers as Kate, wearing a glistening tiara loaned to her by the Queen, diamond drop earrings, and a dress of ivory silk overlaid with lace by Alexander McQueen's Sarah Burton, turned to wave. While Pippa, almost as stunning in a white silk sheath, grabbed the nine-foot-long train of her sister's gown, Kate took her father's arm and strode confidently toward the great West Door of the abbey.

The new Duchess of Cambridge, smiling broadly beneath her veil and clutching a small bouquet, which included Diana's favorite flower, lily of the valley, as well as sweet william, paused before the grave of the Unknown Warrior just inside the abbey doors.

Then, as the choir sang a soaring anthem originally composed for the coronation of Edward VII, Kate glided serenely past the 1,900 assembled guests. Meanwhile William, dressed in the crimson uniform of a colonel in the Irish Guards, and his best man, an equally dashing-looking Prince Harry, waited patiently at the altar.

For the moment, bride and groom seemed calm, even serene. They had reason to be. It was all about to be over. In the nearly five months since they announced their engagement, nearly every waking moment had been devoted to preparing for this one day. "It's a lot like planning a military campaign," William observed to a former fellow cadet at Sandhurst, "only a lot more complicated."

Matters of national pride and even national security were involved—after all, their wedding was of sufficient significance to warrant a national holiday—and William and Kate would be called upon to share the burden of decision making with Prince Charles and the Queen. They would also be required to go through marital counseling with the Archbishop of Canterbury, despite the painfully obvious fact that they were the last two people in the Royal Family who needed it.

Throughout it all, Britain's hyperactive tabloid press made sure there were plenty of distractions. There were the usual, unsubstantiated rumors of a royal pregnancy and baseless speculation that Kate was following in Diana's footsteps with an eating disorder of her own. Pointing to the fact that Charles had to cough up all his available cash—$28 million—to pay for his divorce settlement with Diana led to inevitable talk that there might be a prenuptial agreement. (Ironically, William inherited half that sum when his mother died, and it had grown in value since to an estimated $22.5 million). Since no royal had ever entered into a prenup, William was not about to ask Kate to be the first—and certainly not after she had waited nine years and her parents had generously offered to contribute $500,000 to the cost of the wedding. (The wedding—not counting security, crowd control, and the like—would wind up costing an estimated $34 million).

Planning the Wedding of the Century would not be easy. To make the task even more daunting, everything would have to be done in total secrecy—from the designer of the dress (Alice Temperley and Bruce Oldfield were among the leading contenders) to the bachelor and bachelorette parties and the honeymoon destination.

It seemed nothing short of astounding that, despite the intense scrutiny from the media, Pippa was able to throw a low-key hen night (bachelorette party) without the press ever catching on.

Even more amazing, Harry was also able to pull off a top secret stag party for his brother and twenty-one friends at Lodge Farm, a sprawling $7 million estate in Norfolk. Fleet Street only learned about the party several days after the fact.

They were equally successful at keeping the guest lists to the three main wedding day events confidential. In the meantime, there was endless speculation about who would be among the 1,900 guests invited to the wedding, the 650 guests invited to the wedding breakfast hosted by the Queen at Buckingham Palace, and the comparatively intimate party for 300 Prince Charles was throwing at "Buckhouse" for the newlyweds.

"Who are these people?" Kate might well have been asking herself as she walked up the aisle. There were, of course, the foreign monarchs, heads of state, politicians, military leaders, clergymen, and diplomats invited by the Queen. But there were also rather questionable characters invited by Prince Charles not only to the wedding but to the Queen's reception. These were all either billionaires or near billionaires who had either contributed vast sums to Charles's charities or given him the use of their private jets and yachts—or both.

In this eyebrow-raising group was Timur Kuanyshev, a Kazakh billionaire once allegedly stopped at the Moscow Airport with his wife and accused of trying to smuggle $1 million in cash out of the country in their underwear. German industrialist-turned-playboy Jurgen Pierburg headed up a family firm, DVG, that was instrumental in building Hitler's war machine. His uncle, an SS colonel, was sentenced to twenty-five years in prison for war crimes.

Also on Charles's list of generous pals was a Florentine

nobleman, Vittorio Frescobaldi, who was accused of faking the labels on the wines he produced—a charge he denied—and "Rear Admiral" Sir Donald Gosling. Sir Donald was no admiral at all—he enlisted in the Royal Navy as a seaman and never left enlisted ranks. But Gosling, who built a $500 million empire on turning bomb sites into parking lots, was given the honorary rank of admiral in recognition of his contributions to navy charities. Charles and Camilla used Sir Donald's $80 million yacht to cruise the Caribbean in 2008.

Another curious choice was Lily Safra, who was at the center of one of the most notorious homicide cases in recent memory. Her fourth husband, international banker Edmond Safra, died in a fire at their lavish Monaco apartment in 1999 under mysterious circumstances. Lily, who accumulated a total net worth in excess of $1 billion, was another generous contributor to Charles's causes.

So too was Texas billionaire and frequent Highgrove guest Joe Allbritton, who with his wife Barbie once owned Washington, D.C.–based Riggs Bank. Although he denied any wrongdoing, the bank was fined $25 million after a congressional investigation into suspicious transactions at the bank. Allbritton frequently loaned his private jets to Prince Charles; and in fact, after his son's wedding, Charles was flying to the United States aboard Allbritton's plane—the first time an heir to the throne was permitted to make an official state visit aboard a private aircraft not owned by the Crown.

There were also those conspicuous by their absences. That Barack and Michelle Obama were not invited was ameliorated somewhat by the fact that they would be arriving on a state visit scarcely a month after the wedding.

Though she once enjoyed a sisterly bond with Diana, Sarah

Ferguson was not surprised when the gold-embossed invitation never came. But Kate's uncle Gary Goldsmith, who had been caught in a headline-making drugs and sex sting by the very same tabloid reporter who exposed Fergie's solicitation of a $770,000 bribe, found himself not only invited but seated with his daughter near the front of the abbey.

Less understandable than Fergie's absence was the snubbing of former Prime Minister Tony Blair and his successor, fellow Laborite Gordon Brown. Since both Margaret Thatcher and John Major—two Conservative prime ministers—had been invited (at eighty-five Thatcher was suffering from a variety of ailments and politely declined), it was assumed the Crown was merely showing its Tory leanings. The Palace rejected this, however, explaining that Thatcher and Major held the highest rank of Knights of the Garter, and Blair and Brown didn't.

Yet no manner of excuse could explain why Blair, who had been close to Diana and her sons and shepherded the nation through its grief over Diana's shocking death, was not invited. After all, it could be argued that, had Blair not been instrumental in convincing the Queen to return to London from her holiday at Balmoral, fly the flag at half-mast, and express her own sadness to her people, there might not be any royal wedding—or, for that matter, any monarchy at all.

Thanks in part to Blair's persistence—and perhaps to the Windsors' innate lack of sensitivity—the monarchy was indeed now seemingly on the brink of a new and promising era. Kate was certainly being groomed for her role as helpmeet to the future king.

There were the accoutrements and honors that might on the surface seem trivial but would help William and Kate forge their way as royal personages in their own right. In addition to the titles bestowed by the Queen on the morning of their wedding (a particularly prestigious title she had saved for William since his birth)—the Duke and Duchess of Cambridge—William and Kate had their coats of arms impaled (merged) on the sovereign's command.

Michael Middleton had actually secured the family's coat of arms weeks before. Since the family's aptly named home in Berkshire, Oak Acre, was surrounded by oak trees, Kate selected three acorns and oak sprigs to represent herself and her siblings. A gold chevron running across the center was a nod to mother Carole's place at the heart of the family and to her maiden name, Goldsmith. The fact that the chevron cut through the middle also alluded to the family name—Middleton.

Despite such trappings, William and Kate took care to be more democratic in selecting those who would attend the wedding and the events afterward. First, they invited the childhood friends, schoolmates, and university chums who were at the center of their tight circle of confidants.

Familiar names like Guy Pelly—the "Royal Jester" who had once been accused of turning Harry on to marijuana—sidekick Thomas van Straubenzee, the van Cutsems, Lord Freddie Windsor, the Palmer-Tomkinsons, and of course Camilla's children Tom Parker Bowles and Laura Lopes were all there.

Most strikingly, perhaps, were the exes included on the guest list: at least seven of William's (most notably Jecca Craig and Arabella Musgrave) and two of Kate's (Marlborough College beau Willem Marx and the St. Andrews student she was dating when she met William, Rupert Finch).

There were a multitude of other anomalies. Earl Spencer, whose moving eulogy for his sister in this very place included a thinly veiled attack on the Royal Family, was present on the bride's side of the aisle with his and Diana's sisters Lady Jane Fellowes and Lady Sarah McCorquodale.

What might Diana have thought of the presence of Tiggy Legge-Bourke Pettifer, the former nanny she once so bitterly resented but who came to the young princes' emotional rescue following their mother's death? In a nod to the place Tiggy still occupied in William's heart, her eight-year-old son Tom was one of two pages in the wedding party. (Although the other page was ten-year-old Billy Lowther-Pinkerton, son of the princes' private secretary Jamie Lowther-Pinkerton, all the bridesmaids were to the manor born: Prince Edward's daughter Lady Louise Windsor, seven; the late Princess Margaret's only granddaughter Margarita Armstrong-Jones, eight; Camilla's granddaughter Eliza Lopes, three; and William's godchild three-year-old Grace van Cutsem.)

And just as she had been seated so prominently among the royals at Diana's wedding in 1981, Camilla—next in line to be queen—now occupied her rightful place as stepmother of the groom. Were she alive today, would Diana have chosen to sit with the Royal Family—or with Kate's?

At the bride's insistence, the Middletons had invited those people who had been a part of her life growing up in Bucklebury. The local butcher, grocer, mailman, and convenience store clerks—not to mention the landlord of their favorite pub, the Old Boot Inn, were all there. So, too, were those who had made the Middletons' vacations on Mustique so enjoyable: Basil's Bar owner Basil Charles, as well as the island's yoga teacher, tennis instructor, and even the office manager who handled rentals at the resort.

Similarly, William invited all twenty-seven of his fellow squadron members and their significant others, along with the survivors of fellow Sandhurst cadets killed in Iraq and

Afghanistan. Also invited were representatives of several charities William had become patron of following his mother's death, including the London homeless shelter Centrepoint, the African wildlife group Tusk Trust, the wounded soldiers organization Help for Heroes, and the Child Bereavement Charity for families who have lost children and children who have lost family members. In lieu of gifts, the bride and groom asked that donations be made to these and other charities they supported.

Kate was scarcely halfway up the aisle when Harry turned to look and then grinned as he whispered to his brother. William, staring straight ahead, did not succumb to the temptation to turn and look at his bride.

When Kate arrived at the altar, William greeted her with a Diana-worthy bashful smile. "You look beautiful," he told her. The groom then leaned over to the father of the bride. "I thought," William cracked, "this was supposed to be a small family affair."

Unlike Diana, who transposed two of Charles's names during the exchange of wedding vows, both Kate and William performed flawlessly ("I, Catherine Elizabeth, take thee, William Arthur Philip Louis, to my wedded husband.") In one thing Kate did follow Diana's lead: omitting the word *obey* from her vows.

Outside the abbey, a cheer went up when Kate uttered the words "I will." There was an even louder cheer when the Archbishop of Canterbury pronounced them "man and wife."

There would be only one slightly tense episode, when cameras zoomed in on Kate's hand and it appeared for one horrifying instant that perhaps William might not be able to get the ring over his bride's knuckle. The unflappable Kate merely giggled, unwilling to have this moment spoiled by anything.

Once the prayers were read and the hymns sung and everyone

(except for the monarch, who never does) joined in an especially spirited rendition of "God Save the Queen," the fanfare sounded and William and Kate made their exit to the strains of William Walton's "Crown Imperial."

Emerging from the West Door to the thunderous cheers of the crowd gathered outside, the happy couple climbed into the same horse-drawn open landau that had carried Charles and Diana from St. Paul's Cathedral thirty years before.

Settling into the carriage, Kate said to William, "I'm so happy."

Making their way past the one million people who lined the wedding route from Westminster Abbey to Buckingham Palace, William and Kate smiled and waved until they reached the palace. Entering the inner sanctum, Kate bowed her head as William snapped off a salute.

Minutes later, they were standing on the balcony with the rest of the royal wedding party, facing a throng of nearly 500,000 gathered directly in front of Buckingham Palace. Following a tradition established by Charles and Diana, they quickly kissed, surprising—and perhaps to some extent disappointing—the crowd. Not long after, they delivered a bonus balcony kiss—this time one that lingered just long enough to satisfy their future subjects.

After the wedding breakfast and official photographs of the newly blended family taken in the Throne Room, William and Kate took the media by surprise when they drove out of the gates of Buckingham Palace with the Duke of Cambridge behind the wheel of a blue Aston Martin Volante convertible decorated with Mylar balloons and bearing the license plate JU5T WED. The Duchess—since she was not born a princess, Kate would not be known as Princess Catherine but as Catherine, Princess William of Wales—waved at astonished onlookers as she and William drove to nearby Clarence House to rest before that evening's big reception.

At 7:30 p.m. Kate, dazzling in a long white satin strapless Sarah Burton evening dress worn with a white angora bolero cardigan, emerged with her tuxedo-clad husband and her new in-laws. By the time they arrived at Buckingham Palace, the party in the newlyweds honor was already in full swing.

The Ballroom, largest of Buckingham Palace's 775 rooms, was the early focal point of the reception, which spilled over into the White Drawing Room, the Blue Drawing Room, the Music Room, and the State Dining Room. The high point of the evening was Harry's long-anticipated best man's wedding toast, in which he repeatedly called them "the dude and the Duchess," offered dead-on impressions of Kate calling his brother "Billy" and his brother calling her "Baby," and apologized to his new sister-in-law for having to "marry a bald man."

There were touching moments, too. Once again Harry proclaimed that he loved Kate like a sister, and brought many in the room to tears when he concluded, "Our mother would be so very proud of you."

After the requisite speeches, everyone was led to the Throne Room, which had been converted into a nightclub. There, when they weren't downing flutes of Laurent-Perrier champagne or the couple's favorite crack baby cocktails (a lethal blend of vodka, passion fruit juice, raspberry liqueur, and champagne), guests danced to music that ranged from the Beatles to rap. At one point, William and Kate danced to "You're the One That I Want" from *Grease* and were then hoisted on the shoulders of friends and paraded around the room.

No one outdid Prince Harry, however. The newlyweds doubled over with laughter watching the Spare, his shirt unbuttoned and clearly drunk, climbing onto windowsills and diving into the crowd. When the festivities finally came to an end with a 3 a.m. fireworks display on the grounds of the palace, Harry threw his arms around the newlyweds—and burst into tears. "Obviously," said one of their St. Andrews pals, "it has been a very emotional day for everybody." While Kate and William went home to Clarence House, Harry took a shuttle bus to the Goring Hotel and partied on with friends until 5 a.m.

For those who knew them well, it came as little surprise that Kate and William did not follow the usual course when it came to their honeymoon. Charles and Diana had had their honeymoon laid out for them by the Men in Gray—a few days at Lord Mountbatten's estate Broadlands, followed by a lengthy Mediterranean cruise aboard the royal yacht *Britannia*, and a few days at Balmoral.

William and Kate would take only a few days off before returning to North Wales. They would eventually have their honeymoon, to be sure. But for now they needed to return to their lives—as an RAF search-and-rescue helicopter pilot and his wife—that helped them stay grounded, even as they prepared to undertake two of most high-profile jobs on the planet.

Diana, more than anyone, would have been amazed at the phenomenally poised, strong-willed yet kind young woman who had won the heart of her "little old wise man." There would be much talk of who would be training Kate for her role as princess, although to all who knew her it was evident that she was probably better equipped for the job than the royals themselves. Diana would have been no less impressed that William, while remaining true to his Windsor heritage, had never forgotten the lessons of the heart she had taught him.

When it was all over, the world that had watched William grow to manhood now rooted for the remarkable young woman he had chosen to share his life and the crown. What they had all expected—and got—was the Wedding of the Century. Now they realized this was all merely prelude to something far more important: the first epic love story of the twenty-first century.

Acknowledgments

"When I was born, I was unwanted," Diana once poignantly re-marked. "When I married Charles, I was unwanted. When I joined the Royal Family, I was unwanted. I want to be wanted." This was the overarching irony of the princess's brief and tragic life—that Diana, the most idolized woman on the planet, felt un-loved. It was a feeling that she was determined her sons—William in particular—would never know.

While writing my previous bestselling books about the Royal Family, *The Day Diana Died* and *Diana's Boys*, as well as *Vanity Fair*'s twentieth-anniversary-issue cover story on Prince William, one thing became painfully clear: the monarchy-rocking melo-drama played out by Charles and Diana could have been avoided entirely if only the Prince of Wales had married the woman he truly loved in the first place. Instead, as one wag put it, Charles made the mistake of "marrying his trophy wife *first*."

After watching the private pain and sordid public spectacle of his parents' doomed marriage, William was not about to offer the world a repeat performance. Nor was he about to be rushed into making the kind of heart-and-soul commitment that he fully intended to last a lifetime.

In this, William would defy a centuries-old tradition of care-fully orchestrated royal marriages. To further complicate mat-ters, the woman he fell in love with was a commoner—although clearly not just *any* commoner. In biding her time for nearly a decade—all the while negotiating the treacherous currents of royal protocol and public opinion while never losing her enthusiasm or her allure—Kate proved herself worthy of a king.

William and Kate is the culmination of nearly thirty years spent covering the Royal Family, starting back in the 1980s when as senior editor of *People* magazine I edited numerous cover stories on the Windsors—including our special issue announcing William's birth on July 21, 1982. To hedge our bets, we had two covers mocked up and ready to run—one proclaiming IT'S A BOY! and the other IT'S A GIRL! Fortunately for Kate, it was a boy.

William and Kate also marks a homecoming of sorts to Simon & Schuster, which published my first book in 1976. Once again, I am fortunate enough to be working with some of the finest talents in publishing. I am especially grateful to my editor, Gallery Books Senior Editor Mitchell Ivers, for bringing his skill, insight, and passionate dedication to the project. I am also indebted to the entire Simon & Schuster family, especially Louise Burke, Carolyn Reidy, Jennifer Bergstrom, Jennifer Robinson, Felice Javit, Jean Anne Rose, Lisa Keim, and Jessica Webb.

As both agent and friend, Ellen Levine is simply the best. We've worked together for twenty-seven years, and I look forward to another twenty-seven—if, Ellen, you think you can bear it! I owe an added debt of thanks to the Trident Media Group, and in particular to Ellen's associates Claire Roberts, Margie Guerra, and Alanna Ramirez.

I am obviously also deeply grateful to my parents, Commander Edward F. Andersen and Jeanette Andersen, a remarkable woman who passed away suddenly and unexpectedly during the early stages of this book, and to whom it is dedicated. Her granddaughters, Kate and Kelly, are also remarkable women—brilliant, gorgeous, and accomplished. They get it all from their mother Valerie. This book is all about having the sense to keep your soul mate once you've found her or him. I was lucky enough to find mine in the fall of 1967 on the campus of the University of California at Berkeley.

Additional thanks to Richard Kay, Jules Knight, Peter Archer, Emma Sayle, Alan Hamilton, Beatrice Hubert, Lord Mishcon, Mimi Massy-Birch, Dr. Frederic Mailliez, Guy Pelly, Hugh Massy-Birch, Janet Jenkins, Philip Higgs, Andrew Gailey, Lady Elsa Bowker, Elizabeth d'Erlanger, Hamish Barne, Andy Radford, Vivienne Parry, Lady Yolanda Joseph, Jules de Rosee, Richard Greene, Adrian Munsey, Josy Duclos, Thierry Meresse, Jeanne Lecorcher, the Countess of Romanones, Ezra Zilkha, Harold Brooks-Baker, Mark Butt, John Kaufman, Geoffrey Bignell, Remi Gaston-Dreyfus, Natalie Symonds, Rachel Whitburn, Elizabeth Whiddett, Penny Russell-Smith, Delissa Needham, Miriam Lefort, Penny Walker, Claude Garreck, Aide Wimber, Dee Ennifer, Patrick Demarchelier, Dudley Freeman, Peter Allen, John Marion, Angela Nutt, Fred Hauptfuhrer, Jessica Hogan, Betty Kelly Sargent, Tom Freeman, Gered Mankowitz, Vivian Simon, Elaine Wells, Michelle Lapautre, Alain-Phillipe Feutre, Mary Robertson, Tom Corby, Cecile Zilkha, Kevin Lemarque, Pierre Suu, Hazel Southam, Ray Whelan Jr., Matthew Lutts, Vincent Martin, Everett Raymond Kinstler, Andy Rouvalis, Scott Burkhead, Bill Diehl, Tim Graham, Tiffany Miller, Simone Dibley, Daniel Taylor, Ray Whelan Sr., Paula Dranov, Rhoda Prelic, Liz Miller, Steve Stylandoudis, Tiffney Sanford, Amber Weitz, Julie Cammer, Marcel Turgot, Mary Beth Whelan, David McGough, Yvette Reyes, Charles Furneaux, Connie Erickson, Mark Blumire, Alec Michael, Mel Lyons, Lindsay Sutton, Francis Specker, Walter Neilson, Hilary Hard, Stephen Daniels, Scott Burkhead, John

Stillwell, James Price, Elizabeth Loth, Ian Walde, Wolfgang Rattay, Richard Grant, Mick Magsino, Lawrence R. Mulligan, Tasha Hanna, Jane Clucas, David Bergeron, Art Kaligos, Gary Gunderson, the Press Association, St. James's Palace, Clarence House, Windsor Castle, Buckingham Palace, Kensington Palace, Downe House, St. Andrew's School, Marlborough College, Eton, Ludgrove, St. Andrews University, Sandhurst, the BBC, Sky Television, Channel Four Television Ltd., the *Times* of London, the *Daily Mail*, the New York Public Library, the Boston Public Library, the Bancroft Library of the University of California at Berkeley, the Litchfield Library, the Gunn Memorial Library, the Brookfield Library, the Silas Bronson Library, the Reform Club, the Lotos Club, the Lansdowne Club, the *New York Times*, the Associated Press, Bloomberg, Reuters, Gannett, Associated Press Images, BEImages, Rex USA, Getty Images, Alpha Photos, Retna, Sipa Press, PRPhotos, Infoto, Xposure, BigPicture, Corbis, Bauer-Griffin, and Globe Photos.

Sources and Chapter Notes

The following chapter notes have been compiled to give an overview of the sources drawn upon in preparing *William and Kate*, but they are by no means all-inclusive. Certain key sources at Buckingham Palace, St. James's Palace, Clarence House, Kensington Palace, Sandringham, Highgrove, Balmoral, Windsor Castle, Eton, Sandhurst, and Scotland Yard—as well as relatives, friends, acquaintances, schoolmates, and employees of both the royal and Middleton families—agreed to cooperate only once they were assured their names would not be mentioned. Therefore, the author has respected the wishes of the many interviewed sources who wished to remain anonymous and has not listed them either here or elsewhere in the text. Over the years countless articles and news reports concerning William and Kate have appeared in such publications as the *Sunday Times* of London, the *New York Times*, the *Guardian*, the *Wall Street Journal*, the *Washington Post*, the *Daily Mail*, the *Boston Globe*, the *Los Angeles Times*, *Time*, *Life*, *People*, *Newsweek*, the *New Yorker*, *Vanity Fair*, *Paris Match*, *Le Monde*, the *Times* of London, and the *Economist* and been carried over the Associated Press, Bloomberg, and Reuters wires.

CHAPTERS 1–2

Interview subjects included Alan Hamilton, Dr. Frederic Mailliez, Beatrice Humbert, Jeanne Lecorcher, Richard Kay, Thierry Meresse, Richard Greene, the late Lady Elsa Bowker, Peter Archer, Ezra Zilkha, Harold Brooks-Baker, Andy Radford, Mark Butt, Claude Garreck, Josy Duclos, Remi Gaston-Dreyfus, Peter Allen, Barry Schenck, Miriam Lefort, Janet Lizop, Pierre Suu, and Steve Stylandoudis. Published sources included Amar Singh, "The Battle to Protect Kate," *Evening Standard*, January 9, 2007; Kira Cochrane, "In Diana's Footsteps," *Guardian*, January 9, 2007; Annick Cojean, "The Final Interview," *Le Monde*, August 27, 1997; "Charles Escorts Diana Back to a Grieving Britain," the *New York Times*, September 1, 1997; Anthony Holden, "Why Royals Must Express Remorse," *Express*, September 3, 1997; Robert Hardman, "Princes' Last Minutes with Mother," *Daily Telegraph*, September 3, 1997; "The Princes' Final Farewell," *Sunday Times* of London, September 7, 1997; Alan Hamilton, Andrew Pierce, and Philip Webster, "Royal Family Is 'Deeply Touched' by Public Support," *Times*, September 4, 1997; "Diana, Princess of Wales, 1961–1997," *Week*, September 6, 1997; "The Nation Unites Against Tradition," *Observer*, September 7, 1997; Lord Stevens of Kirkwhelpington, *The Operation Paget Inquiry Report into the Alle-*

gation of Conspiracy to Murder Diana, Princess of Wales, and Emad El-Din Mohamed Abdel Moneim Fayed, December 14, 2006; "Farewell, Diana," *Newsweek*, September 15, 1997; John Simpson, "Goodbye England's Rose: A Nation Says Farewell," *Sunday Telegraph*, September 7, 1997; "Driver Was Drunk," *Le Monde*, September 3, 1997; Andrew Morton, *Diana: Her True Story*, (New York: Simon & Schuster, 1997); Pascal Palmer, "I Gave Diana Last Rites," *Mirror*, October 23, 1997; Robert Jobson and Greg Swift, "Look After William and Harry," *Daily Express*, December 22, 1997; Christopher Andersen, *The Day Diana Died* (New York: William Morrow, 1998); "Flashback to the Accident," *Liberation*, September 2, 1997; Howard Chua-Eoan, Steve Wulf, Jeffrey Kluger, Christopher Redman, and David Van Biema, "A Death in Paris: The Passing of Diana," *Time*, September 8, 1997; Wendy Berry, *The Housekeeper's Diary* (New York: Barricade Books, 1995; Thomas Sancton and Scott MacLeod, *Death of a Princess: The Investigation* (New York: St. Martin's Press, 1998); James Hewitt, *Love and War* (London: Blake Publishing, 1999); Marianne Macdonald, "A Rift Death Can't Heal," *Observer*, September 14, 1997; Tess Rock and Natalie Symonds, "Our Diana Diaries," *Sunday Mirror*, November 16, 1997; Simone Simmons, *Diana: The Last Word* (New York: St. Martin's Press, 2005); Deirdre Fernand, "The Girl Who Would Be Queen," *Sunday Times*, December 31, 2006; Claudia Joseph, "The Making of the Middletons," *Mail on Sunday*, December 30, 2007; Rosa Monckton, "Time to End False Rumors," *Newsweek*, March 2, 1998; and Jerome Dupuis, "Diana: The Unpublished Report of Witnesses at the Ritz," *L'Express*, March 12, 1998.

CHAPTERS 3–5

For these chapters, the author drew on conversations with Peter Archer, Jules Knight, Mimi Massy-Birch, Lady Yolanda Joseph, Emma Sayle, Guy Pelly, Lady Elsa Bowker, Hamish Barne, Hugh Massy-Birch, Countess Mountbatten, Delissa Needham, Elizabeth d'Erlanger, Alice Tomlinson, Richard Greene, Geoffrey Bignell, Penny Walker, Lord Mishcon, Jules de Rosee, Richard Kay, the Countess of Romanones, Farris Rookstool, Fred Hauptfuhrer, Cecile Thibaud, David McGough, Hazel Southam, Charles Furneaux, Evelyn Phillips, Susan Crimp, Elizabeth Widdett, Janet Allison, and Mary Robertson. Among the published sources consulted are David Leppard and Christopher Morgan, "Police Fears over William's Friends," *Sunday Times*, February 27, 2000; Barbara Kantrowitz, "William: The Making of a Modern King," *Newsweek*, June 26, 2000; Claudia Joseph, *Kate* (New York: Avon, 2009); P. D. Jephson, *Shadows of a Princess* (New York: HarperCollins, 2000); Robert Hardman, "Just (Call Me) William," *Daily Telegraph*, June 9, 2000; Alex O'Connell, "Prince Chases Adventure in Remotest Chile," September 30, 2000; Andrew Pierce and Simon de Bruxelles, "Our Mother Was Betrayed," *Times*, September 30, 2000; Michelle Tauber, "Speaking His Mind," *People*, October 16, 2000; Richard Kay, "William Stalked by His Uncle's TV Crew," *Daily Mail*, September 27, 2001; Bob Colacello, "A Court of His Own," *Vanity Fair*, October 2001; Warren Hoge, "Charles's Response to Use of Drugs by Son Is Praised," *New York Times*, January 14, 2002; J. F. O. McAllister, "Once Upon a Time, There Was a Pot-Smoking Prince," *Time*, January 28, 2002; Antony Barnett, "Prince Taken to Drink and Drugs Rehab Clinic," *Observer*, January 13, 2002; Ben Summerskill, "The Trouble with Harry," *Observer*, January 13, 2002; Warren Hoge, "Royal Palace Is Roiled Again by New Round of Revelations," *New York Times*, November 11, 2002; Joan Smith, "Prince Charles: What a Guy! What a Boss! What?" *Independent*, March 12, 2003; Tom Rawstorne, "William: In His Own Words," *Daily Mail*, May 30, 2003; "William 'the Young Yob': Charles Forced to Apologize for His Son's Road-Rage," *Daily Mail*, June 16, 2003; Christopher Morgan and David Leppard, "Party Girl in William's Circle Snorted Cocaine," *Sunday Times*, February 26, 2000; Christopher Andersen, "The Divided Prince," *Vanity Fair*, September 2003; Matthew Bailey and Andrew Pierce, " 'I'm Sorry for Wearing Nazi Swastika,' Says Prince Harry," *Times*, January 13, 2005; Susan Schindehette and Allison Adato, "Princess in Love," *People*, August 8, 2005; Nicola Methven, "Hypno-Di-Sed: Hewitt Put in Trance," *Mirror*, September 19, 2005; Michelle Green, "Is She the One?" *People*, October 17, 2005; Andrew Pierce, "Cameron's Royal Link Makes Him a True Blue," *Times*, December 5, 2005; Richard Palmer and Lizzie Catt, "William and Kate on Ibiza 'Rave' Holiday," *Daily Express*, September 2, 2006; Robert Jobson, *William's Princess* (London: Blake Publishing, 2006); Mazher Mahmood and Amanda Evans, "I Called Wills a F***er," *News of the World*, July 19, 2009; Sandra Laville and Owen Gibson, "Scooped by His Own Mobile Phone," *Guardian*, November 30, 2006; Alex Tresniowski and Ashley Williams, "Will & Kate: The Perfect Match," *People*, December 11, 2006; Emily Nash, "Diana: The Verdict," *Mirror*, December 11, 2006; "Prince William Graduates as an Officer," *Guardian*, December 15, 2006; Chris Hughes, "Salutes You, Sir," *Mirror*, December 16, 2006.

CHAPTERS 6–8

Information for these chapters was based in part on conversations with Richard Kay, Emma Sayle, Philip Higgs, Mimi Massy-Birch, Peter Archer, Lord Mishcon, Alan Hamilton, Guy Pelly, Alex Shirley-Smith, Lady Elsa Bowker, Grigori Rassinier, Richard Greene, Ezra Zilkha, Geoffrey Bignell, Aileen Mehle, Janet Lizop, Muriel Hartwick, Sioned Compton, Gared Mankowitz, Cecile Zilkha, Natalie Symonds, and Hugh Massy-Birch. Published sources included John Elliott, "Charles Plans a Mansion Fit for Lovebirds," *Sunday Times*, December 17, 2006; Frances Gibb, "Lawyers Planning Test Case to Stop Paparazzi Hounding Kate Middleton," *Times*, January 9, 2007; *"News of the World* Journalist Jailed," Reuters, January 26, 2007; Don Van Natta Jr., Jo Becker, and Graham Bowley, "Tabloid Hack Attack," *New York Times Magazine*, September 5, 2010; Oliver Marre, "Girl, Interrupted," *Observer*, March 18, 2007; Nikhita Mahajan, "He Was Touchy Feely," *Sunday Mirror*, March 25, 2007; Duncan Larcombe, "Wills & Kate Split," *Sun*, April 14, 2007; Laura Collins, Katie Nicholl, and Ian Gallagher, "Kate Was Too Middle Class," *Mail on Sunday*, April 15, 2007; David Smith, "Royal Relationships: The Breakup," April 15, 2007; Zoe Griffin and Grant Hodgson, "Wills & Kate 2002–2007: The Fairytale's Over," *Sunday Mirror*, April 15, 2007; Rajeev Syal, "Tony Blair: Let Them Be, They Are Young," *Times* of London, April 16, 2007; Victoria White and Stephen White, "Life After William,"

Mirror, April 21, 2007; Katie Nichol and Amy Hanson, "Flirty Kate Had Designs on Me," *Mail on Sunday*, April 22, 2007; Laura Collins and Louise Hannah, "As Kate Re-Emerges More Tanned and Confident, a New Middleton Girl Takes a Bow," *Daily Mail*, May 27, 2007; Karen Rockett, "It's Back On," *Sunday Mirror*, June 24, 2007; Eva Simpson and Sarah Tetteh, "Thrills & Kate: Exclusive," *Mirror*, July 3, 2007; Richard Woods, "Leave Us Alone," *Sunday Times*, October 7, 2007; Andrew Alderson, "Prince Eyes Legal Action," *Sunday Telegraph*, October 7, 2007; Sarah Knapton, "Prince Denounces 'Aggressive' Paparazzi Pursuit," *Guardian*, October 6, 2007; Lisa Sewards, "The Day Prince William Pulled a Gun on Me," *Daily Mail*, December 28, 2007; Robert Jobson and Keith Dovkants, "Kate, the 'New Royal,' Gets Her Own Bodyguards," *Evening Standard*, January 9, 2008; Andrew Pierce, "Prince's Lawyers Warn Paparazzi Off Stalking Middleton," *Daily Telegraph*, February 23, 2008; Rebecca English, "William Landed His Air Force Helicopter in Kate's Garden," *Daily Mail*, April 21, 2008; Aislinn Simpson, "William Flies into a Storm," *Daily Telegraph*, April 21, 2008; "William's Training Cost 162,000 Pounds," *Birmingham Post*, May 8, 2008; Ben Guy, "Will Finds a Way to Get to Church on Time—in a Helicopter," *Newcastle Journal*, April 23, 2008; BBC News, "William and RAF Sorry for Prince's FIVE Chinook Joyrides," April 23, 2008; Fred Redwood, "Helicopter Stunt that Put Kate's Home on the Map," *Sunday Telegraph*, May 18, 2008; Lucy Cockcroft, "Prince William's Chinook Flight to Stag Party Costs 8,716 Pounds," *Daily Telegraph*, June 30, 2008; Alan Hamilton, "A Feather in His Cap: Young Prince Is New Recruit to the World's Oldest Order of Chivalry," *Times* of London, June 17, 2008; Sri Carmichael, "Prince William: Drug Buster," *Evening Standard*, July 2, 2008; Simon Perry, "Prince William's Ship Seizes $80 Million in Drugs," *People*, July 2, 2008; Richard Kay, Geoffrey Levy, and Katie Glass, "Wild Side of Kate's Family," *Daily Mail*, August 9, 2008; Nick Owens, "Crown Sugar: Jagger Sings for Wills & Kate on Mustique Love Trip," *Sunday Mirror*, August 10, 2008; Duncan Larcombe, "Exclusive: The Kate Frame Robbery," *Sun*, September 1, 2008; Vicky Ward, "Will's Cup of Tea," *Vanity Fair*, November 2008; Richard Eden, "Kate's 'Vulnerable' Mother Speaks Out for the First Time," December 7, 2008; Charlotte Hunt-Grubbe, "Inside the Sex Club for Girls," *Sunday Times*, March 15, 2009; Geoffrey Levy and Richard Kay, "How Many MORE Skeletons in Kate's Closet?" *Daily Mail*, July 22, 2009; James Whitaker and David Collins, "One's Been Frozen Out: Queen Tells Kate It's Family ONLY at Sandringham This Christmas," *People*, December 20, 2009; Liz Hoggard, "Let Them Eat Cake," *Evening Standard*, February 18, 2010; Alex Tresniowski, "A Royal Love," *People*, May 3, 2010; ABC News, "Duchess of York Scandal," May 24, 2010; Vanessa Friedman, "Fantasy Matrimony," *Financial Times*, May 29, 2010; Ed Pilkington, "Sarah Ferguson on *Oprah*," *Guardian*, June 2, 2010; David Stringer, "Prince William Makes First Royal Rescue for RAF," Associated Press, October 5, 2010.

Bibliography

Allison, Ronald, and Sarah Riddell, eds. *The Royal Encyclopedia*. London: Macmillan, 1991.

Andersen, Christopher. *The Day Diana Died*. New York: William Morrow, 1998.

———. *The Day John Died*. New York: William Morrow, 2000.

———. *Diana's Boys*. New York: William Morrow, 2001.

———. *After Diana: William, Harry, Charles, and the Royal House of Windsor*. New York: Hyperion, 2007.

Barry, Stephen P. *Royal Service: My Twelve Years as Valet to Prince Charles*. New York: Macmillan, 1983.

Berry, Wendy. *The Housekeeper's Diary*. New York: Barricade Books, 1995.

Boca, Geoffrey. *Elizabeth and Philip*. New York: Henry Holt and Company, 1953.

Botham, Noel. *The Murder of Princess Diana*. New York: Pinnacle Books, 2004.

Bradford, Sarah. *Diana*. New York: Viking, 2006.

Brander, Michael. *The Making of the Highlands*. London: Constable and Company, 1980.

Bryan, J., III, and Charles J. V. Murphy. *The Windsor Story*. New York: William Morrow, 1979.

Burrell, Paul. *A Royal Duty*. New York: New American Library, 2004.

———. *The Way We Were*. New York: William Morrow, 2006.

Campbell, Lady Colin. *Diana in Private*. London: Smith Gryphon, 1993.

Cannadine, David. *The Decline and Fall of the British Aristocracy*. New Haven: Yale University Press, 1990.

Cannon, John, and Ralph Griffiths. *The Oxford Illustrated History of the British Monarchy*. Oxford and New York: Oxford University Press, 1992.

Cathcart, Helen. *The Queen Herself*. London: W. H. Allen, 1983.

———. *The Queen and Prince Philip: Forty Years of Happiness*. London: Hodder and Stoughton, 1987.

Clarke, Mary. *Diana Once Upon a Time*. London: Sidgwick & Jackson, 1994.

Clifford, Max, and Angela Levin. *Max Clifford: Read All About It*. London: Virgin, 2005.

Davies, Nicholas. *Diana: The Lonely Princess*. New York: Birch Lane, 1996.

———. *Queen Elizabeth II*. New York: Carol Publishing Group, 1996.

———. *William: The Inside Story of the Man Who Will Be King*. St. Martin's Press: 1998.

Delderfield, Eric R. *Kings and Queens of England and Great Britain.* London: David & Charles, 1990.

Delorm, Rene. *Diana and Dodi: A Love Story.* Los Angeles: Tallfellow Press, 1998.

Dempster, Nigel, and Peter Evans. *Behind Palace Doors.* New York: Putnam, 1993.

Dimbleby, Jonathan. *The Prince of Wales: A Biography.* New York: William Morrow, 1994.

Edwards, Anne. *Diana and the Rise of the House of Spencer.* London: Hodder and Stoughton, 1999.

Ferguson, Ronald. *The Galloping Major: My Life and Singular Times.* London: Macmillan, 1994.

Fisher, Graham, and Heather Fisher. *Elizabeth: Queen & Mother.* New York: Hawthorn Books, 1964.

Foreman, J. B., ed. *Scotland's Splendour.* Glasgow: William Collins Sons & Co., 1961.

Fox, Mary Virginia. *Princess Diana.* Hillside, NJ: Enslow, 1986.

Goldsmith, Lady Annabel. *Annabel: An Unconventional Life.* London: Phoenix, 2004.

Graham, Caroline. *Camilla: The King's Mistress.* London: John Blake Publishing, 1994.

———. *Camilla and Charles: The Love Story.* London: John Blake Publishing, 2005.

Graham, Tim. *Diana: HRH the Princess of Wales.* New York: Summit, 1988.

———. *The Royal Year 1993.* London: Michael O'Mara, 1993.

Gregory, Martyn. *The Diana Conspiracy Exposed.* London: Virgin, 1999.

Hewitt, James. *Love and War.* London: John Blake Publishing, 1999.

Hoey, Brian. *All the King's Men.* London: HarperCollins, 1992.

Holden, Anthony. *Charles.* London: Weidenfeld and Nicolson, 1988.

———. *The Tarnished Crown.* New York: Random House, 1993.

Hough, Richard. *Born Royal: The Lives and Loves of the Young Windsors.* New York: Bantam, 1988.

Hutchins, Chris, and Peter Thompson. *Sarah's Story: The Duchess Who Defied the Royal House of Windsor.* London: Smith Gryphon, 1992.

Jephson, P. D. *Shadows of a Princess.* New York: HarperCollins, 2000.

Jobson, Robert. *William's Princess: The Love Story That Will Change the Royal Family Forever.* London: John Blake Publishing, 2006.

———. *Harry's War.* London: John Blake Publishing, 2008.

Joseph, Claudia. *Kate.* New York: Avon, 2009.

Junor, Penny. *Charles.* New York: St. Martin's Press, 1987.

———. *The Firm.* New York: Thomas Dunne Books, 2005.

Lacey, Robert. *Majesty.* New York: Harcourt Brace Jovanovich, 1977.

———. *Queen Mother.* Boston: Little, Brown, 1986.

Lathan, Caroline, and Jeannie Sakol. *The Royals.* New York: Congdon & Weed, 1987.

Maclean, Veronica. *Crowned Heads.* London: Hodder & Stoughton, 1993.

Martin, Ralph G. *Charles & Diana.* New York: Putnam, 1985.

Montgomery-Massingberd, Hugh. *Burke's Guide to the British Monarchy.* London: Burke's Peerage, 1977.

Morton, Andrew. *Inside Buckingham Palace*. London: Michael O'Mara, 1991.

——. *Diana: Her True Story*. New York: Simon & Schuster, 1997.

——. *Diana: In Pursuit of Love*. London: Michael O'Mara, 2004.

Pasternak, Anna. *Princess in Love* London: Bloomsbury, 1994.

Pimlott, Ben. *The Queen: A Biography of Elizabeth II*. New York: John Wiley & Sons, 1996.

Reese-Jones, Trevor, with Moira Johnston. *The Bodyguard's Story*. New York: Warner Books, 2000.

Sancton, Thomas, and Scott MacLeod. *Death of a Princess: The Investigation*. New York: St. Martin's Press, 1998.

Sarah, the Duchess of York, with Jeff Coplon. *My Story*. New York: Simon & Schuster, 1996.

Seward, Ingrid. *The Queen and Di*. New York: HarperCollins, 2000.

——. *William & Harry: The People's Princes*. London: Carlton Books, 2009.

Simmons, Simone, with Susan Hill. *Diana: The Secret Years*. London: Michael O'Mara, 1998.

——. *The Last Word*. New York: St. Martin's Press, 2005.

Smith, Sally Bedell. *Diana in Search of Herself*. New York: Times Books, 1999.

Snell, Kate. *Diana: Her Last Love*. London: Granada Media, 2000.

Spencer, Charles. *The Spencers: A Personal History of an English Family*. New York: St. Martin's Press, 2000.

Spoto, Donald. *The Decline and Fall of the House of Windsor*. New York: Simon & Schuster, 1995.

——. *Diana: The Last Year*. New York: Harmony Books, 1997.

Lord Stevens of Kirkwhelpington. *The Operation Paget Inquiry Report into the Allegation of Conspiracy to Murder Diana, Princess of Wales, and Emad El-Din Mohamed Abdel Moneim Fayed*. London: December 14, 2006.

Thornton, Michael. *Royal Feud*. London: Michael Joseph, 1985.

Wade, Judy. *The Truth: The Friends of Diana, Princess of Wales, Tell Their Stories*. London: John Blake Publishing, 2001.

Wharfe, Ken, with Robert Jobson. *Diana: Closely Guarded Secret*. London: Michael O'Mara, 2003.

Whitaker, James. *Diana v. Charles*. London: Signet, 1993.

Wilson, Christopher. *The Windsor Knot*. New York: Citadel Press, 2002.